Jono Lineen is a writer, curator and public speaker whose passion for landscape and humankind's connection to it inspires his writing. He worked for years as a project manager for Médecins Sans Frontières in war and disaster zones around the world. Currently he is a curator at the National Museum of Australia. He is the author of *River Trilogy: Travels Down Three of the World's Greatest Rivers*.

www.jonolineen.com

TO NICHOLAS

Into the Heart of the
HIMALAYAS

Alone across the highest mountains on Earth

JONO LINEEN

ENJOY THE JOURNEY
ALL THINGS CREATED MUST PASS.
'WALK ON'
jono.

MELBOURNE UNIVERSITY PRESS

MELBOURNE UNIVERSITY PRESS
An imprint of Melbourne University Publishing Limited
11–15 Argyle Place South, Carlton, Victoria 3053, Australia
mup-info@unimelb.edu.au
www.mup.com.au

First published in Canada 2012 by Pottersfield Press
This edition published 2014
Text © Jono Lineen, 2012

This book is copyright. Apart from any use permitted under the *Copyright Act 1968* and subsequent amendments, no part may be reproduced, stored in a retrieval system or transmitted by any means or process whatsoever without the prior written permission of the publishers.

Every attempt has been made to locate the copyright holders for material quoted in this book. Any person or organisation that may have been overlooked or misattributed may contact the publisher.

A donation from the proceeds of the sale of this book will be made to the Australian Himalayan Foundation in acknowledgement of the work the undertake across the mountain range. www.australianhimalayanfoundation.org.au

Translation of traditional song on page 258 courtesy Anjali Capila, Associate Professor in Development and Communications, Lady Irwin College, New Delhi

Cover design by Nada Backovic
Printed in Australia by McPherson's Printing Group

National Library of Australia Cataloguing-in-Publication entry

Lineen, Jono

Into the Heart of the Himalayas: Alone Across the Highest Mountains on Earth/Jono Lineen.

9780522866001 (paperback)
9780522866018 (ebook)

    Lineen, Jono—Travel.
    Hiking—Himalaya Mountains Region.
    Himalaya Mountains Region.

915.496

For Gareth

If we were doomed to live forever,
we would scarcely be aware of the beauty around us.
—Peter Matthiessen, *The Paris Review*

CONTENTS

Prologue – Gareth   1

MUSLIM HIMALAYAS   7
    Chapter 1   Live as Best You Can   8
    Chapter 2   Turquoise and Coral   32

BUDDHIST HIMALAYAS   57
    Chapter 3   In the Steps of the Yak   58
    Chapter 4   Dreams and Truth   89
    Chapter 5   Dangerous Places   130
    Chapter 6   Finding Gods   158
    Chapter 7   Harvest   189

HINDU HIMALAYAS   221
    Chapter 8   Religion in Landscape   222
    Chapter 9   Balance   243
    Chapter 10   Skirmishes   272
    Chapter 11   Gratitude   301

PROLOGUE
Gareth

August 7

The jeep taxi dropped me at my starting point, the confluence of the Indus and Astore rivers in the Northern Areas of Pakistan-administered Kashmir. It is a tumultuous landscape, where three of the world's greatest mountain ranges – the Himalayas, the Karakoram and the Hindu Kush – collide. The result is a labyrinth of peaks and valleys, a terrain wrenched by earthquakes, glaciers, and ceaseless erosion. Beyond the rivers that surged at my feet, the valley rose into hills and those hills climbed further into some of the highest peaks on earth: Nanga Parbat, K2, Gasherbrum, Masherbrum, Broad Peak. It was a big landscape, a setting that could eat away at your confidence.

I lifted my pack from where the jeep's twelve-year-old ticket collector had flung it to the ground. Dust pirouetted in miniature tornadoes around my feet. Using one knee and both hands I swung the pack up and onto my back. I felt its weight settle evenly between my shoulders. Its top-heavy pressure weighted my lungs and tightened the muscles in my chest and stomach. I adjusted the straps until it balanced on the ridge of my spine. I gently shook the load back and forth until the backpack wrapped me like a turtle shell, heavy but snug. The pack was my household – bedroom, kitchen, dining room – so I needed it to be comfortable.

I put one foot in front of the other, focusing on the rocks beneath my feet and the tightness in my muscles. I gasped, struggling for oxygen in the altitude-rarified air. A wind brushed my cheeks, dry from the mountains, wet from the rivers. The raw, early afternoon sun brought out a sweat that hung under my arms and spread across my chest. I was anxious about what lay ahead, but within minutes apprehension was overwhelmed by the joy of movement. I was walking, performing a simple action with a clear mind. I was where I wanted to be – at the beginning. The beginning of a four-month, 2,700-kilometre solo trek through the Western and Central Himalayas.

There are events in life that consume you. This walk and my brother Gareth's death are such occurrences for me, and with the clarity of retrospect I realize just how intimately they are connected. I know now it was Gareth who brought me to the Himalayas.

On a cold January night my little brother drowned in Elk Lake, British Columbia.

He had gone there that afternoon to train with the University of Victoria rowing team. Two eighteen-metre, eight-man-plus-coxswain rowing shells set out onto the water. It was breezy but there was nothing threatening about the conditions. Then around five p.m. a sudden ferocious storm blew up off the Pacific Ocean to the southwest. The crews in the two shells pulled madly on the oars to make it to shore but quickly one of them was swamped by the rising waves. The motorized coach boat picked up that first crew, but the four-and-a-half-metre, aluminum-hulled runabout was hopelessly overloaded and it too was swamped near the lake's edge. The rowers struggled onto dry land through vicious surf. It was now 5:30 p.m. and winter darkness had fallen.

On the lake Gareth's boat had taken on water and was sinking. The nine-man crew was holding onto the broken, upturned hull and being washed over by two-metre waves. The lake was four degrees Celsius. It took three-quarters of an hour for hypothermia to take my brother. I'm told it's a peaceful way to die. In the cold and chaos of the storm he slipped, unseen by his struggling crewmates, from the wreckage. I still think about his perfect, lean body floating inert on the furious surface of the lake and then quietly dropping, like an autumn leaf, to the lake floor.

The following day would have been Gareth's birthday. He was with us only hours short of nineteen years. He was a gentle, good-hearted soul, someone you could wish no harm towards and I was blessed to have him in my life. I can't think about him without seeing his big-toothed, face-consuming smile. He was the kind of person who fit in anywhere because he found the fun in every situation, not brimming with confidence – at eighteen years old he hadn't hit his stride yet – but someone who made you feel welcome. He was nearly two metres tall, a thin, gangly kid still growing into his body, but there was an emergent stability about him; you could feel the confidence of manhood rising. He was handsome with a narrow classically proportioned face, blue eyes sparkling with energy, and a lean strength in his frame.

I was his older brother, four years difference, and for most of my teenage years he was the little brother with too many questions and too many requests to tag along. Sometimes I treated him harshly, scolding words and cold shoulders and in that there's regret for me, but Gareth has taught me many lessons, the first of which is that remorse can be the catalyst for great change.

Losing Gareth was something more distressing than I could ever have imagined. Two years of aimless wandering consumed me following his death. Cross-country ski racing, which for years had been my passion, held no attraction. At university I drifted and my studies suffered. Relationships dissipated before anything solid could develop. I had little interest in my own future, never mind one involving someone else. Without the structure that training for ski racing had given me I slid into apathy. I needed a focus and slowly the dreams of my childhood resurfaced.

I have always had a fascination with the Himalayas, and had devoured Chris Bonington's, Doug Scott's and Reinhold Messner's mountaineering books with awe. The Himalayas were my dream mountains. The aftermath of Gareth's death was all dreams and nightmares.

I went to the Himalayas for a single season's trekking, but that transformed into eight years amongst those magnificent peaks. By the time I started my solo trek I had already spent five seasons in the Himalayas. My time was split between forestry work in Northern Canada from April until August and autumns and winters in the mountains of South Asia. While in India and Nepal I worked occasionally as a trekking guide, but since I made enough money from forestry most of my time was spent hiking alone, studying Buddhism and learning Hindi and Tibetan languages.

Over those years, the Himalayas developed as my sanctuary and in a quiet way walking became the means through which I could fathom my loss. Walking induces clarity; its pace and simplicity engenders contemplation. In the conscious motion of my footsteps was heightened awareness. Walking became my filter – the goodness I experienced in the Himalayas came to me from the ground up.

But after five years I saw that immersion was the only means by which I could integrate the decency I had found in the mountains. So I decided to connect the pieces of the

Himalayas' cultural and geographic jigsaw puzzle in one long, uninterrupted, solo trek. I planned a walk that would take me from the Indus River in the west to the Mahakali River in the east, from Northern Pakistan through India to the western border of Nepal.

It would be a trip through seasons, landscapes and religions. Over the course of 2,700 kilometres I would meet Muslims, Buddhists, Hindus and animists; traverse jungle, desert and high alpine areas; climb to over 5,000 metres; and descend into rain forest-shrouded canyons. But most importantly the walk would let me be one-on-one with the people who make those mountains so magical.

MUSLIM HIMALAYAS

CHAPTER 1
Live as Best You Can

August 7

The path into the mountains followed the steep-walled gorge of the Astore River. Thousands of years of unceasing white water had carved the broad fissure through shaly, Paleozoic rock. The sun was framed by the canyon's ochre walls. Its heat worked deep into the chasm.

I was following the only road up the valley, and at times the route was cut directly into the walls of the canyon. By the river it was hot and wet, but when the track pulled up and out of the gorge the air was desert dry. In the eight hours I spent on that first day's trek I saw no one walking; a few jeeps rumbled past me, blowing their horns and spewing thick, altitude-choked clouds of exhaust, but I was the only person on foot along that desolate stretch of road. Even in the small village of Mangdoian the houses appeared deserted, no sign of even a tea stall. But I was not alone. Himalayan marmots chirped from the scree slopes above, and by the river there were birds. A few hours into the walk a red start landed on a nearby boulder, bowing, flaring its ruby tail. Shimmering black choughs

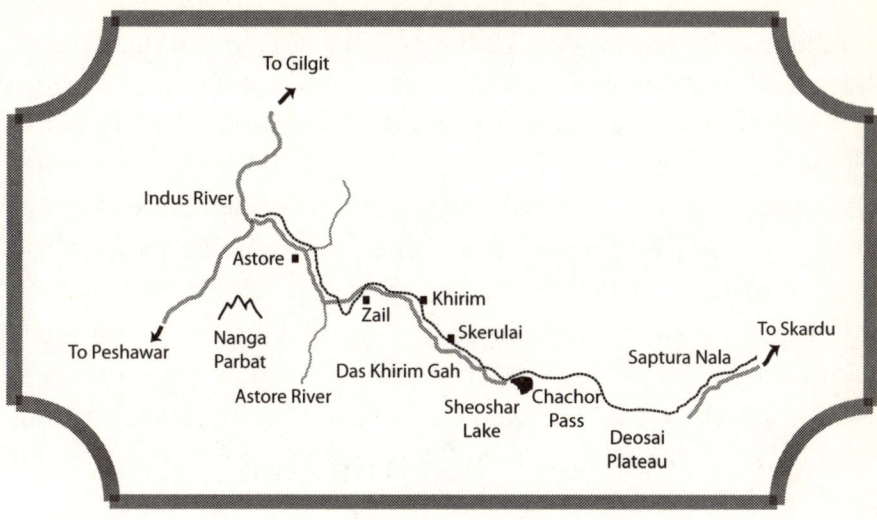

GILGIT, NORTHERN AREAS, PAKISTAN

followed, three in a pack, their scarlet beaks chattering. Not long after, six pigeons swooped by centimetres from my head.

Late in the afternoon the Astore Valley's first significant greenery appeared. Poplar trees were planted in straight lines, their heart-shaped leaves already tinged in gold, the first signs of fall at 2,500 metres. Not long after the plantation I saw the outskirts of Astore village. Astore is a ragged collection of low, mud-brick houses interspersed with a few corrugated steel government buildings: warehouses, the post office, a telephone exchange. Barbed wire was everywhere – by the side of the road, between the walls of houses and around irrigation canals and barns. I rounded another bend and saw the village bazaar, a cluster of small one-storey buildings balanced ten metres above a broad alluvial fan of river stones on the water's edge.

I took a room in Astore's only guest house then went to explore the village. The few dusty alleys, the vegetable bazaar and half a dozen flat-roofed shops took only a few minutes to browse. A mosque, a bank and a gun shop stood out as the most diligently maintained buildings. I lingered by the gun shop. It was an anomaly, clean, orderly and fronted with a self-closing aluminum and glass door. Its neatness attracted me, but it was fear that pulled me inside.

As a child in Belfast I remember watching British Army patrols on the streets; the men, drawn out in single file, moved in unison, quickly, stealthily, doorway to doorway, while my friends and I played scrappy soccer in the rain. To us kids the soldiers always looked the same: bulky flak jackets, helmets, pale faces drawn in concentration, eyes flicking back and forth – snipers or anonymous bombers were the constant threat – and always their hands gripped tight to matte black self-loading rifles. Maybe the real draw of the Astore gun shop was its potential for me to trace an old fear to its source.

I left the garbage-strewn alley; inside the place was all leather and steel. Along one wall, to the rear of a wood and glass counter, the goods were tidily displayed – Russian, Chinese, American, German and Pakistani automatic, semi-automatic, and bolt-action rifles – all arranged as to calibre, nationality and price. There was a greater selection of weapons at the gunsmith's than of vegetables in the bazaar.

The owner sat behind the counter, his generous girth smothering the stool beneath him. He wore a spotless shirt and trouser suit, the traditional salwar khamiz. His face was covered by an unruly black beard glistening from an application of coconut oil. His close-cropped head was crowned by a flat-topped woolen hat.

He smiled in the effortless way of good salesmen, not appearing surprised at all by the arrival of a foreigner. He asked if I wanted tea and motioned for me to sit. I dropped onto a cheap white plastic patio chair and he ordered a boy outside to fetch us tea. Mr. Abdul Salim introduced himself, adding in accented English,

"Welcome to my shop. How can I help you?"

I lied about my reasons for being there, feigning a hunter's interest in his guns. Abdul nodded, but I could tell he was suspicious and in way of compliment I inquired why his business was so much better kept than its neighbours. This was the segue he needed to launch into an explanation of local gun culture. Handling a gun in Pakistan, he explained, is a man's rite of passage, a part of every male's role in defending his family's honour.

Pakistan is an area of terminal instability and defending your family in such an environment means possessing a weapon. The Northern Areas' recent history is particularly violent. In 1889 the principality of Gilgit fell under British rule and, as it straddles the border between India and Afghanistan, became a strategic outpost of British India. When British rule came to an end in 1947, the region was handed over to the state of Kashmir. This was the year of independence and partition for India and Pakistan. Maharaja Hari Singh of Kashmir delayed his decision in joining his Muslim-majority state with Pakistan or India. In Gilgit a battalion of the British Indian Army (soon to be absorbed into the Pakistani Army), the Gilgit Scouts, mutinied and declared the area a republic. A few days later Pakistan declared the entire Northern Areas within its borders and invaded the valley of Kashmir from the west and north. Maharajah Hari Singh asked for India's assistance and the Indian Army reached the valley before the Pakistanis and held off the invasion. The result was the traditional borders of Kashmir were sliced in two and the whole of northwestern India and Pakistan have been in a state of flux ever since.

Mr. Salim told me his was the largest weapons market in the area. I was shocked there was more than one. It was disturbing to think that a village of Astore's size needed such an array of firepower. The recent tide of surplus weapons from Afghanistan, he said, had put sophisticated weaponry within reach of many villagers.

I asked if he thought there were negative aspects to the number of guns in the district.

He looked at me, furrowing his brow.

"Allah does not love the aggressor, my friend," he said. "But a man must defend his family. This is his duty."

To move the discussion away from such a delicate subject I asked how business was. He smiled and admitted that, with the ongoing troubles in Kashmir and Afghanistan, "demand was up."

Mr. Salim was generous with his time. He showed me dozens of weapons, disassembling the guns with the precise snap and click of a man comfortable with his goods. My reticence in handling them amused him.

I told him of my plans to walk to Nepal and immediately he offered me a gun at a bargain price. I declined the antique, wooden-stocked, bolt-action rifle; it would have been comically conspicuous strapped to my backpack. Abdul shook his head in disbelief. He could not comprehend someone undertaking such a journey without a weapon.

By the third cup of tea it was obvious I was not a customer and our conversation petered out agreeably. We shook hands, I stepped outside and an old man in an undyed woolen cloak brushed past offering me the traditional Muslim words of greeting,

"*A Salam Alaykum.*" May peace be upon you.

That first night I stayed in the town's single guest house. The front desk was a table in the dining room on which I signed multiple forms, all of which asked for my father's name in full.

The owner sat unmoving on the other side of the table. He was a large man with the requisite beard and salwar khamiz. In my short time there I never saw him without a scowl on his face. He didn't offer his name and I didn't ask. I was the hotel's only guest.

In the narrow concrete-walled bedroom two single beds, steel cots really, were pushed against opposite walls. I dropped my pack onto one and the metal frame groaned. Pencilled onto the plaster behind the headboard were a few pieces of graffiti in elegant Urdu script, but one phrase, just above the pillow, in off-kilter, thickly printed English stood out: GOD IS GREAT, SUPER GREAT.

As instructed, at six p.m. I went to the empty dining room. Only one table was set with cutlery. I looked over the menu, where meat dishes dominated the hand-written single sheet of cardboard. I usually don't eat meat. When the owner asked for my preference I ordered rice and lentils. He wrote out the request, stopped writing, paused a second, and asked, "And what kind of meat?" I repeated I just wanted rice and lentils. He looked up from his dog-eared notepad, sucked on a strand of beard he had dragged to his lip and stared at me. I tried to ignore him.

In two minutes a child no more than eight years old brought the meal from the kitchen; the rice was hot, the lentils cold.

August 8

I was up before the sun, but the manager was there in the dining room reading an Urdu newspaper. I asked if I could have coffee and some toast, both of which had been on the menu I'd seen the night before. He nodded, went to the kitchen and in a short time returned with tea and chapatis, the ubiquitous round, unleavened bread of the subcontinent.

From Astore I moved south in the direction of Tarshing village, but ten kilometres before it I turned southeast up the valley of the Das Khirim River. This is the route to Deosai Plateau and farther on to the Indus River. Nanga Parbat, the ninth highest peak in the world, lay over the ridge to the west. The valley walls obscured the view, so I decided to climb in search of the mountain. At the hamlet of Zail I crossed the river on a tottering log bridge and began the ascent.

The trail was steep and passed through golden terraces of wheat. The grain waved in the breeze, the stalks bent in tunnelled patterns, serpent traces swept through fields and disappeared into the surrounding forest.

After about fifteen minutes I realized I was the focus of two pairs of eyes. On my left two small boys, half-hidden in the paddies, stared at me. They had followed me from the village. I looked over and they glanced at the ground, avoiding eye contact, too shy to talk. Their hair was the colour of wheat, their eyes that of the sky. According to local legend, blond-haired Baltis are the distant offspring of Alexander the Great's army that had fought its way from Macedonia to the banks of the Indus 2,400 years ago.

At the age of those boys Peter, my older brother, Katrina, my younger sister, Gareth and I had had the same blond hair and blue eyes. We were inquisitive, irrepressible children. Belfast was rife with prejudice and hatreds but in truth we'd had a secure and carefree childhood. We'd amused ourselves with wooden guns, played daily games of IRA versus the British Army, all the while knowing that in our Presbyterian world the Brits had to win. When we ventured downtown with my mother we ogled the soldiers, simultaneously scared and impressed by them. We never saw the IRA. They were everywhere and nowhere.

During lunch hours we fought Catholic boys from the denominational school built directly behind our public one. It was absurd that a Catholic institution had been constructed just across the fence from our Protestant one because in the sectarian cauldron of Northern Ireland it was inevitable the students would clash. There was no reason for those confrontations beyond the untried, deep-seated assumption by us Protestant kids that Catholics were bad. Now it's awkward for me to think of those senseless brawls. But through it all my brothers and sister and I thrived. We genuinely enjoyed each other's company.

Gareth was the baby. Katrina as the only sister warranted special behaviour but Gareth was exceptional by being the last in the line. He was always the last one picked in teams for our mock battles or endless football games, but at the same time we knew that he, as the baby, should not, could not be hurt. Maybe it was fear of our mother's wrath – "Don't you dare hurt the baby!" – or just an innate sense of protectiveness, but Gareth rarely got injured in our skirmishes and in the full-contact nature of our childhood that was something special. I like to think it was because we loved him for what he was, the "wee man," the "littlest one."

Halfway up the ridge I rested on a flattened boulder. A shepherd came silently from the far side of the creek and sat close to me. We nodded; no words were exchanged. I could smell woodsmoke on his frayed shirt, the manky trace odours of his flock and the sprig of mint perched behind his left ear. We watched the river. He nudged me. I turned to see his hand brimming with tiny apricots. He smiled, revealing a file of broken teeth. The fruit was firm, the flesh juicy, the transparent amber skins dappled in red. We saved the pits so he could later extract their almond-like kernels. I washed the sweetness down with ice-cold water and said "Shukria," thanks.

The shepherd spoke little Urdu, only the local Tibetan-related, Balti language. The year before I had spent three months at a language school in the Indian Himalayan hill-station town of Mussoorie intensively learning Hindi, which is related to the Pakistani national language, Urdu. So far I had been able to communicate with most of the people I had met. However, in situations such as with the shepherd, where spoken language was stymied, body language took over.

Before us the steep path continued. The shepherd motioned that he was heading for his flock in the high meadows and would guide me up. It was obvious the older man was used to the grade. With a ten-kilogram sack over one shoulder and tattered canvas sneakers dangling from his feet he skipped from rock to rock, negotiating the precipitous track with well-worn grace. It was his land; I was a stumbling apprentice.

As the trail levelled we emerged from the pine forest and before us stretched a small, thickly grassed field. On the far side, tight into the hillside, lay the shepherd's hut, a stone shanty with thin, vertical, slit-hole windows and a low-angled wood-shingle roof patched with moss. Between us and the cabin lay a narrow pond, the water motionless in the ridge's wind shadow. Above us the hill rose another two hundred vertical metres and beyond the crest, squarely behind the hut, peeked the icy summit of Nanga Parbat.

The shepherd busied himself cleaning the hut, sweeping the slate floor with a whisk of birch twigs and rearranging his meagre kitchen utensils on a stone shelf above the soot-blackened fireplace. Within minutes he had built a fire and was boiling water. In the doorway of the shack the shepherd prepared tea, a strong bitter brew, black and unsweetened. On the smooth rock of his front step we drank in silence. He indicated he wanted me to stay for dinner, but I was anxious to reach the ridgetop and set up camp before nightfall. With my hands I asked where the trail was and he opened his arms wide, demonstrating that on the thinly forested ground above us the way to the ridgeline was whichever way I chose.

Another hour of heart-pounding scrambling and I reached the summit. I sat down breathlessly on a boulder jutting horizontally from the slope. To the south, in the dying light, the Astore River cut a jagged path down the wide basin, a silver thread stitching together patchworked fields. Along Nanga Parbat's base the valley floor was checkered with green and gold paddies, their colour dependent upon the ripening barley. Tracks and mercurial streams broke the cultivated geometry. Human sign was muted, fused with the earth. A few single-storey dwellings dotted the landscape, insignificant against the great mountain's massif. The peak's face was sheer and immensely broad, its shoulders flexed outwards, pushing against the sky. It was not an inviting mountain; it was imposing, a convoluted mass of stone and ice that demanded respect.

The summit was wreathed in erratic cloud. Behind it the sun eased to the horizon, its descent accompanied by laser-rays of sunlight, emanating from the peak itself, breaking the clouds in every direction. It was a vast Japanese ink-brush fantasy.

Two hundred metres ahead of me, out over the valley a silver-black lammergeier, a bearded vulture, circled, scanning the fields below for carrion and small animals. In the last light it was searching for its evening meal. The sunset wore on, the flush transformed to gold, to carnelian, to bloody red, and then, as suddenly as the magical light had developed, it disappeared and the valley fell to darkness.

I set up my tent in pitch black, a two-man tunnel design rated to withstand four seasons of inclement weather. It was forest green and sat tight to the earth like a mossy boulder. I liked it because it was functional and strong. Lying down on my sleeping bag I felt as if I was in an emerald cave, safe and warm. On the inside of the roof I'd tied strings of Tibetan prayer flags, red, green, blue, yellow and white. When the tent was erected, the lines of flags drew taut and the interior was imbued with a faint sanctity.

I pitched the tent by touch. Without looking I let my fingers slip the thin aluminum poles into the nylon sleeves that wrapped the shell. These were my house's skeleton and skin. The pole ends I inserted into the floorsheet grommets and voila! Like an instantly inflated hot-air balloon the tent took its half-shell form. Each end of the swaying structure was pegged to the ground and my home was ready. I unrolled a thin yellow foam mat and laid my sleeping bag on top of it. Inside it smelled, not unpleasantly, of old summer sweat, cedar wood and the paraffin edge of ski wax.

At its front the tent sported a small vestibule, just big enough for my boots and cooking gear. From my sleeping bag I could operate the one-burner kerosene stove and each morning I treated myself to instant coffee in bed with dry biscuits.

That night I cooked by the light of a single candle. Dinner was what had become the staple of my time in the Himalayas, rice and dal, the characteristic boiled and spiced lentils of India and Pakistan, cooked together in a compact two-litre pressure cooker. At 2,700 metres the only way to cook hard grains like rice is under pressure. Almost every meal I enjoyed in those great mountains was serenaded by the squeal and whistle of the pressure cooker's off-let steam.

August 9

In the morning I descended back to the Das Khirim River. In the lower meadow the shepherd had left to tend his flock. In the valley the main trail pushed southeast, against the water's flow, up towards the plateau.

I passed three small villages through the afternoon, each huddled into the hillside seeking refuge from the downvalley wind and wintertime avalanches. Early that evening, while I was passing a one-room house on the edge of Khirim village, an old man called me over. He waved his hands, shouted jovially in Urdu and pointed at the door of his shack. I answered with a few words of Urdu and probably gave him the false impression I knew more.

We shook hands and he indicated by holding his forefinger and thumb up to his mouth that he wanted to make me tea. Inside his hut I sat on an uncovered mud-brick bench. Drinks were served with no attempt at conversation and the man immediately returned to the fire to prepare dinner. I realized the sweet, milky tea was just a beginning. He boiled sweet, thumb-sized new potatoes and drizzled them with fresh butter spiced with parsley and chili. We ate in silence. With each bite small clouds of fragrant steam escaped my mouth.

He took my plate and handed me more tea, the fresh milk on its surface pooled in oily bubbles. The plates were washed in a battered aluminum basin then carefully placed above a homemade table near the fire. Finishing this he moved across the room and sat on a metal cot in the far corner. Still he made no effort to talk. I became a little nervous, for although I don't speak much Urdu I wanted to communicate. I was getting up the courage to speak when from out of his robes he pulled a rosary of wooden beads and worked them between his fingers. His lips moved in a quiet address to God and within minutes the evening call to prayer came from the village mosque.

"La Ilaha Illa La." There is no God but God.

In Khirim the mullah's minaret was the second-storey balcony of a log house and it was the power of the priest's own lungs that brought the words of the prophet to the village.

I listened and watched as the old man prostrated, dropping from the straight-backed form of an individual to the crouched position that spoke of our insignificance before God. Every movement was performed with great consciousness. There was a simple decency about the action, his prayer in time with breath and gesture. It was relaxing just watching him perform his prostrations. The food, the mullah's call, the prayers and in the background the river moving ceaselessly to the ocean – for those few minutes in the old man's shack everything was moving as it should.

Northern Pakistan's religious history is as complicated as its geography, and the Northern Areas are a mosaic of beliefs. The region's original animist and pre-Buddhist Bon traditions were absorbed into the wave of Buddhism that overtook the region when it came under control of the Tibetan king Songsten Gampo in the seventh century.

To this day Northern Pakistan is a treasure house of early Buddhist art. A bedraggled American I met in Islamabad, who described himself as a part-time art dealer, told me he had met farmers in the Swat Valley to the southwest of Gilgit who still, when plowing their fields, occasionally unearthed ancient Buddhist statues.

Islam arrived in the fifteenth century with the Iranian Sufi saint Amir Kabir Syed Ali Hamadani. Other Sufi saints followed, including Shah Syed Muhammad Noorbakhsh, and soon the entire area had converted to the Noorbakhshi order of Sufism. Sufism is Islam's more esoteric school. The aim of Sufis is to let go of all notions of duality, including the idea of self or God, and realize a divine unity. Sufism is still a controversial subject within Islam. However, during the nineteenth century the majority of the local population converted again, this time to the Sunni and Shia schools. Now the Baltis are Shia dominated with smaller minorities of Sufi and Sunni followers.

With his responsibilities complete the old man tucked away his rosary and pointed towards a bench in the opposite corner of the shack. He was inviting me to stay the night. It was pitch black outside, too late to find a decent camping spot. I had no choice and so unfurled my mat and sleeping bag. He sat by the fire poking the embers, and as I drifted off to sleep the mullah again launched into the call to prayer and the man unrolled his faded prayer mat.

Wild mountains, the thin, sparkling air and careening rivers are what had initially drawn me to the Himalayas but it was the people that pulled me back again and again. The old man was the latest in a long line of inordinately generous people who had gifted me with unfailing hospitality over the previous five years. In my time in the mountains I had lost track of the number of people who had offered tea, cooked meals and prepared sleeping spaces for me. I had bedded down in kitchens and barns, with horses and sheep, on roofs and verandas. It was an ongoing marvel that I could walk into a village, sit on anyone's mud step and within ten minutes a resident or neighbour was offering me a warm drink.

In Pakistan it was always men who invited me to their homes. In India and Nepal old women, children, men returning from the fields and pregnant women with toddlers in tow offered great kindness. These people rarely asked for payment, and I knew from having asked a few times that offering money was scorned, but often I would leave a concealed offering on the bed where I slept or with the dishes I had eaten from.

August 10

Not surprisingly, I woke to the call to prayer and the old man dropping his brittle frame to the hut's dirt floor. It seemed improper, almost sacrilegious, to interrupt his religious duties and so, feeling like an accidental voyeur, I waited, with one eye closed, in my sleeping bag. When he finished his prostrations he sat meditating, praying and running his prayer beads through his hands. Then he rose and walked out the door. I wasn't sure whether to leave or wait for him to return. I packed my sleeping bag, rolled up my mat and ate some biscuits. He still hadn't returned so, making sure the door was well latched, I left.

As the rough four-wheel-drive track climbed towards the Deosai Plateau the villages petered out. I was reaching the limit of fertile land. Skerulai, at 3,700 metres, was the last settlement before the barren tundra of the high plains. It was hard to believe people eked an existence from such steep, rocky terrain. Just fifty metres above the houses the alpine zone's band of broken stone began.

Skerulai looked temporary. There was no shop, no post office, not even a mosque. It was a migrant camp for those pushed to the edge of the cultivated world.

On my arrival children emerged from behind houses and boulders. They were thin, rough-clothed boys and girls. Seeing a foreigner they charged me en masse. Eerily none asked for the usual pens or rupees or sweets. They gathered in a circle around me and stared. Then one child cupped his hands in the supplicating gesture of Muslim prayer and begged me to take a photo of him. Why did he want a photo? Was it something solid he needed, his face immortalized on film? I didn't take the picture. I didn't take my camera out of my pack. I knew I would never send the image back to Skerulai. When I left, the boy and two friends followed me out of the village. Silently they tracked me for over a kilometre, wiping the snot from their noses with the caked backsides of their sweater sleeves and talking quietly amongst themselves.

An hour out of the village I encountered my first rain. A gentle fog embraced me, loosened, rose and transformed into dark-cored rain clouds. Scree slopes and creeks drifted by in breaths of mist. It was pleasant precipitation until near Chachor Pass. There the hills opened out and the wind picked up. By the time I reached Sheoshar Lake the needles of rain were driving straight into me.

I pitched my tent in the lee of a hillock and climbed, soaking wet, into the nylon shell. From my pack I pulled my kitchen gear, kerosene stove, pressure cooker, pot, water bottle, Swiss Army knife, teaspoon, tablespoon and neat little nylon sacks of food. The stove was in three pieces. I screwed them together and into the small brass cup below the burner poured a few tablespoons of fuel. I set alight a twisted up piece of newspaper and laid it in the bowl. In thirty seconds the burning kerosene had heated the line leading to the burner and vaporized the fuel. I turned the valve, lit a match and *whoosh*! In a contained blast of blue flame the stove jumped to life.

I put the pot of water on to boil. On the ground beside it I measured one cup of rice and half a cup of lentils in the pressure cooker. I added double the amount of water, some salt, a teaspoon of chili and a few pinches of pepper. Taking the boiling water off the flame, I added a tea bag and let it steep off to one side near my boots. The rice pot went on the stove. I laid out my sleeping bag and mat and in the mesh pockets hanging off the wall of the tent stored a flashlight, toilet paper and matches in preparation of a late night call of nature. After adding sugar and milk powder, I relaxed with my cup of tea and waited for the rumble of pressure to build up inside the cooker. Twenty minutes later the hiss of steam and the clatter of the pot's top valve signalled dinner was ready. Into the rice and dal I stirred two tablespoons of butter and straight from the pot I ate my meal accompanied by a cacophony of rain drumming on my fabric roof.

August 11

I was up early, rolled out of my sleeping bag and unzipped the two front panels of the tent. Outside the storm had blown itself out, but fragile clouds gathered around the lake. Sheoshar is not much more than a pond and in the calm after the squall it was mirror flat. As I made breakfast the clouds climbed to a horizontal band fifty metres above the lake. Emerald earth and an azure sky framed a line of white-clad mountains to the northwest. Two crows hopped silently along the lake's far shore, their eyes on me. Marsh marigolds and primulas peeked from the watered draws. The light was sepia-toned, the air dead still. The only sound was the steady, steam engine chugging of my stove. Coffee would soon be ready.

From the lake I trudged northeast over hummocky, rain-soaked grassland. The ground squelched underfoot. The clouds had lifted but the sun was blurred by a thin residual fog. All around were green hills, one-dimensional in the dull light. I could hear the air expanding and contracting through my chest.

It was a dense internal atmosphere, but any loneliness I might have felt disappeared as I topped the next ridge.

Below me was a line of four trucks, stationary on a muddy trail. The front two vehicles were hopelessly mired in the bog. A small crowd had gathered by the lead jeep, watching a single shovel-wielding man do battle with the encasing muck.

I made my way down the hill and at one hundred metres from the vehicles the group turned and stared at me. An excited chatter swelled from the crowd. A man stepped forward and introduced himself. "Sergeant Major Muhammad," he said with his hand outstretched. The soldier explained in English that they were members of a Pakistani Army regiment in the midst of maneuvers, a common event in Northern Pakistan, sandwiched as it is between India, China and Afghanistan. Kashmir, which lay just to the south, had become one of the most hotly contested regions of the world, a place so steeped in nationalistic myth that it had become symbolic to both India and Pakistan's identity.

The 1947 partition of India and Pakistan created the border problem that dogs Kashmir to this day. The once idyllic valley has over the past sixty years, and the last twenty-five in particular, degenerated into a long-term, low-intensity battleground.

In 1987 Muslim political parties complained that the state legislative assembly elections had been rigged by the ruling, pro-Indian, Jammu and Kashmir National Conference party. Losing faith in the democratic process the Islamic parties formed militant wings. Some groups demanded independence for the state of Jammu and Kashmir while others called for union with Pakistan.

Pakistan gave its support to the movement, calling for the issue to be resolved via a United Nations-sponsored referendum. But the government of India maintained that Pakistan supported the insurgency by training and supplying weapons to militant separatists and repeatedly called for

Pakistan to cease the "cross-border terrorism." India also claims that in 1989 Afghanistan mujahideen entered the valley at the end of the Soviet-Afghan war. These seasoned, fanatical fighters dramatically increased the insurgency's violence. The situation in Kashmir has only deteriorated since then. Well over 160,000 Hindu residents have fled, and human rights abuses are common amongst the insurgents and the Indian Army. The Indian government now claims that 65,000 people have died in the conflict.

The army four-by-fours were buried to the floorboards. The soldiers were digging out the space in front of the wheels hoping to drive through the bog. From years of forestry work I knew that the best approach would be to back out of the soft muck and try crossing again on a more stable piece of ground. I suggested this to the sergeant major and offered my assistance. He happily agreed.

We jacked the lead vehicle's front wheels from the mud, pushed it backwards off the pivot, then repeated the action. With each rise and fall we gained six inches. After an hour of hard work the first truck was able to drive around the sinking ground and then drag the second jeep through. It in turn pulled the third vehicle across and the action was repeated until the entire convoy was clear.

The drivers were ecstatic. Their job was to set up the camp before the main body of troops arrived; we had avoided their worst embarrassment, being caught by the infantry. In addition, just as the towrope was unhitched from the last vehicle the commanding officer arrived. Everyone stood ramrod straight, fists clenched by their sides. From the passenger seat of his gleaming jeep the officer gave a token inspection of the churned-up swamp. He called out, "Good driving boys, good driving," not knowing it had taken two hours to navigate the 200-metre section.

The sergeant major stepped up and gave an account of our labours. I recognized my name amongst the patter of Urdu. The colonel looked me up and down, motioned me over to his jeep, said he was grateful for my contribution and invited me for afternoon tea.

The officer's four-by-four pulled off the track a hundred metres past the bog. From a second jeep soldiers extracted wicker hampers and large tin boxes. Within minutes they had assembled an impressive picnic: thermoses of hot drinks, sandwiches, rice, meats, curried vegetables, biscuits and cakes, all laid out on a handwoven, tribal-patterned, woolen mat.

The colonel had been writing notes in his jeep and when a junior officer told him, "Snacks are ready, sir," he stepped out, walked over to the picnic and lay on the grass off to one side of the rugs. He looked every bit the latter-day pasha. He was a handsome man in his early fifties with thick black hair and a deftly trimmed moustache. He wore the requisite officer corps aviator sunglasses, a freshly ironed shirt and well-creased trousers. As we began the meal, the infantrymen started to pass us on the trail. Some looked bedraggled, others exhausted, but all of them straightened their backs and regained some sense of formation before throwing a salute as they passed the colonel.

What a scene – me in a grubby black T-shirt and greasy hair, the colonel in immaculate khaki sitting together sipping tea in the most isolated corner of Pakistan while platoon after platoon of Islamic warriors marched before us.

Throughout the "snacks" Colonel Ikram lectured me on how his religion had developed in a time of social and political disorder on the Arabian Peninsula. The Prophet Muhammad, he told me, was a stabilizing force and the army in Islam had become an instrument to insure that stability.

"We are the tools of Allah," he said, gesturing with his open Swiss Army knife towards the passing soldiers.

The colonel was a God-fearing man, and when I let slip that I was interested in all religions, he started into a spontaneous denunciation of Hinduism. "It is a colourful belief with all those bright gods," he said, going on to describe Hindus as "children only able to concentrate on the deity that was before them."

The meal finished and the peons cleaned up. The colonel stood, delicately brushing bread crumbs from his shirt. He offered me a lift and what he promised would be a "proper" dinner in his regiment's next camp. I politely declined.

August 12

Knotted clouds pitched across the morning sky. To the west the high Himalayas were bright with fresh snow. The sun emerged from behind bristly peaks. Light and shadow wove in spotlight sweeps across the grasslands. In the shadow of clouds the scene was ashen and then, in the blink of an eye, the sun was released and insipid colours were shot neon.

I headed for the 4,500-metre Malak Mar Pass on the northwestern edge of the plateau and along the way Deosai produced new surprises. The west of the plateau was abloom in an ocean of knee-high wild flowers. The breeze lifted waves of colour. I found myself wading through rainbows of gentians, primulas, irises, violas and asters – magentas and golds, violets and jades, ruby and indigo. The earth trembled with colour.

Close to the pass I came upon a large shepherd camp. A tall man with a Romanesque nose and eyebrows like two hairy black caterpillars walked parallel to me. He intentionally crossed my path and nodded dourly. Then, in answer to my jaunty head shake, he smiled and in decent English invited me for tea. He held out his hand, made the tiniest of bows and introduced himself as Karim.

I was hesitant. I had consciously avoided the few groups of shepherds I had seen in the area. This was the legacy of a tale told to me by a friend who had guided in the region for many years. An acquaintance of his, an experienced trekker, had been solo walking on Deosai when he was set upon one evening by a group of herdsmen. They had looted his camp. The main gang had left, but three men stayed on and when their accomplices were out of earshot, had pinned him to the grass and raped him.

In the five years I had spent in the Himalayas I had never had anything but extreme generosity from the people I met. I didn't want this to be any different. Down a small hill I followed Karim to a hut that was larger but of the same flat-roofed, mud-cemented stone construction as the shepherd's above the Khirim River. Woodsmoke wafted from holes in the roof. Karim pulled aside a filthy shard of blanket that acted as a door and I crouched to enter the hovel.

It was dark, but three shafts of light fell from the openings above the fires. The one large room was less than a metre and a half tall. I stood hunched over. The air was thick with a fug of livestock, musty sweat and rancid milk. My eyes adjusted slowly to the dim light. Eventually, I could see a half-dozen shepherds squatting on worn stones against the walls. They were a dishevelled gang, their features hardened by the sun. Everyone wore the shepherd's garb, undyed homespun cloaks over western-style shirts and baggy pajama trousers. Most sported the ubiquitous flat-top Balti hat tilted at a different rakish angle. I shook the hands that were presented out of darkness. Thick fingers, lanolin soft, smothered mine.

I was offered a seat, a flattened boulder near the fire. Tea was offered. I had an audience and felt uneasy, too conscious of my differences and of being the centre of attention. But conversation evolved naturally. Karim translated – how accurately I will never know. At one point an elder spoke for two minutes, and Karim's translation was, "He says he's very old."

I was told that more than sixty men from Satpura village, the closest settlement to the east, spend their summers on Deosai. From mid-June to the start of September they tended their flocks on the plateau. After the snow melts the ground is waterlogged but with the summer sun a deep carpet of grass covers the plain, perfect fodder for thousands of goats and sheep that are herded up from the valleys. The shepherds' days are spent following their animals, but evenings are passed smoking the hookah pipe, drinking strong tea and, most importantly, telling stories.

By the second cup of tea the shepherds' tales had begun. As an outsider possibly they saw me as some kind of confessor because immediately they launched into the difficulties involved in the changes that had recently overtaken their traditional lives: falling prices for mutton and goat; rising prices for wheat, rice and kerosene; the number of villagers moving to the city; the warmer, drier winters in their villages. It was the kind of recounting of woes I'd heard from aunts and uncles as a child in Ireland; start by telling how bad things are and the yarn can only get better.

Then the trajectory of the storytelling changed and they began to tell me about the Himalayan brown bears that live on the plateau. For centuries the bears and the shepherds have been adversaries. The bears stole sheep and the shepherds guarded against them. Over the previous decades the herds of livestock, which were increasing in size, had had to move farther inside the bear's range. More sheep and goats were disappearing and more tension had developed between predator and protector. The shepherds conceded that they would be happy if there were no bears on the plateau at all. Yes, they admitted they had killed bears, but the bears killed their sheep and had, according to legend, killed humans, although no one in the hut could recall any victims. They were frustrated that the government had declared the southern part of the plateau a wildlife reserve. There had been no consultation with the shepherds. But more annoying for them was the bureaucracy that came with the park, another layer of governmental interference.

One of the younger shepherds, an energetic guy with a baseball hat amateurishly printed with the logo PAKISTAN CRICKET, piped up. "The army is here. Why don't they administer the park?"

An old man, one of the few who had not engaged in the conversation, laughed and said a few sentences in Balti. Karim said, "He's laughing because he's seen army officers out shooting bears."

The only time I had ever seen a Himalayan brown bear was in New Delhi. I was walking through the faded Edwardian grandeur of Connaught Circle on a sticky-hot monsoon evening when a chained and toothless bear had staggered onto the sidewalk in front of me. Its fur was matted, it walked with a painful hobble, its claws were snipped. The owner trailed at the far end of a chain; his yellowed teeth and weepy eyes matched the bear's uncared-for appearance.

With an unctuous grin he asked if I wanted to see the bear dance then poked the listless animal with a stick. The scene was pathetic. I quickly moved on, not saying a word, but couldn't help staring back at the sorry pair.

I left the shepherds giving thanks, shaking hands and declining a dinner invitation. There was no sense of threat but an uneasiness lingered, the residue of old stories impossible to forget.

I pitched my tent far from their camp and lay that night with my Swiss Army knife close at hand. Bears came to me in my dreams. Fear, in all its forms, was something I had come to the Himalayas to face.

Gareth's passing had evoked a previously unknown fear in me – that of untimely death. The thought of not living eighty fruitful years was something that had rarely crossed my mind until then. My grandparents had all died after long and fulfilling lives. I can only remember them smiling and full of enthusiasm. Gareth's death was abrupt and terrifyingly final. I realized the same could happen to me. It wasn't that I was scared of death, but I was afraid that there was so much more to live for and that at any moment it could be taken from me. In the years after his death I had been without moorings. I drank and experimented with drugs partly to ignore his absence. What was the point in focusing on the future when it was so uncertain? I know now that much of the lethargy that drew me down through those years was a result of not finding motives to push past life's unpredictability.

Walking in the Himalayas opened me up. The flip side of Gareth's passing was the understanding of the urgency of this life. "Live as best you can" were the words that summed up how I wanted to lead my life after I slowly found my footing in the wake of his death. It became my mantra, something I repeated on buses and in bookshops, at dinner and as I fell asleep. Living a good life was my way forward.

CHAPTER 2
Turquoise and Coral

August 13

My route down off the Deosai Plateau followed the Satpura River. From its wellspring on the northeast corner of the plateau it meanders to the edge of the tableland, drops abruptly into a steep canyon and hurtles to meet the Indus at Skardu, the largest, most important town in Baltistan and the strategic lynchpin of the region.

For millennia shepherds had led their flocks up narrow trails through the gorge, but now the Pakistani Army has sliced a tenuous four-wheel-drive trail along its banks. The river, however, is undaunted and in the rainy season it presses with even greater force through the breach.

After the silence of the plateau the water's constant roar was intrusive. Slowly, over a day of walking beside it, the river's hum absorbed me. Everything else became peripheral. I lost track of time; the sun moved overhead. I focused on the single footstep ahead of me and gradually, from behind the rush, a rhythm evolved. It was not water or wind; it was a thumping

Turquoise and Coral   33

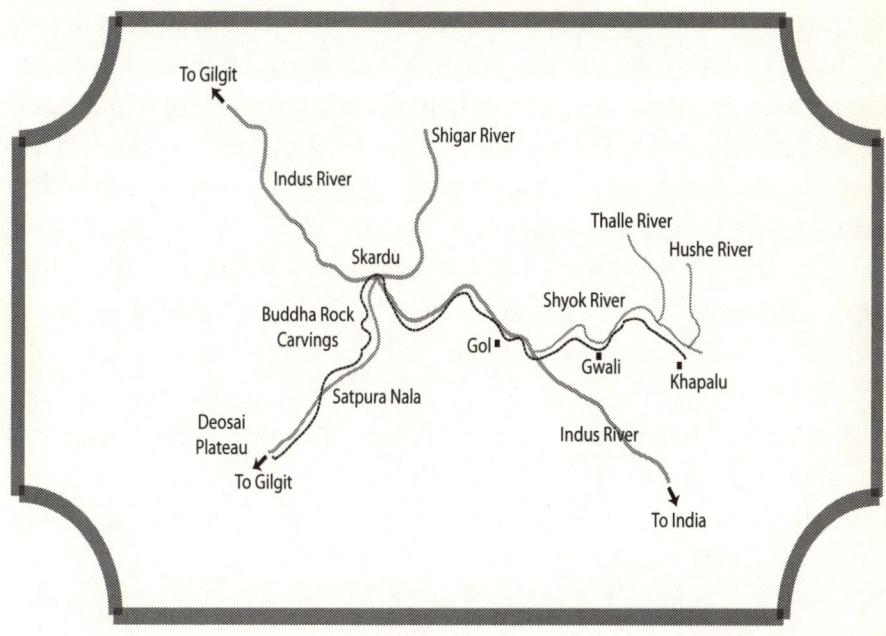

SKARDU, NORTHERN AREAS, PAKISTAN

pulse. *Whuuuump, whuuuump, whuuuump.* I would stop, shake my head, but the beat continued. I let my pace work with the sound, let my mind drift, until ten kilometres farther on the canyon opened out onto a stony plain and the river slowed its pace. The echoing walls of the gorge gave way to weather-beaten, boulder-strewn flats and the expanse ahead absorbed the water's music.

Water was the last sound Gareth heard. The lake roaring, a northeast wind whipping the caps off two-metre-high waves. The boys in the water knew they had to stay in contact. The boat was upturned and snapped in two, and there was the worry that the crew would drift apart. So they called out their seat numbers, one to nine, rotating around the shell. Human sound was the verification they were all still there, still alive. The cold leeched into them; no one had more energy than what they needed to call out that single-syllabled number. Eventually, Gareth lost the energy to call his number; he lost his sound, and slipped from the smooth fibreglass hull. Underwater I imagine he wouldn't have heard the crash of waves and the howl of the wind. Maybe there in the cool, peaceful, enveloping blackness he would have heard the same pulse that tracked me down the Satpura, the subliminal thump, pulsing gently, merging with the slowing beat of his own heart.

On the riverbed five kilometres before Skardu, I diverged from the main trail in search of a rock carving that a man selling camping gear in the Gilgit bazaar had brought to my attention the week before. On the map I'd bought from him he had pointed to the spot on the unfolded paper where it roughly lay and described it as a "great example" of Baltistan's Buddhist history, a ten-metre-tall miniature copy of the Bamiyan Buddha carvings in Afghanistan.

Half an hour of exploration and I found the stonework. It was half the size the man claimed, about five metres tall, a granite boulder sitting alone, well removed from a cliff to the west. On its sheer northeast aspect was a large, full body carving of a Buddhist bodhisattva, a great teacher. The chiselwork was mellowed by two thousand years of wind and rain but still you could see the folds in the monk's robes and the elongated node on top of his skull, one of the eighty-four signs of a Buddha. The image was surrounded by Apsaras – Buddhist angels – and a scrolled frame of Sanskrit writing.

Until Islam arrived in the eighth century Buddhism had been south-central Asia's dominant religion. In the early years after conversion Islam eradicated Buddhism's physical remnants – monasteries, shrines and temples – but simple, village stonework, too modest to challenge new powers, has endured. The Bamiyan Buddhas in Central Afghanistan were the best example, until they were blown up by the Taliban in 2001.

Thin clouds stirred above the carving. A rhododendron bush flashed scarlet in the ribboned sunlight. A thicket of wild rose at the stone's base swayed, heavy with bloom. Two magpies, iridescent black and white, leaped from rock to rock, eyeing me suspiciously. Cirrus clouds crossed the sun, shadows gathered on the stone, the bodhisattva's body darkened and lost definition.

For Buddhists, the body is a shell, a flimsy layer of skin and bone that decays second by second from the moment we are born. The corpse is merely a vehicle in which the soul travels through this life. My life, up until Gareth's death, had been focused on my body. The muscles and mind I had been gifted were well suited to the long-distance pain of cross-country ski racing. I had loved what I could do: run for hours through forests and over mountains, ride my bike across entire continents. On and on and on – I was an endurance machine. In those days my body was a vehicle for the discovery of the outside world, not a vessel for my mind. But in the end, when it needed to prove itself the most, it had let me down.

The night Gareth died I was in Sweden. I had been training since September in the Alps and later in the Arctic Circle in Scandanavia. It was my year, the year I would race my first Olympics. I was a full-time cross-country ski racer. The two previous years I'd spent competing on the World Cup circuit. Like my brother I was a dedicated athlete.

The same afternoon as Gareth's accident the team coach and manager, Christer and Hugo, called me into their office in the small town of Idre Fjall. I sat in a beaten old armchair, its innards bursting from frayed corners and edges. They looked nervous. Christer had flecks of Swedish chewing tobacco stuck to his teeth. Hugo didn't look me in the eye.

"Jono," said the manager, "I'll get to the point. You won't be racing in the Olympics."

He said he wasn't happy with the decision but word had come from higher up the sporting hierarchy that my times in the qualifying races were not up to the standard. I had been cut. After years of training focused on a single goal this was like telling me I needed to have a limb amputated. I was in shock. I complained I was still moving towards my season's peak performance and that selections should be decided closer to the Olympics, but my protests were met with embarrassed silence.

I stepped outside into the freezing midday sun of northern Sweden. I was numb on the outside, hollow on the inside. I had to lean against the wooden panelling of the cabin and I still had no idea that my brother was dead.

A few of my teammates walked by without a word. They knew already. It was as if I was a leper. Being cut from the Olympic squad was the plague none of them could risk catching.

I went back to my room, curled up on the single bed and cried. Ten years I'd committed, a decade of getting faster and faster, my body modifying itself, becoming a machine to move fast and long, and yet the transformation was incomplete; when I needed it the most, during the selection races, my body didn't have the extra centimetres of speed I needed. I couldn't help but feel that ten years had been wasted.

Yes, the body is a vessel gradually changing with time, but Gareth's body had gone through an infinitely more tragic transformation. It had shut down in the brutal cold of Elk Lake. His thin film of insulating fat had done nothing to stave off the deadly grip of the freezing water. In less than an hour he had changed from an almost perfect human body to a lifeless husk.

August 14

The Skardu plain is one of the few broadenings of the Indus during its passage through Northern Pakistan. As the flattest, most fertile land in the region, the forty-kilometre stretch of ground at the confluence of the Indus and Shigar rivers has been of strategic importance to every invader with a claim to the region. The area is littered with their relics: the Buddhist stone art of the Greeks, Kushan, and Ghandaran eras, the lonely hilltop forts of Sikh and Dogra invaders from the Punjab and Jammu in the south, and now the Pakistani Army's long rows of corrugated steel Quonset huts.

In Skardu you realize the extent of the military's power in South Asia. The army is everywhere. Soldiers are conspicuous on the streets, every fourth vehicle is painted khaki and sandbagged sentry posts stand at every intersection. The area is constantly on the verge of conflict. Baltistan was the scene of intense fighting during the India-Pakistan wars of 1947, 1965 and 1971. In 1999 a border war broke out between Pakistani irregulars and the Indian Army forty kilometres south of Skardu near the Indian town of Kargil. This was the first fighting between the two countries after they had each tested nuclear bombs in May 1998. Over a period of fifty days the Indian Army gradually pushed back the intruders. In Pakistan, the aftermath caused major instability and on October 12, 1999, a coup d'etat by the military elevated army chief Pervez Musharraf to power.

In 2001-2002 a huge military buildup occurred in the region in response to a terrorist attack on the Indian Parliament on December 13, 2001. India blamed Pakistan for supporting the Lashkar-e-Taiba and Jaish-e-Muhammad Islamic fundamentalist groups who initated the attack and in a show of force amassed 500,000 military personnel along the border. Pakistan replied with 120,000 soldiers. It was the largest buildup of troops since the 1971 war. The tension de-escalated following diplomatic pressure and a speech by President Musharraf promising a crackdown on Islamic extremists groups in Pakistan.

This brinkmanship plays into the hands of both countries' security forces. Since both countries are created entities – India is an amalgamation of more than five hundred princely states and Pakistan was arbitrarily sliced from the right flank of India – a common enemy has proved useful in the creation of national identities. In India, with its multicultural chaos, to be Indian is to not be Pakistani, and in Pakistan to be Pakistani is to be Muslim and not Indian.

I arrived in Skardu from the south on a rough road that followed the Satpura River. After the quietude of the Deosai Plateau Skardu seemed a lively, bustling town. In the summer dozens of mountaineering expeditions gather to organize on their way to the great 8,000-metre summits of K2, the Gasherbrum group and Broad Peak. The area has one of the densest concentrations of spectacular peaks in the world and during the dry season Skardu is filled with height-crazed adventurers.

In the main bazaar, a fly-infested, blue and green tarp-covered sprawl of wooden stands and shabby shopfronts, I met such an explorer. I stumbled upon Michel while locating parts for my dysfunctional kerosene stove. He knew the bazaar and led me directly to a man who could repair it. I invited him to lunch in one of the market's open-fronted restaurants. We sat at an unsteady, plastic-covered wooden table between the tandoori oven and the rush of market-goers on the path outside.

He was a fiftyish climber from Chamonix in the French Alps, but in his cut-off T-shirt and hiking shorts you could see he had the body of a thirty-year-old. His face had been tanned and tightened by years in the sun and his shoulder-length greying hair was swept back in a way that made you think he'd just arrived from some windblown cliff. It was a long lunch, with Michel leading the conversation.

The conversation revolved around the Himalayas. Michel said he loved the mountains and couldn't bear to be away from them. Purgatory for him were the planar landscapes of Holland, Belgium or Luxembourg. "The high places are my home," he said, sweeping his hand out towards the snow peaks that surrounded the valley. The Karakoram were his chosen range. This was his fourteenth trip to the area. When I asked him why, he said because "they are the most beautiful, and the most dangerous." K2 and Nanga Parbat, he said, have some of the highest death rates amongst the world's highest peaks.

The answer hinted at a machismo that didn't fit with the selfless impression he had given me. I asked him, if the Karakoram were so dangerous then did he harbour a death wish?

"I climb in dangerous, beautiful places to be close to God."

I looked up from my rice and lentils.

Michel went on to explain how he considered himself a climbing Sufi. Sufis are followers of an esoteric form of Islam whose goal is, through intense practice, to have contact with Allah in this life. It was God, he said, who brought him to the summit. Danger, he said, was the catalyst for his practice. Climbing was the medium through which he could connect with God. In the midst of a technical climb, in the interzone between life and death, Michel believed he had contact with Allah.

I didn't ask how Michel had developed this philosophy and I have no idea how traditional Sufis would feel about his interpretation, but over that lunch with the great moutains all around us he seemed a man at peace with himself.

In our comfortable suburban existences it's strange to think about danger, but in the end it's unavoidable. I remember once at university walking back to my dormitory and seeing a group of people milling around a flight of concrete steps near the gym; some of them were crying. It was raining, the concrete was stained dark grey, but I could see darker marks on the lower steps, as if something had been spilled. I asked what was going on and a guy from my economics class told me a student had died there just an hour before. He had been jogging, tripped at the top of the stairway and hit his head on the edge of one of the steps. That was it – a simple fall and he was dead. For weeks afterwards I thought about it constantly. I'd never met the guy but I'd run and walked those steps dozens, possibly hundreds of times. I'd never fallen. I'd never even thought about falling. It was just another flight of stairs. But he had fallen. He'd fallen and he was dead.

In that vein you don't think of rowing as a dangerous sport. Well, maybe crossing the Atlantic in an open shell, but not training on Elk Lake on the outskirts of Victoria. Pulling oars with seven other guys in a twenty-metre-long rowing shell, on a two-kilometre by one-kilometre freshwater lake, surrounded by comfortable neighbourhoods, it's not a picture of great risk.

Gareth's death was a tragic, one-in-a-million accident. I accepted it was something larger than the individual; the weather, water, wind, preparations on the lake and the combined power of nine men were involved. Gareth was one small element. Maybe there were reasons for it, but if there were they existed on a universal scale, a dimension to which my background had given me no insight.

August 15

Along the Indus River heading east I walked the road that connects Skardu to the disputed border with India. Again I was struck by the number of soldiers. Every ten kilometres I was stopped at a checkpoint and asked by a young man with a rifle for my passport and to verify, in writing, my nationality and purpose in Pakistan. Every hour or so convoys of camouflaged trucks rolled by, their covered cargo decks bursting with raucous infantrymen headed for the battlefields of Siachen glacier. At one point a soldier leaned out the back of one of the transports, holding onto the truck with one hand and waving his burgundy beret with the other. "Hop on," he shouted in respectable English. "It's a one-way trip to the snow."

The twenty-year-old battle for Siachen glacier, a snaking tongue of snow and ice at 5,000 metres, may be the epitome of the nonsensical war. In the 1960s and 1970s the United States Defense Mapping Agency, with no legal authority, began showing the area on its publicly available maps as part of Pakistan. The Pakistani government's claim to the area was bolstered by its issuing of permits to international climbing expeditions throughout the 1970s and 1980s.

Eventually, in 1984, the Indian government decided to act and Operation Megdhoot was launched. The military airlifted three hundred men onto the glacier and in what became a race for the peaks they secured two of the three major passes and two-thirds of the glacier's area before Pakistan could get its troops into place. Since then the two armies have been stalemated; India controls much of the high ground but Pakistan has much easier access into the area. Neither country can reduce the number of troops on the glacier for fear that the other side will attack and twenty years of intense labour and hard-won propaganda will be lost. So the soldiers wait on a frozen wasteland as the two armies face off at 5,600 metres, squabbling over a piece of rock and ice so desolate that no mammal can survive on it. On Siachen, the sad truth is that more men are squandered to the whims of altitude and cold than to the bullet.

A friend of mine, a porter from the remote Zanskar Valley between Ladakh and Kashmir, worked on Siachen in the mid-1990s carrying loads for the Indian Army. It is a well-paid job for porters. I asked him if he would go back there again. "No, it is a too much dangerous place, always people shooting and bombs going off."

Near the small village of Tampa I passed fields thick with ripened barley. The irrigation ditches by the road were lined with fleecy capped heracleum. A man on the other side of the canal walked towards me through the stubbly field. He drew close and swung the shovel he was using as a walking stick over his shoulder. His fingers, broad and sinewy, wrapped easily around the wooden handle. There was the smell of mustard flowers about him. He said hello and asked me to join him and his son on a blanket by the canal. He spoke English well and we made small talk about weather and crops.

Muhammad Khan was a government official in the village, but his long woolen robe and rubber boots were reminders that during harvest everyone was needed in the fields. He was eager to have me home for dinner; he had never talked with a foreigner. I knew I would simultaneously be guest and entertainment but still accepted.

Muhammad's family had lived in the valley for centuries and his home reflected that longevity. It was a massive mud-brick construction of three stories. Many of the rooms were unused, the family concentrated in only four: the kitchen, an adjoining dining room, and two bedrooms. The rooms were barely illuminated by tiny windows glazed with opaque glass. The walls were castle-like, one metre thick. The atmosphere in the dining room was comfortable, where woolen carpets lay patchworked on a dirt floor and low, brightly painted tables were constantly stacked with cups of tea and plates of biscuits.

Muhammad's young son and a male friend from the office joined us. During a lull in the conversation I asked about his wife and daughter. Muhammad shrugged and replied, "They are in the kitchen."

I then made a faux pas by asking him if he did not think they would enjoy participating in our conversation. At this Muhammad chuckled and responded as if talking to a child who posits unanswerable questions. "My friend, it would be uncomfortable for her to be here."

His friend and son nodded in agreement and it was true.

For the sake of dinner I pulled back from my line of questioning. But it was too late, and the meal thereafter was a tightwire affair with the height of manners observed on both sides.

Normally, someone such as Muhammad would have invited me to stay the night, but after my question he wasn't quite sure of my personality and so, before it became too uncomfortable, I excused myself after the meal. I threw my pack back on and trudged another few kilometres southeast of the village until I found a pleasant campsite on a stony flat amongst trees by the river. I didn't bother setting up my tent. Instead, I laid out my mat and sleeping bag, climbed into the downy cocoon, and let the rustle of the poplars' leaves lull me to sleep.

August 16

Ten kilometres farther east up the Indus River, a broadening in the valley is watered by a stream running from furrowed peaks to the south. The creek irrigates Gol village's many layers of paddies. Every sliver of practical ground has been adapted to agriculture; barley and wheat grow to the edge of the road and up the hillsides to the band of fields where the soil turns to stone. Between the houses, sheds, barns and walls the broad leaves of cauliflower, spinach, potato and cucumber blossomed. The harvest looked ready, as heavy sheaves of golden grain and the deep, dusty green of late summer vegetables dotted the view. But Gol is a land on the edge of fertility. Altitude and topography work against crops and this is in stark contrast to the valley's swelling population. In the previous five years I'd walked through dozens of valleys such as this and asked myself many times where the ever-expanding population will fit into such a crowded land.

At the tea shop in Gol – a one-bench, polyethylene tarp-covered addition to an existing mud-brick house – I put the question to the only other customer that afternoon. Iqbal Jafaar looked to be in his sixties, and though his weather-beaten face and hands were those of a farmer, his clipped English and neatly trimmed moustache were those of a bureaucrat. Dressed in a traditional ankle-length dark woolen robe, cinched at the waist by a purple silk sash, he looked every bit the Balti patriarch.

Mr. Jafaar was the father of five and the grandfather of nineteen. His family, he told me, was the village's last surviving "old" clan, all of whose members still lived in the area. He estimated that three-quarters of the young male population had moved south to Islamabad, Lahore and Karachi in search of work. Mr. Jafaar lamented that the passage was not just a migration of opportunism but a cultural exodus because the young men left Baltistan with the traditions they had absorbed and those customs were lost in the chaos of Pakistan's megacities.

He had not wanted his children to move south, for he believed that a good family equalled a good life. Although all three of his sons had said they would like to move south, he had encouraged them to stay and admitted that as a government official he could afford school fees and had promoted education. He boasted that each of his sons used newly developed seed and fertilizers and were able to independently feed their families as well as hold down government jobs. Now, with so many villagers reappearing from the city empty-handed, he was confident that his stubborn decision not to let his sons leave had been a sound one.

My family had moved to Canada for some of the same reasons that the young men of Gol moved south: opportunity, security, expectations. Belfast was the past, a place steeped in gloomy history and deep-seated hatreds. When we left in the early '70s Northern Ireland's economy was in ruins. All my cousins have worked overseas at one time or another.

Canada had security, not just economic stability but distance from Northern Ireland's troubles, but unfortunately even on the other side of the world there were relics of the past. The first summer we were in Canada my family went to the annual twelfth of July celebrations put on by the Northern Irish community in Vancouver. Considering the history of that particular day – a remembrance of the Battle of the Boyne in 1693 where the pro-Catholic Jacobite forces of King James II of

England were defeated by the pro-Protestant forces of William of Orange – maybe it was inevitable that history would creep up on us.

It was a hot day by Burnaby Lake. The men in typical Irish fashion were drinking heavily and the air was thick with the smell of whiskey, beer, barbequed meat and the acidic trace of vomit. The lake was surrounded by maple trees and freshly cut grass. My brother Peter and I were sitting close to five men, all in unbuttoned marching band uniforms. They were gathered around a huge bass drum, a metre and a half in diameter. We were interested in their drunkenness, their movements smooth and jerky at the same time, their speech and facial expressions labouring in slow motion. We wanted to laugh but knew it was the height of bad manners to laugh at anyone drunk and still standing.

The man in the centre of the group had a shock of dark hair hanging over one eye. All of a sudden he stood up straight, shouted, "C'mon, lads." He threw back his Brylcreemed Elvis hair and started thumping the drum, *booom, booom*. It was the kind of bass that settles under your skin and gets the hair on the back of your neck stiff and tingling. For me it was the thud of marching season in Belfast, a sound that accompanied thousands of tramping feet and days of shouting. It was a sound loaded with emotion and Peter and I were mesmerized. The leader started singing, and he'd only gotten a few words in before his mates joined him.

> *If I had a penny I tell you what I'd do,*
> *I'd buy and rope and hang the Pope.*
> *Yes, that is what I'd do.*

And the chorus went on and on. The drunken antics of the crew halted and the four of them stood up straight, arm in arm, swaying to their tune and wailing to the treetops. Peter and I would have liked to join in – they were happy men singing a song with a catchy chorus, and we knew that "Pope" was a word that never failed to generate a reaction in the adults – but before we could get caught up in it my mother was striding towards us.

"Right, you two. Time to go." She pulled me to my feet and tossed a withering look at the oblivious crew of fundamentalist choristers.

The last thing I remember as we were dragged towards the car was my dad's rugby-playing, beer-loving friend Mr. Pye shouting at the four singers, "You're a bunch of fucking idjits. It's a different country. Let it go."

August 17

Five kilometres from Gol the Shyok River merges with the Indus, which has flowed north from the border with India. I followed the Shyok another twenty kilometres east to the small village of Gwali. The place bustled with activity, for the first wheat and barley were being gathered. Around the apricot trees planted between the fields, the earth was littered with fruit and bandy-legged goats feasted on the decaying pulp. A wetness blew off the river, and on its banks grew wild asters, everlasting and pedicularis. Busy people worked the fields, too engaged in their work to notice a single man tramping the periphery of their paddies.

The downy shade of the fruit trees bordering the road encouraged me to extend my lunch. There, under the poplar trees' branches, in the village's open-air tea shop I met another elder of the district. Mr. Khan was an older, more wizened version of Mr. Jafaar from Gol. He wore the same ankle-length, rough woolen robe held at the waist with a tie-dye patterned sash, his flat, woolen cap hung low over his forehead and his face was creased like old brown paper.

Mr. Khan spoke no English but the young man making chai translated for us. The elder initiated the conversation with a slight bow of his head and the offer of a cup of tea for a "weary traveller." Quickly, though, after polite introductions and small talk about the weather, he turned to what was most important in his life, Islam. It seemed important for him that I understand his devotion. He told me that after a life devoted to his family and his land, now he was an old man and had the time to commit himself to his religion. After that first cup of tea I realized I was in the presence of a gentle missionary. Islam, Mr. Khan insisted, had an answer for everything. The prophet Muhammad had spoken on all aspects of life. "Why look elsewhere for the answers?" he asked me.

I asked what motivated his conviction. He said life in Baltistan was "short and full of hardship," but his reward for a life lived within the prescripts of the Koran would be a "glorious hereafter." Living long enough for his family to support him meant he could absorb himself in practice. His one great remaining aspiration was to complete the Haj, the Muslim pilgrimage to Mecca.

I mentioned how I too was on a pilgrimage, a solo one with no set goals. As Mr. Khan looked at me, his old eyes caught a spark and he began to laugh. The young shopkeeper raised his eyes and translated as Mr. Khan spoke.

"He says that you are on a long walk, not a pilgrimage. Pilgrimage is about drawing close to Allah. About working with your Muslim brothers. There must be compatriots and a focus on God for it to be a pilgrimage."

My shoulders drooped. I could have replied that Muhammad, Jesus and the Buddha had all undertaken individual quests in the wilderness, removed from their everyday lives, each had found what he was looking for.

The wanderings of the prophets have inspired a lineage of disciples: Sufi travellers, the dervishes who used walking, Siyahat, to detach themselves from the world and lose themselves in Allah; the ancient Christian church's *ambulare pro Deo*, "wanderers for God," roaming mendicants imitating the trials of Christ in the desert; and the Hindu saddhus, travelling ceaselessly over a landscape imbued with their faith. The last words the Buddha uttered to his closest disciples were, "Walk on!"

I mentioned none of this to Mr. Khan. He had deeply held beliefs, a confidence in one answer to every question. Religious journeys to Mr. Khan occurred within a tightly regulated framework. His God was a man of discipline and strength. There was no point in arguing with someone so close to his final goal.

For the four months I spent walking in the Himalayas I'd believed I was on a personal pilgrimage. I had convinced myself the trek was part of the research for a book on landscape and religion, a pilgrimage towards knowledge. But I never asked myself the basic question of why I wanted to write about those subjects.

It wasn't until five years after the trek that I understood the deeper motivation for my obsessive walking. I was in Kathmandu after another season in the Himalayas. I had already written three drafts of *Into the Heart of the Himalayas*. I knew the walk was a great story, but I had been unable to tell it the way I had felt it. Then I gave the manuscript to a friend, a carpet entrepreneur and an astute reader. She read the book and her first comment was, "There's something missing in this story. There's something more going on behind the scenes."

I disagreed. To me it was simple. It was a book on landscape and religion, an intelligent adventure tale about walking through the highest mountains in the world and trying to understand the religions I was moving through. After all, I had written the book, so I should know what it was about.

A few weeks later I was rewriting the manuscript again. I was working on the section where I arrive at Gaumukh, the source of the Ganges River. It read like this:

"I approached the glacial source of the River Ganges as the sun set. I was alone. I had walked for eight hours that day. I had been walking for three months, eight hours everyday. My body was tuned to the rhythm of my steps. Every part of me wanted to walk. I hummed in time with my steps, up and down, passes and valleys, rivers and peaks. I had traversed the length of the range from the northern edge of Pakistan to the Hindu heartland of the Indian Himalayas.

"Before me the azure and white of sky and snow merged with the setting sun. The valley was shot with the colour of coral. In the near distance Gangotri glacier's icy frontal wall shimmered in turquoise. Coral and turquoise are the protective stones every Tibetan child receives in a necklace at birth. The land glowed in that soft, pre-sunset light. I reached the glacier's snout, the point of emergence for the nascent river, the place called Gaumukh, the Cow's Mouth. In Hinduism the cow is the personification of maternal energy. At the birth of that great river I was immersed in a compassionate landscape. I was exhausted and at ease.

"By the ice cliff, on the bank of the stream I unslung my pack and sat down. The shaly earth was cool, the air stirred by a fresh breeze blowing from the west off the glacier. I breathed deeply. I was wearing a T-shirt and a fleece vest. The skin on my forearms prickled. The world slowed and that composure filtered into me. The wind stilled. Everything was quiet. The boundary between me and the world outside slipped. Tears welled up, stumbled off my cheeks and fell to the dark sand. I was crying."

For years after the trek the thought of those tears returned to me again and again. Initially I'd attributed them to being in a landscape infused with the religion of a billion people and to sitting quietly at the birth of the one of the world's greatest rivers. But when I went back over that passage in Kathmandu a sense of déjà vu filled me. When was the last time I had felt that same calm, that chill, the quietude? It came to me – the same cold clarity was there when I had seen Gareth's body in the hospital morgue in Victoria.

It was more than a week before Gareth was recovered from Elk Lake. Every morning dedicated navy scuba divers combed the storm-churned lake floor looking for the anomalous silty hump that would be my brother's body. On the ninth day of searching they found him.

Mum, Katrina and I went together to the hospital when we heard his body had been found. The room, somewhere in the building's concrete rabbit warren of a basement, was dim and very still. The air was cool and the light fluorescent. Gareth, his long body shrouded in a white sheet, lay on a stainless steel table. The nurse motioned us one at a time up to his side. When it was my turn she pulled back the covering. I let out a half breath. He was a handsome man with curly blond hair and thin, perfectly proportioned features. I had always envied his looks. He appeared so peaceful, his skin slightly freckled and very pale, his eyelashes thick, his lips thin and blue. It was a face without any of the fear that Western society associates with death.

With that connection, the stillness in Gangotri and the quietude of the morgue, whole pieces of my life fell into place; the trek, the meetings, the landscape, all the thoughts and ideas in those four months of walking that in small ways had scared me, started making sense. I had been crying at Gangotri because of Gareth. The trek was about the search, a quest through the ideas that inspired me – landscape, religion and walking – to come to terms with my brother's death. I saw that the reason I wanted to write a book about those subjects was because subconsciously they were tools to help me move through the loss of Gareth. Gareth was the catalyst and eventually he became the endpoint of my pilgrimage.

August 18

I saw Khapalu, the capital of Ghanche District, from a distance, a green mottling against a steep earthen backdrop. As with all the villages along the Shyok River, it is as an oasis in the high desert with its abundant orchards of apples and apricots, fields laden with barley and vegetables, sheep and goats dotting the pastures. In the gardens close to the village, finches and buntings darted to and fro, gorging themselves on the harvest's leftovers. It was a vision of plenty in a land of parched grass and vertical sandstone.

I quickly found a guest house in the village, laid out my sleeping bag on the thin bed and had a lunch of rice and dal at a café across the road. In the afternoon I walked up to the Mir's palace on a path lined with stone walls and apricot trees. It was a trail of lingering village smells, fermenting stone fruit, the stench of goat, soils rich with decaying compost.

Khapalu is, after Skardu, the largest settlement in the region and before the subcontinent's partition in 1947 it had been the second most powerful principality in Baltistan. After partition, the area came under control of the Azad (Free) Jammu and Kashmir (AJK) government, but in 1949 the AJK government officially delegated powers to Islamabad. The arrangement was unfortunately very similar to the one in existence during the British colonial times, with the local Rajas and Mirs allowed to maintain their power and continue to tax their subjects, but in the 1970s Prime Minister Zulfikar Ali Bhutto removed the Mirs' oppressive system of land revenue. The role of the hereditary monarch has been greatly eroded and the Northern Areas are controlled, to a greater extent along the eastern border with India and to a lesser degree along the western border with Afghanistan, directly from Islamabad.

That afternoon, in the gravelled widening of the road that is the parking lot for the Mir's palace, I came across a young man leaning into the engine compartment of a late-'80s model Toyota Corolla. The car was black and yellow with jagged rust holes eating at the wheel wells. In a previous life it may have been a taxi in Lahore or Karachi. The man heard me coming and pulled his head out from under the hood. His smile was open, disarming in a way, and we started talking. He was a pleasant, modern young man in his late teens or early twenties. He wore jeans and a polo shirt. Ahktar was his name, and he told me he was in charge of the Mir's interests "in the tourist industry."

I looked at the old taxi and he smiled. He invited me for tea and from the front seat of the car he took a stainless steel thermos and poured me a plastic tumbler of steaming chai. The chai was sweet and hot, maybe too much of both for a warm day. After our drink he offered to show me around the buildings, telling me that he had grown up there.

The palace is a rambling two-storey structure of mud-brick and sagging applewood beams. The central feature, situated over the main entrance, is an impressive octagonal balcony; its filigreed windows are carved with a skill that would be difficult to find today. Ahktar said the building had been constructed by multiple generations of imported Kashmiri artisans, but now the grand residence is a shell; years of vacancy have drained it of life. The overall effect is of a majestic relic – the walls falling in on themselves, doors crooked in their frames, the woodwork decomposed to a state of blurry recognition.

The palace is 230 years old, its style of another age, yet twenty-five metres away across a flat, parched lawn sits a substantial house curiously in the fashion of British Indian hunting lodges. Two buildings of such differing provenance I would have expected in the old Indian hill station towns of Darjeeling or Shimla, but not in Khapalu. Without my asking Ahktar explained that it was the "new" palace, built for the wife of the current Mir's great-grandfather. The Mir's wife, he proudly pointed out, had been English. The story was something of a local myth as Akhtar continued on. The Mir and his future wife had met in Srinagar, Kashmir, a holiday spot for British Raj administrators and rulers of the princely states. The monarch had swept his bride off her feet with "his horsemanship and manliness." The couple had wed in Kashmir and soon after returned to Khapalu.

The lady would have had little knowledge of the land she married into; in the nineteenth century only a handful of Westerners had been to the area. Baltistan's precipitous high desert was geographically and climatically removed from the soft, green hills of Kashmir. Ahktar said the princess disliked the drafty, old palace and had demanded a new home. The hunting lodge could not compare in splendour to its architectural neighbour but was eminently more practical for the winter cold and biting wind that rips down the Shyok Valley.

I imagined the princess sipping tea in the evening, prints of fox hunting on the walls, a silver tea set on a walnut table, a crackling apricot wood fire in the fireplace and outside in the bitter Balti winter, the temperature dropping to minus thirty Celsius. The doors of the lodge were locked, the windows boarded up, but Akhtar said the Mir still stays there when he returns to Khapalu.

August 19

At first light the next morning I packed my bag and made my way to the Shyok River. I left my pack on the gravelly bank and climbed a large, smooth boulder to get a better view upstream. On the far shore people were moving to the fields. I could hear the low chanting of their harvest songs. A lizard appeared on the mica-peppered rock by my feet, warming itself in the early sun, a tangerine rosette on its flanks moving in quick time with its breath. Two brown dippers flickered restlessly close by, their tail feathers bobbing with every twist of their heads. Anxious for morning food, they were concentrated on the river's back eddies. The river swept by, gently, smoothly, the water turquoise and turbid, swirling with muddy debris. The sun caught the surface obliquely and glinted metallic.

The Shyok is a river that cuts its way aggressively through the deep valleys of Baltistan until it meets the Indus east of Skardu. The Indus flows west for 250 kilometres then turns south and wanders through the heartland of Pakistan to the Arabian Sea. It is the economic engine of the country. The Indus is also one of the seven sacred rivers of Hinduism and, through the Harappan culture that flourished along its banks from 3300 to 1700 B.C.E., one of the cradles of human civilization.

The river's source is northeast across the Greater Himalayas near Mount Kailash, the holiest mountain in Buddhism and Hinduism, and the Kailash area is the source of a matrix of rivers that spread across the entire subcontinent. From its southern slopes the Indus winds west and south; the Tsangpo River pushes east through Tibet, then as it turns south it becomes the Brahmaputra and carves a path through India and Bangladesh; the Ganges and Yamuna rivers press south and then east from Kailash; the Sutlej River, the fastest running in the Himalayas, drives west then drops off the Tibetan plateau to flow south; and the Mahakali, the final destination of my own pilgrimage, parallels the Sutlej's course through the highest mountains in the world. I felt a humble connection to the wild water and mountains that stretched for 3,000 kilometres to the east.

I removed my shoes and socks and dipped my feet in the water; the glacial melt was numbing. The water was beyond borders.

Water: soothing, moving, giving, all-encompassing, without ego, an altruistic medium. We are fifty to sixty percent water and without ingesting three litres a day we will slowly die. We can't live without it. But water at two degrees Celsius is deadly because immersed in it for anything more than a few minutes the body becomes hypothermic. When the body's temperature drops by one or two degrees below normal you enter the first stage of hypothermia. You start to shiver, and breathing becomes quick and shallow. As body temperature drops by three or four degrees you enter hypothermia's second stage; miscoordination becomes apparent, your movements become clumsy and you are mildly confused. If your body temperature drops below thirty-two degrees Celsius you have entered the third, possibly lethal stage of hypothermia. You have difficulty speaking. You are unable to use your hands. Below thirty degrees Celsius the shivering stops. Around this time major organs fail and with that your body dies. Strangely, though, because of the slowed metabolism, the brain continues to function for a short time. For a frightening moment you are that rarest of entities, a mind devoid of a body.

Gareth went through those stages. The water leeched away his warmth, his life. It took him without a thought as to who he was, who he could have become. Lucky, unlucky? Water doesn't care. Water has made me believe in karma, in fate, in the difficulty of changing that universal hand of cards. Water. I used to love it but now I fear it. Maybe that's why mountains have become my sanctuary.

BUDDHIST HIMALAYAS

CHAPTER 3
In the Steps of the Yak

August 29

The seat was hard; coconut husk stuffing burst from the vinyl upholstery. The bus's suspension had long ago collapsed, but there was a soothing, maritime sway to the way the vehicle rolled down the road. It was five a.m. and in the moonglow, thin alpine grass outside shivered in the silver light. I felt the stub of the ticket I had bought to get on the bus. I was tired, still half-asleep and a fragile memory came to me in a rush.

A few summers before, Gareth had impulsively bought me a ticket to join him at a rock concert. I had just returned from a long summer of working in a remote bush camp and was about to leave for Europe and the ski-racing season. There was no time to go to a concert with my younger brother. I was too cool, too full of my own importance – too much ego hung on my body. The recollection came in a flash of images and in the darkness of that frigid bus it felt like such a wasted opportunity. My body trembled and the emotion overcame me,

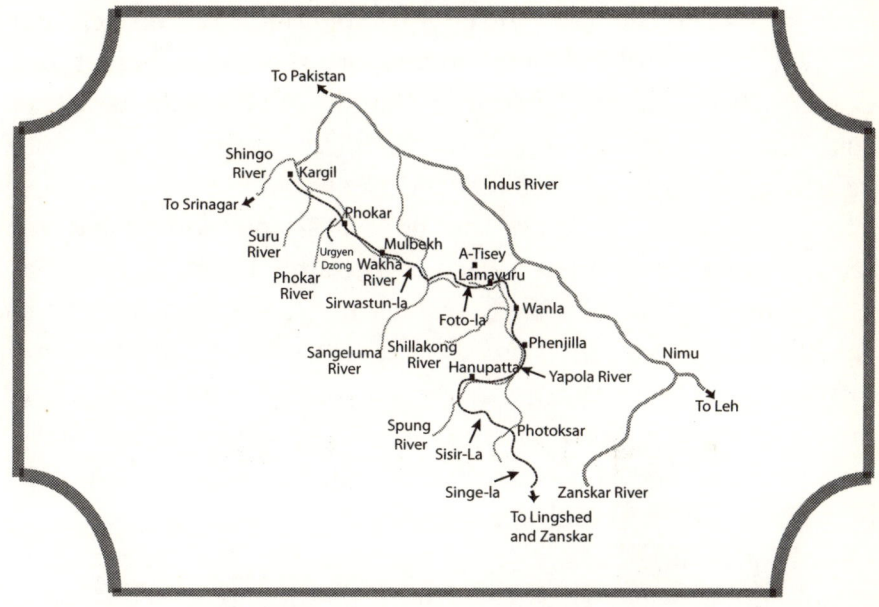

KARGIL DISTRICT, JAMMU AND KASHMIR, INDIA

and I cried for what could have been. I cried silently, holding it to myself.

In the seat beside me an ancient Ladakhi lady stared straight ahead. She had skin like old leather and burgundy robes that smelled of butter and dried grass. I was embarrassed by the tears and tried harder to hold them back, but it was impossible and my body shook more. Silently the old lady moved her hand on top of mine. Her palm was like paper. She didn't try to hold on; she just left it there and the dry warmth was all I needed to know I wasn't alone in the universe.

The bus was headed from Leh, the capital of Ladakh district in the Indian state of Jammu and Kashmir, 234 kilometres west to Kargil, the small capital of its namesake district in the same state. As the crow flies Kargil is only sixty kilometres from Khapalu, the village in Pakistan where I had left off my trek, but Kargil sits on the Indian side of the disputed Line of Control while Khapalu is on the Pakistani

Four times in the past fifty years fighting has broken out between India and Pakistan over where the "true" border lies. Consequently, the land between Kargil and Khapalu is a "hot zone," a territory of confused sovereignty criss-crossed with minefields, firing lines, bunkers and trenches.

It's impossible to cross this no man's land, so to make the sixty-kilometre trip from Khapalu to Kargil I had to travel by jeep from Khapalu to Gilgit, by bus to Rawalpindi and on to Lahore, then across the border by train to New Delhi to board a plane to Leh on the northern side of the Himalayas. There finally I caught another local bus to Kargil. That's how a sixty-kilometre walk became a convoluted journey of more than 3,000 kilometres. The trip took me a week.

My plan had been to take the overnight bus from Leh to Kargil, then walk southwest from Kargil along the Wakha River and cross a mountain pass to the Sangeluma River. From there I wanted to cross another pass to reach the monastery of Lamayuru and head south following rivers and crossing passes until I reached the Zanskar Valley.

I'd counted on that section of the walk taking me about two weeks, so when I reached Leh I was taken aback by news of political problems in Zanskar. To pressure the state government of Jammu and Kashmir to grant more autonomy to the remote valley – a Buddhist enclave in a majority Muslim district – the Zanskaris were denying access to foreigners. After four days of frustrating delays in Leh, I decided it was better to risk the circumstances than to jeopardize my walk. So, under bright moonlight, I boarded a local bus and rumbled off into the night.

August 30

Kargil sits at the confluence of the Suru and the smaller Wakha rivers. It is a town of 10,000 people and is similar to many of its sister villages across the border in Pakistan with mud-brick, flat-roofed houses, concrete-block government buildings, a noisy bus park and a coating of dust on everything. But Kargil seemed a particularly dirty place. Maybe there was more traffic, and so more diesel exhaust stains on the walls and pools of oil by the side of the road, but there was also bright plastic garbage blowing in the wind and the laundry I saw flapping in the breeze was speckled with soot. Kargil is the last Muslim town before the shift to Buddhism and the town closest to the disputed border. It is a place on the frontier of religious and political divisions. Some residents resent the fact they are controlled by the Indian Army. As one man with a full beard, grimy jeans and the smell of old tobacco about him whispered to me in a tea shop by the bus park, "We are occupied by a force of idol worshippers and dark men."

The place was not inviting, so after that quick cup of tea, during which I felt that half the men in the crowded chai shop were staring at me, I walked southeast down the Wakha Valley. I passed a few small villages along the way and after about twenty kilometres reached the confluence of the Wakha and Phokar rivers where I turned south and soon came to Phokar village, the first Buddhist community on my trek. Families were in the fields harvesting barley and because of the altitude, 3,200 metres, for the first time I saw yaks instead of goats grazing on the leftover stubble. I later learned the animals at Phokar were in fact a cross between yaks and cows called a dzo, bred for their higher milk production and more manageable demeanour.

The pungent smell of dung fires lingered in the air. The village looked prosperous. Every few hundred metres I passed two-storey mud-brick mansions with walls a metre and a half thick and flat roofs piled high with tight sheaves of freshly cut barley. The whitewashed walls were rubbed with diamond-shaped, blood-red markings, which I was to learn were protection from the evil spirits that many Buddhist Ladakhis believe lurk behind every ill-considered action. On the roofs of the houses, above the front doors, conical, one-metre-high terra cotta incense burners billowed out peppery, juniper wood smoke; locals believe the particular smell attracts benevolent energies.

The majority of Ladakhis follow a Tibetan style of Buddhism which traces its local history back to the eighth century when the region was caught in the midst of the clash between Chinese and Tibetan expansionism. Control of the region moved back and forth between the two powers but in 842 Nyima-Gon, a Tibetan royal representative, took advantage of the chaos surrounding the separation of the Tibetan empire and annexed Ladakh for himself. This initiated a period of Tibetanization that has continued to this day. In the fourteenth and fifteenth centuries Ladakh was invaded multiple times by Muslim armies. It was splintered but never completely conceded its independence and in 1470 King Lhachen Bhagan united the state and founded the Namgyal dynasty that still exists. In 1834 the Dogra army from Jammu successfully invaded Ladakh and made it part of Kashmir. During partition in 1947 Ladakh was invaded by the Pakistani Army. Kargil and Zanskar were occupied but eventually, after the Namgyal king signed the Instrument of Accession, which made the area an official part of the new Indian state, the Indian Army repulsed the invaders.

The trail up through the village was lined with stupas, earthen domes built upon square mud-brick pedestals and topped with brick or brass spires. Some were crumbling, while others seemed freshly painted. The stupas came in all sizes, some smaller than an upended shoebox, others more than seven metres high. Stupas were the earliest Buddhist religious monuments. Initially they were built to house what were thought to be relics of the Buddha. Over time they changed from being reliquaries to being objects of veneration themselves. Stupas came to be propitiated not for what they may have contained, but for what they represented. They have become architectural manifestations of the Buddha.

I tried to imagine the stupa as a devoted Buddhist might: the square base stepping upwards like a mind logically moving through levels of realization towards a state of enlightenment; the spherical core, both expansive and receptive, like the knowledge of the Buddha; and atop the dome a spire, a needle of fierce mind reaching for the highest state of consciousness.

By the roadside and scattered around the stupas were boulders, rocks and pebbles each chiselled with the ubiquitous Tibetan mantra, *Om Mani Padme Hum: Om* – the jewel inside the lotus flower – *Hum*. I found myself repeating it in time with my steps. *Om* – stride, *Mani* – stride, *Padme* – stride, *Hum* – stride. I had learned the mantra years before in Kathmandu and it had become a peaceful mumble that, to this day, sneaks up on me unconsciously.

I played with the words, quickened my pace and the mantra sped up. I slowed and the prayer lingered, working its way like a bass tone into my chest, sound and movement working together.

I bent down and picked up one of the mani stones. It was flattened and water-worn, a perfect river skimmer, smooth on one side, rippled with chisel work on the other. I slipped it into my trousers and felt it rubbing through the thin cotton of my pocket against my thigh.

I pitched my tent that night a few kilometres beyond Phokar in the lee of a wall constructed of thousands upon thousands of hand-carved mani stones, a work of devotion generations in the making. As I lay in my sleeping bag, a breeze blew through the stones, generating an undulating moan. The prayers serenaded me to sleep.

August 31

I slept in late, knowing I had only a five-kilometre walk up a side stream of the Phokar River to reach Urgyen Dzong, a cave where legend has it the eighth-century Buddhist saint Padmasambhava, also known as Guru Rinpoche, "the Lotus Born One," spent time in meditative retreat.

Padmasambhava's life is a rich mixture of myth, legend and archeological fact. Born in the Swat Valley in what is now Northwestern Pakistan, he became a great scholar of the esoteric school of tantric Buddhism and was renowned for his ability to memorize religious texts and put the teachings immediately into action. His fame reached the Tibetan king, Trisong Detsen (742-797), who invited Padmasambhava to Lhasa, Tibet's capital, to overpower what he believed was a demonic force that was draining the life from his country. Legend has it that Guru Rinpoche overthrew the demons not by eliminating them, but by using tantric practices and redirecting their negative energy for the cause of the good, in this case the diffusion of Buddhism. Padmasambhava is regarded by many Tibetan Buddhists as the second most powerful figure in the religion after the Buddha himself.

For Guru Rinpoche to travel from the Swat Valley to Lhasa he most likely would have passed through the area of the Wakha and Phokar rivers.

To reach the cave hermitage I followed a pebbly stream eastward from the Phokar River to a fifteen-metre chain of ladders that climbed three interconnected waterfalls. At the base of the falls I met a monk headed in the opposite direction. He was a young man with a bouncy step who broke into a broad smile when he saw me. He shook his dripping burgundy robes and water flew everywhere. Grabbing my right forearm with one hand and my right hand with his other he asked me excitedly, "You go to cave?"

I nodded and he shouted, "Good, very good!" then slapped me on the back so hard I lost my breath. He didn't seem to have time for a chat and before I could get a word in he was off towards the village, his waterlogged sneakers squelching with each step.

The canyon walls framing the cascades were carved with mantras and rose far above me on either side. The sound of the creek reverberated all around. The water's spray worked through my shirt and pants, clammy against my skin. Strung across the lip of the chasm were lines of prayer flags – red, green, yellow, blue, and white – all snapping in the breeze, tinting the light that filtered into the depths.

The ladder to the topmost waterfall wobbled as I scrambled up it, so I tried to keep one hand on the algae-slick surface of the cliff wall. At the fall's upper edge the fissure opened out onto a ring of sandstone cliffs surrounding a shaly hillock. On the mound stood a modest temple, and when I arrived I found its door was open. Another small room lay off to one side – the monk's quarters, I assumed. Its door was bolted shut and secured with a large brass padlock.

Inside the temple were the customary triumvirate of Tibetan Buddhist images: the historical Buddha Shakyamuni; Avolaskiteshvara, the many-armed representation of compassion; and, on the Buddha's right side, his eyes wide and all seeing, sat Padmasambhava – Guru Rinpoche.

From the hill I scanned across the cliffs looking for the cave. It took some time to find it. The hollow was so inconspicuous that were it not for the faded ochre paint spilling from its entrance I may never have spotted it.

Two caves, one on top of the other, make up the shrine. Both were much smaller than I expected, and neither was tall enough for my six-foot frame to stand up in. The lower grotto is thought to be Guru Rinpoche's kitchen and the upper one his meditation chamber. A small stupa is built in the highest room. Around it were placed traditional offerings of butter lamps, flowers, silk scarves, pictures of the master or other great teachers and many prayer stones. Each of the items was an offering to the senses: vision, smell, touch.

In the kitchen area, in the shallow dip in the floor that is said to have been the saint's hearth, pilgrims have left bracelets, necklaces, beads and brooches. Fruity aromatic oils had permeated the stone. Himalayan blue poppies and white columbines were arranged off to one side in a pink plastic tumbler. These were women's offerings, intended to draw some of the saint's energy into their own homes.

I pitched my tent near the small temple on the hill. I had thought about sleeping in Guru Rinpoche's kitchen, but the place had been cold and damp and I was nervous I might breach some local custom. It was a strange night, as a wind howled continuously and the circle of cliffs around me amplified the sound. Eventually, I dropped to sleep while a banshee wailed and whipped at the loose ends flapping around my tent. Even with the noise and commotion, I was still glad I hadn't stayed in the cave.

September 1

I retraced my steps back down to Phokar village and the Wakha River, then followed it east another twenty kilometres to Mulbekh, the next large village. I arrived in late afternoon. Most of the day's walk had been on trails close to the main road so I was dusty and tired. I easily found a room in the guest house overlooking its major attraction, a ten-metre-tall sculpture of the future Buddha, Maitreya, carved into a twenty-metre-high finger of stone. Maitreya, like the belief in Christianity of the second coming of Jesus, is the Buddha who will appear when he is needed most. He is the successor to the historical Buddha Shakyamuni (Sage of the Shakyas) who, until he discovered the Buddhist path to higher consciousness, lived as Prince Siddhartha Gautama in Northern India in the fifth century B.C.E.

Strangely, the main road between Leh and Srinagar, the capital of Kashmir, runs directly in front of the statue. It was impossible to sit on the deck of the guest house, sip a cup of tea and take in the statue without being blasted by one of the dozens of trucks that rumbled by that evening.

September 2

The next morning, as the sun rose and softened the thin air's bite, I crossed the road vowing to see the Buddha sculpture before the truck convoys began. The monks who take care of the statue had already opened the door to the compound and from the dusty quadrangle I watched the Buddha stir with the first sign of the sun's ascent. An unhurried golden wave swept over it. The movement was barely perceptible, like tides with the pull of the moon. The sun was performing the statue's morning ablutions, catching the sculpture at shallow angles and highlighting chisel work still deep and defined after 1,400 years.

An inscription to one side of the statue suggested that the Buddha was carved between the seventh and eighth centuries, a time before Buddhism was fully established in Tibet. If that were the case, the inspiration and maybe even the labour would have come from Kashmir, which was a hotbed of Buddhist learning at that time. The sculpture has a distinct Hindu feel to it; the Buddha has long flowing hair and his four hands each hold religious implements, traits associated with the Hindu god Shiva rather than with the more austere Buddha. The statue is a reminder that before he discovered his own path to enlightenment, Buddha was a Hindu.

Maitreya is considered by Buddhists to be a bodhisattva, a key concept in Tibetan Buddhism. Bodhisattvas are individuals who have the ability to reach the stage of full enlightment but delay their progress in order to assist other beings in their quest for the highest state of development. Many Buddhists believe the Dalai Lama is such a bodhisattva – delaying his own enlightenment in order to guide others along the path.

When I became interested in Buddhism I thought of Gareth as my personal bodhisattva, the one who had pushed me out of my old life in search of something more fulfilling. It was an absurdly simplistic interpretation of a difficult concept, but there was a grain of truth to it because through the loss I was forced to study my life intently: what I did and didn't do, what made me happy, what I had regretted. Those considerations pushed me farther towards Buddhism's teachings of self-responsibility, respect for all beings and a life ordered around the twin pillars of wisdom and compassion.

Later that morning I followed the Wakha River east, turned south out of the main valley at the village of Kharl and climbed the Sirwastun-la (la in Tibetan languages means pass) towards Budh Kharbu village. The climb was up a wide, shaly, windblown slope. There were no trees, only tumbleweeds and stub-leafed aromatics – thyme, sage, marjoram – whose fragrance floated in the air, spicing the wind with high-desert incense.

Near the summit I was surprised to see a group of grazing horses, two pale mares and a yearling, just below the ridgeline. I had seen sheep, goats and yaks in my first few days in Ladakh but no horses. Their focus was absorbed in a square metre of plant life directly in front of them. They moved efficiently, slowly, with purpose. The wind caught their manes, throwing them wildly from side to side, then a shift in the wind brought them my scent. They lifted their heads, saw me, and as suddenly as they had appeared they burst from their formation and galloped in a wide vee over the crest of the hill.

Over that next rise, in the wind shadow of the bare ridge, I came upon two men wearing army surplus pants and jackets. They were sitting and chatting outside a tent made from a frayed khaki nylon parachute. Smiling, they waved me over. I joined them by their dung fire, its glowing embers pulsing with the breeze. Over the fire an aluminum pot of arak, the local rice alcohol, was warming. I was handed a battered enamel mug topped with the strong brew, and no words were spoken until we finished our cups. Afterwards they explained in Hindi how they were on a week-long fodder cutting expedition and the horses were theirs. The cups were filled again and the younger man asked in slow English where I was headed. I indicated to the east and using a stick he drew me a map of the route in the sandy soil at our feet.

We talked haltingly in both languages about home and being away from it. The men enjoyed their time in the mountains every summer with only their animals and what they could carry. Summer was about being outside, while winter was about being at home, about telling stories around the kitchen fire and, as the younger man said with half a smile, "making babies."

They insisted I stay for another cup. I did, and joined them for one more after that, but after the fourth I excused myself, having felt the effects of the arak moving hotly down my spine. I rose on unsteady legs and moved out of the hollow back into the dry wind. The men were waving and laughing at my instability. I waved back. The horses were there again, only now instead of running away they stood firm and stared at me until I was out of sight.

I camped that night on the far side of the Sirwastun-la. The sky was cloudless so there was no need to pitch the tent. I laid my sleeping bag on a hard-packed strip of goat-sheared grass overlooking a file of sandstone cliffs. From my nylon cocoon I watched the sun play on the spires, vast, drafty palaces of ochre and purple. Alpine swifts flitted in and out of the recesses that marked the walls, catching the sun in wing-flicked bursts. Night's blackness crept down the rock face, devouring the cliff's colours. Silence and darkness arrived together.

September 3

With sunup I packed my bag and dropped from the pass following the Kharbu River into an arid but well-irrigated valley. Channels of all sizes split and moved the small stream to every accessible patch of fertile ground. The barley fields were almost cropped. Potato flowers bloomed, their purple corollas offset by golden stamens. The dusty path was intersected by stupas and paralleled by walls of prayer stones. The air was touched with dung-fire smoke and sizzling oil, hints of the midday meal. I passed three quiet clusters of mud-brick houses before the trail returned to the road. The smell of simple lunches gave way to the caustic reek of diesel. I was back following the road up the Sangeluma River towards the Foto-la.

The trail to the pass pushed directly up the slope, intersecting the switchbacked road at even intervals. During the afternoon rain started to fall and the grey sky dropped to the earth. I pushed through a mist so dense it felt as though I were in two worlds. By the road, blaring juggernaut trucks came at me, laser-beam headlights cutting the fog, the drivers struggling to control top-heavy loads on the slick ribbon of asphalt. Then the trail would cut away and a blanket of cloud enveloped me. Ahead the green pasture melted into a pale horizon and traffic noise reached me as underwater thunder.

Down the eastern side of the Foto-la I almost ran. The trail was a steady grade and the rain encouraged me to hurry. I entered the monastery village of Lamayuru on the traditional route from the northwest, a path lined with hundreds of metres of chest-high, prayer-stone walls. The legacy of an entire community's devotion, hundreds of thousands of stones were chiselled with Sanskrit and Tibetan mantras, images of the Buddha, wheels of life and simple circular mandalas. More than once I stopped to touch them. The stones were cold and shimmering in the rain. The walls were crumbling, the connecting mortar peeling away. Golden saxifrage flowers bloomed through the relics. The structure was deteriorating but the stones survived.

From that angle the Lamayuru monastery, or gompa in Tibetan, is one of the most impressive in the Himalayas. It sits tottering on an aggregate stone bluff fifty metres above the village. The complex is a huge construction, a hundred metres by a hundred metres, a disintegrating mud-brick fortress. I had seen it before in bright sunshine, when the buildings had been radiant, their walls blistered white, like houses on a Greek island. But the rain had changed its demeanour, and now the gompa looked ominous. Grey and overbearing, it had the air of a sedentary but unapproachable animal. In desert country moisture undermines your understanding of the landscape.

Lamayuru is the oldest and largest monastery in Ladakh. Legend has it that Naropa, one of the great Indian Buddhist scholars, came to Lamayuru in the eleventh century and spent many years meditating in a local cave. At that time the area around the monastery was a lake, but Naropa's meditation practice was so powerful it caused a split in the surrounding hillside, a geological feature that can still be seen today, and the lake emptied through this opening. After the lake drained, Naropa found a dead lion and on this spot the master built the first temple of the Lamayuru complex, the Singhe Ghang (Lion Mound). From that single temple the monastery grew to be the largest in Ladakh. At one time it consisted of five large prayer halls and more than four hundred monks, but now only a single main hall remains and 150 monks reside there.

In Tibetan Buddhism the monastery typically takes the high ground, the site of authority. It looks over its congregation, emphasizing how the building stores the community's knowledge and in a practical sense provides a raised defensive position in time of war. But Lamayuru was now a microscosm of India's changing mores because the highest construction in Lamayuru is no longer the monastery but the road. The highway winds around the mountain high above the village and the gompa. The cloister has been supplanted; the road is the new connection between the people's earthly reality and the heavenly abodes of Delhi and Mumbai.

I stayed in a guest house in the village and after a cup of hot tea I changed into some dry clothes and made my way up the hill to the gompa. A few children were playing in the courtyard. When they saw me they ran off and came back with Karma, a young shaven-headed monk, who spoke much better English than my Hindi. He shook my hand almost violently and while still holding it pulled me towards the prayer hall.

This was the room I was most interested in as it is built around the cave that Naropa had legendarily meditated in ten centuries ago. I had expected the grotto to be in the centre of the room, the focus of the monastery's activity. After all, Naropa is part of a great lineage of Buddhist teachers. His teacher was the master Tilopa, the founder of the Kagyu school of Tibetan Buddhism which the monastery belongs to. Tilopa developed the Buddhist Mahamudra philosophy, a way of knowledge Buddhists consider to be the true nature of the mind.

The prayer hall was the size of a small gymnasium. There were no windows and it took a while for my eyes to adjust. It had the smell of old things, brass and worn wood, burnt oil and ancient bodies. The young monk provided commentary as we circled the room. At the front of the hall was the chest-high wooden throne of the head lama. It was draped in gold and burgundy silk, and large pictures of the Karmapa, the leader of the Kargyu school, were placed above those of the head lama. Karma's explanation over the competition for the seat was, "Lama is great, but Karmapa is greater."

To the right of the throne was a small stupa and statues of Padmasambhava and a former head lama of the monastery. As Karma explained in his succinct way, "Great lama, dead long ago." On the other side were statues of Mahakala, the most fearsome of the Buddhist guardian deities, and a female guardian deity who Karma did not name, but described as "very strong lady." Considering she had what looked like a garland of human skulls around her neck and held a severed skull cap dripping with blood, I had to agree.

Behind the throne and statues were a series of thangkas, Tibetan paintings on canvas, depicting the many incarnations of the Buddha. On the right was a statue of Tara, a female deity considered to be the embodiment of compassion. Karma's comment: "Very beautiful lady."

I was interested in the statues but could see no sign of the legendary cave. I asked Karma about it, and his eyes brightened. "Oh yes," he said, "you know our Naropa?" and pulled me over to a small glass door in a red and gold frame. Behind it was what I would have to describe as a slit in the rock face against which the prayer hall was built. It was small and very narrow, and I don't think even in my most yogic moments I could have fit inside it, but that didn't matter as the space was taken up by three statues, Naropa, and his legendary students Marpa and Milarepa. It would have been a miracle for the great teacher to have spent much time in there, but of course that is the point; somewhere as memorable as Lamayuru really should be founded on a miracle.

September 4

I stayed in Lamayuru another day to take a day walk up a tributary valley to the small monastery of A-Tisey. I started walking through drizzly rain and as I gained altitude the rain transformed to snow. By the time I reached the monastery I felt as if I was floating through a soft blizzard. On the trail I passed stolid yaks with their horns draped in bright silk ribbons, marks of their owner's pride. They stood unwavering, waiting out the hard weather in four-legged meditation. I arrived through fields of snow-blanketed barley. The early snowfall had collapsed hectares of grain and unless the sun returned to evaporate the frozen weight the harvest was doomed. By the scattered houses below the monastery mastiff guard dogs barked and tugged their choke chains to breaking. Past them, in a swirl of mist, trapped at the end of a box canyon, above a trio of farmer's huts, was the gompa.

I climbed the monastery steps but found the prayer hall locked; the local lamas, I later discovered, were helping the villagers clear snow from the ill-fated crop. I returned to the huts below, knocked on doors and eventually, from a one-room house set away from the others, an old man and his wife came to my aid. I explained in a combination of Hindi, English and sign language that I wanted to see the prayer hall and from beneath the purple sash girdling his waist the old fellow produced a cluster of keys so dense it looked like a metallic hedgehog.

We walked back up the trail. Well, I walked; the old man shuffled painfully, which maybe explained his absence from the fields. Fumbling to extract one of the medieval-looking keys, he opened the prayer room door. He turned and smiled; three blackened stubs were all he had for teeth. His face was broad and dark, his skin creased like an ancient cowboy's. Each time I tried to speak he smashed his open palm against my back and let air whistle through his broken teeth.

We took our shoes off at the door, and the cold of the smooth mud floor crept through my woolen socks. The man was keen to show me the prayer hall and even more intent that he, the tiny boy who had followed us and snuck into the temple between our legs, and I should prostrate before the life-sized gilded Buddha that took pride of place on a throne at the head of the room. He was indicating with his hands how the three of us should drop our heads to the floor, but I was unsure. I was stalling.

Was I ready, ready to commit myself to such an act of faith? Having been raised Presbyterian I had never bowed before a statue before. To expose myself in front of an image was something distant for me. But in truth I felt comfortable there, the snow falling outside, the smell of wood and butter all around and beside me a little boy with a baby goat held close to his chest.

Images came to me. The countless prayer stones scattered across the valley. The thousands of stupas, whole plains given over to those reminders of what is important to Buddhists. I thought of the old man's wife, standing in her doorway, waving as we left their house. Her dried-apple smile was as toothless and generous as her husband's.

Through an open window I smelled the snow, the first of the season, fresh as clean paper.

The Buddha sat before us.

Balanced.

His hands, strong and pliable, hovered over bent knees; his eyes, half-open, were those of an adoring mother.

He was perfectly motionless.

The old man was chanting prayers and moving his hands in the tai-chi style gestures called mudras. He started to drop to the floor and I found myself following; three generations dropped our foreheads to the floor. It was a layering of ages. I heard the rustle of the man's heavy woolen robes and the cracking of his ancient joints. To my left the boy's wheezing tubercular breath meshed with my own. I felt the cold, dry mud of the prayer room floor, smooth from afar, but abrasive against my forehead.

Behind me three goats were backlit against the open doorway, their heads cocked, amber slit-eyes staring, unblinking.

The old man mumbled mantras – rough, warm, words.

We returned to standing and repeated the motion. One prostration for the Buddha, another for Avoleskitevara, a last for Guru Rinpoche.

Three completions and I returned to standing – still Jono Lineen, still with both feet on the chilly prayer room floor. I looked at the man and the little boy with a face as smooth as peanut butter, still absorbed in prostrating, not interested in an elated novice.

The old man invited me to his home. In the kitchen we sipped cups of bu-ja, Tibetan salt tea. The old lady had made it when we arrived, pouring boiling water from a kettle on the woodstove into a long wooden tube encased in hammered brass. Then she added chunks of black Chinese brick tea, flakes of salt and a few pats of golden butter. The mixture was churned vigourously in the tube, then the contents poured into the wooden cups laid on the low table before us.

The old lady looked every bit the good witch, her face creased by sun and labour, hair like tufted steel wool protruding from a bright yellow, many-peaked, woolen felt hat. The tea tasted like soup, excellent for the freezing weather. There was no conversation; we smiled at each other. I pointed at the cup, making thumbs-up gestures. Eventually, my sign language grew stale. The lady was ready to brew another batch of tea/soup but I stood, pointed to the door and bowed with insistence. The man escorted me out. His wife waved. Outside snow was still falling.

September 5

Early the next day I left Lamayuru to walk south over the Prinkiti-la for Wanla village at the junction of the Shillakong and Yapola rivers. The bad weather held, wreaking havoc on the trail. In shiny mud I slipped uncontrollably on the way up, but the route down was even worse. Cabin-size hoodoo slabs of silt-stone tumbled from the walls lining the track.

When I reached Wanla, sky and earth were the same dull shade of grey but nearby at the rivers' confluence the mist had risen and shafts of light broke the cloud. The sun struck the dewy landscape, briefly returning harvest colour to the quilt-patterned fields. Beyond the village were more signs of the rain's destruction. Puddles gathered where almost ripe barley should have been and tattered, blue plastic tarpaulins covered the circular, hard-packed threshing grounds by every home. The hamlet's small gompa, a series of low one-storey buildings, sat high upon a razor-backed ridge north of the village. The mud-brick buildings were so close in colour to that of the land they looked to be sprouting organically from the hill. Only the cream and carmine washes around the windows and doors distinguished them from the earth.

I made lunch under a tree and some villagers, a bedraggled trio of men on their way to survey damaged crops, stopped to talk. They told me how the rain was destroying the trail to Zanskar. Only a single group had gotten through the gorge from Hanupatta village the day before and that passage was won only after hours of rebuilding the path and with the loss of one precious horse; in seconds the poor animal had slipped in the mud, gone over a cliff and been taken by the river. Until the rain ceased and there were three days of sun, the villagers said, they would not move their livestock from the secure high pastures. I asked if they thought a single man could make it through the gorge and an old fellow in a threadbare burgundy hat and rubber boots three sizes too big for him piped up in English, "You're crazy enough, you'll make it!"

The start of the trail up the Yapola River was dotted with craters, the result of rain-loosened boulders toppling from the cliffs. The walls on either side of the river were unstable conglomerate stone, remnants of the 600-million-year-old Tethyan Sea floor which, over time, the earth's tectonic plates had pushed 5,000 metres towards the sky.

Farther on the canyon narrowed, and in the distance, through curls of mist, I saw boulders somersaulting over the trail. Strangely, the wallop of the careening rocks carried above the water's roar. Near Phenjilla village, half way to Hanupatta, a drowned yak floated by, its dark coat glistening on a bloated corpse. Its stiff legs caught in the branches of a half-submerged tree. The right front hoof wagged in the current, a taut, controlled movement, like the queen waving from her golden coach.

Then, three kilometres after Phenjilla, I was faced with the inevitable. Before me, a gaping metre-and-a-half-wide hole had severed a section of the trail that had been built with wood and stone directly into the cliff wall. The narrow path was disintegrating. Loose stone on either side of the breach framed the river. The water below was dun-coloured and frantic. I had to decide, forward or retreat. Any other route to Zanskar would be longer and just as dangerous. My mother whispered in the back of my head, "Turn around, be safe," but not for the first time I foolishly ignored her.

Stepping back twenty paces, I took a running leap. My body rose. I hung for a millisecond and landed – *bam* – two feet on solid ground, my nervous knees hammering like a sewing machine. I breathed deeply and leaned against the cliff to regain some composure.

I set off again, now dwelling in the sharpness that follows difficult experiences. The river was louder, the tenuous light gave the moist cliffs an even sheen, raindrops flickered on their descent.

A kilometre farther on my resolve was tested again. As I edged across a sloughing section of open trail the mucky surface moved, shifting towards the creek. I was moving with it. Simultaneously, from above, I heard the rifle crack of falling stone. I was trapped. If I moved I might destabilize the slope, but if I stayed where I was the falling rock could smash my skull. I couldn't look up and lose my footing and in that moment of absolute exposure there was only one choice – faith.

I pressed my face into the mud, praying for protection, forgetting the Lord's Prayer of my youth and repeating instinctively the only mantra I knew, *Om Mani Padme Hum*.

One second, maybe two, and a trio of rocks whizzed by, inches on either side of me. I glimpsed them landing, contained splashes in the churning river.

I waited and waited, still praying. The slope stopped moving and I pulled my mud-caked boots from the coagulated mess. Another hour of tense walking and the canyon opened out. The wind eased and my heart rate slowed.

I pitched my tent at the junction of the Yapola and Spung rivers on a small plateau close to the water – not too close as I was fearful of a sudden rise in the water level, but still far enough away from the cliffs and their falling debris. I set a pot of water boiling on the stove – coffee was what I really wanted. I sat just inside the vestibule of my tent, sipping the hot brew and listening to the crack and roar of water and stone hurtling down the canyon.

September 6

I was up early as I had a long day's walk ahead. After instant coffee and oatmeal with lumpy milk powder and lots of sugar, the kind of breakfast that kept me going for hours, I packed quickly. It was almost automatic now how everything I needed was assembled, disassembled and neatly put away. By seven a.m. I was walking. The trail followed the Spung River west towards Hanupatta.

All morning the rain fell but by the time I reached the village, with the gain in altitude, it was falling as plump, billowing flakes of wet snow. The valley was blanketed with a pristine cover of white. I stopped in search of a hot drink, but at the tea stall people were too busy clearing the storm's slushy mess to concern themselves with a thirsty foreigner.

The young owner of the tea stall pointed me towards a house where he said they would make me a hot drink. I wandered in the open door and found the old owner and his wife huddled in the only dry corner of their kitchen. Their hands clasped steel mugs of steaming rice wine, or chang as it's known in Ladakh. They offered me a cup and I stayed for two. Two men and a woman, the grown sons and daughter, wandered in and out surveying the damage to the walls. None of them seemed to care that a stranger was in the family home drinking chang with their parents.

Ladakhi houses are built to endure cracking cold. Metre-thick mud-brick walls create massive insulation and tiny windows hamper the entry of winter's bitter winds. Adobe is the perfect material for that environment, but precipitation, a rarity on the north side of the Himalayas, is as decimating to earthen homes as fire is to wooden ones. In Hanupatta the houses were collapsing. Waterlogged roofs trembled on their birch branch trusses. The two old people were quiet, but I felt the need to reciprocate their hospitality with conversation and asked in Hindi about the state of the village. The old man broke into a grin, wrinkles multiplying around his mouth and eyes. "Rains come and some houses will break," he said, "but we can build them again." When I left they smiled and waved, shockingly nonchalant about their house disintegrating around them.

I stopped at the stupa on the edge of the village and was overtaken by a fast-walking man, his son and their four donkeys. The man stopped to catch his breath and sat on the stone bench at the base of the monument. When I asked why he was in such a hurry, he said his animals were needed in Photoksar, the next village, to assist in a relative's barley harvest. He was in a rush. He stood to leave and I joined their modest procession.

Donkeys are not all-weather animals. With their knobby knees, tiny hoofs and swollen bellys, they look desperately out of place in a winter landscape. Any time we stopped the little beasts shivered uncontrollably.

It is twelve kilometres from Hanupatta to Photoksar and to help the little animals through the deepening snowdrifts the man was shovelling off the top six inches of cover. In such weather it seemed a manic trek, but the relative's harvest would begin as soon as the melt was on and the man had promised to help.

It was five kilometres from Hanupatta just to the base of the 5,000-metre Sisir-la. We started the long climb but within an hour it became obvious the donkeys were reaching their physical limit. They would stop mid-trail breathing heavily, their eyes closed as if the view ahead disturbed them. Only stern words from the farmer moved the group onwards.

The trail steepened. Donkeys and humans were breathing in time.

The young boy rode the lead animal. He was as quiet as his father was vocal.

Sometime in that second hour I heard a soft thud behind me. I turned to see the third animal in the line collapsed in knee-deep snow. The man shook his head, turned around and dropped to his knees. He murmured words of encouragement but the animal only replied with wheezing gasps. Its leg muscles were contracting violently. The father began to massage the donkey's legs and talked to it as if addressing an injured child. The son sat calmly on his mount, unblinking. The three other mules stared mutely at their compatriot. Eventually, the broken donkey climbed gingerly to its feet, snow hanging in clumps from its matted coat. It was the end. The man looked at me and raised his hands, palms to the sky. He had to surrender to the elements. If the donkeys were to die there was no point in going on. So, with a shake of his head, the entourage turned and moved in slow motion back the way they came.

In silence I continued on, following the hoofprints made by a yak the day before through deeper and deeper snowdrifts. It was late afternoon, the sky had cleared and shadows were becoming long and distorted. The top of the pass was nowhere in sight.

The tracks became my focus. I followed them doggedly, one foot in front of the other, each step gaining altitude, each movement requiring more and more effort. I felt a symbiosis between my breath and the steps. At the start of the climb I had been taking one strong breath for every two steps, then it was one breath for every single step. Eventually, with the altitude, I was breathing during the step and then breathing again before initiating the next motion. I was moving slower and slower but the pace didn't bother me; it was a meditation.

I imagined the freezing air making the transition from atmosphere to energy, first passing the moist channels of my nose and mouth, travelling down the fleshy passage of my trachea, filling my lungs and then, in the tiniest recesses of the capillaries and alveoli, transferring oxygen into blood and bringing energy out to my energy-starved legs. At that altitude I recognized inhalation as a nurturing pulse through my thighs and calves.

On what I thought was the last pitch to the summit, the yak prints veered left and moved away perpendicular to the fall-line of the slope. Even the yak had decided that reaching Photoksar was not worth the effort. I was alone, plowing through thigh-deep snow in the mellow light before sunset.

Where the yak had turned was not the last pitch; it took another hour to reach the ice-crusted stupa that marked the divide. I was drained. I sat on the monument's top step to catch my breath. I stood up, took off my pack, lay down on the ice-crusted snow and from there watched the last minutes of the sun's descent. Copper-pink wisps of cloud flitted north. The sun edged behind a line of guardian crags. In its wake a frigid border swept across the tilted plane of the pass and then there was darkness.

The temperature dived. I threw on my pack and raced straight down from the pass. Gravity was working with me. The energy I had lost on the climb returned in the thrill of the descent. I threw myself down the hill, using the metre of fresh snow as a brake. With each step my feet drove deep into the drifts and my body leaned forward against the packed snow. The moon had pulled up from behind the ridge and the slope was bathed in a pale glow. I was being pulled as fast as my legs would carry me. If I fell it was a soft landing, and I would let out a whoop, roll over the top of my pack and be thrown back to standing.

I reached an open stream, the first signs of the Photang River, and followed the trickle to an open patch of shaly ground. The ascent had taken five hours, but I reached the campsite only forty minutes after leaving the pass.

I pitched my tent by touch, scooped frigid water to make my rice and dal, then wrapped my sleeping bag around me as I ate. The temperature was still falling and if I concentrated I could hear the snap and crack of stones and plants, the water in them freezing and expanding, pushing out against minerals and living cells. Even in that frozen space the world was moving.

September 7

I woke without hearing the tinkling of the creek. It was the first week of September and already moving water was freezing. I slept until nine a.m. – today would be an easy fifteen-kilometre trek. I had learned from crossing the Sisir-la that it was folly to attempt the next pass, the even higher Singe-la, in the slushy conditions of late afternoon. Instead, I would camp at the base and climb the next morning at first light on the icy crust.

I arrived at Photoksar to clear skies and sunshine, made doubly bright by the veneer of snow. The village is the most spectacular on the northern route to Zanskar. It clings precariously to a cliffside above the turbulent Photang River and looks ready to crash into the gorge with the slightest shudder of Mother Earth. Pragmatism is behind its positioning; the most fertile land lies behind the village and so, to optimize cultivated space, homes have been moved to the edge of the abyss.

Photoksar had suffered badly in the storms. I saw, in open areas, stalks of barley crushed under the weight of drifts. On the slopes people were shovelling snow to expose patches of grass for hungry goats. The animals had, for the past three days, been on minimal diets culled from stocks set aside for the long winter and now, with the change in weather, every effort was being made to provide fresh feed. Any pasture exposed now meant another day's fodder during the lean days on the far side of the cold season.

I thought about stopping in Photoksar but the village was empty because everyone was in the fields so I kept walking. Just east of the village the Photang River joins the larger Yapola River and I followed it south towards the Singe-la.

I topped a small hill not far out of the village that offered views down the broad valley towards the base of the pass. Knowing I didn't have to race the sun to the top made for an easy walk. I stopped frequently, caught in the silence, so quiet after the residents' frenetic activity in Photoksar and my own efforts climbing the Sisir-la. Nothing stirred in the rock-walled amphitheatre; there were no echoes from far-away cliffs, not even the rush of a river. Between the rocks, deep pink clusters of stonecrop bloomed.

Overhead ravens soared, jet-black spirits, spiralling up and down on invisible drafts. Usually they are raucous aerial gymnasts, but that day even they were silent. I tracked them skywards until their silhouettes disappeared into blue. From that height they must have been able to see from the Indus to the Vale of Kashmir. That was fitting because in Tibetan culture ravens are far-seeing clairvoyants, oracles with the ability to predict the future, and in every village there are men and women skilled at interpreting the black bird's mystic utterings.

My thoughts were broken close to the end of the valley as two Zanskari men caught up to me. Tenzin was headed to Lingshed village and Padma to Nerax. Both planned to tackle the pass at dawn. We pushed on together.

Zanskar is the farthest western extent of Tibetan Buddhist influence. Zanskari is a Tibetan dialect and Buddhism originally came to the valley from Kashmir possibly as early as 200 B.C.E.. The earliest stone carvings have been traced to the Kushan period (100 B.C.E. to 500 C.E.). But Zanskar (and Ladakh) were overrun in the seventh century by pre-Buddhist Tibetans from the west who imposed their animistic Bon religion.

The influence of Buddhism was revived in Zanskar in the eighth century when Tibet was converted to Buddhism. Between the tenth and eleventh centuries, two lineages of monarchs were established in Zanskar and the major monasteries of Karsha and Phuktal were founded. This independence lasted until the fifteenth century when the valley came under the influence of Ladakh, and when Ladakh became part of the state of Jammu and Kashmir in 1842, so too did Zanskar.

It was good to be with two such cheerful men. Padma, the younger, had just returned from New Delhi and was eager to practise his English. He chatted away with little regard for grammatical intricacies. I liked his rendering of the language, as he crafted spontaneous constructions anytime the English eluded him. Our discussion became an exercise in improvised vocabulary.

"Mr. Jono," he would say, "we are hoping with most gandatca that you will Apti be coming with Tenzin and muchta to our homes."

I rolled his words over my tongue, imagining new meanings, searching for linguistic relationships, replaying the game that must have initiated my own first understanding of the language forty years before.

Padma and Tenzin were planning to camp in a small shepherd's hut and invited me to stay with them. When we arrived I saw the shelter was four walls of loose stone. The roof was strung with branches and the men had brought their own tarp to throw on top of it. I declined their offer as the size of the hovel would have meant we would be sleeping on top of one another. But I happily joined them for dinner.

I pitched my tent, laid my sleeping bag out and returned to the hut. Tenzin stoked the yak dung fire until bitter, white smoke obliterated our view of each other. Then he got down to the business of making thukpa. Thukpa in Zanskari means soup but it covers a wide variety of the dish, from fragrant glass noodle broths to the doughy mass of yak cheese stew my friend prepared that night. The meal was complemented by two bottles of chang that Tanzin produced from his rucksack.

We laughed and joked late into the night; the men were full of stories. Any impressions I may have harboured about the peaceful Buddhists of Ladakh and Zanskar were comically challenged that night as Padma told me of his favourite brothels and prostitutes in New Delhi and Tenzin, with Padma interpreting, gave us stories of his time in the Indian Army and the regular alcohol-fuelled brawls he had gotten into with other soldiers. Exhausted, I excused myself long before they were ready for bed.

Outside silver-fringed clouds drifted by a gibbous moon. In my slightly drunken state I searched for ravens, winged silhouettes against the pale light. I breathed deeply, cold air touched by ice, the taste of glaciers. I slipped into my nylon cocoon. Padma and Tenzin's rowdy shouts quietened as I drifted to sleep.

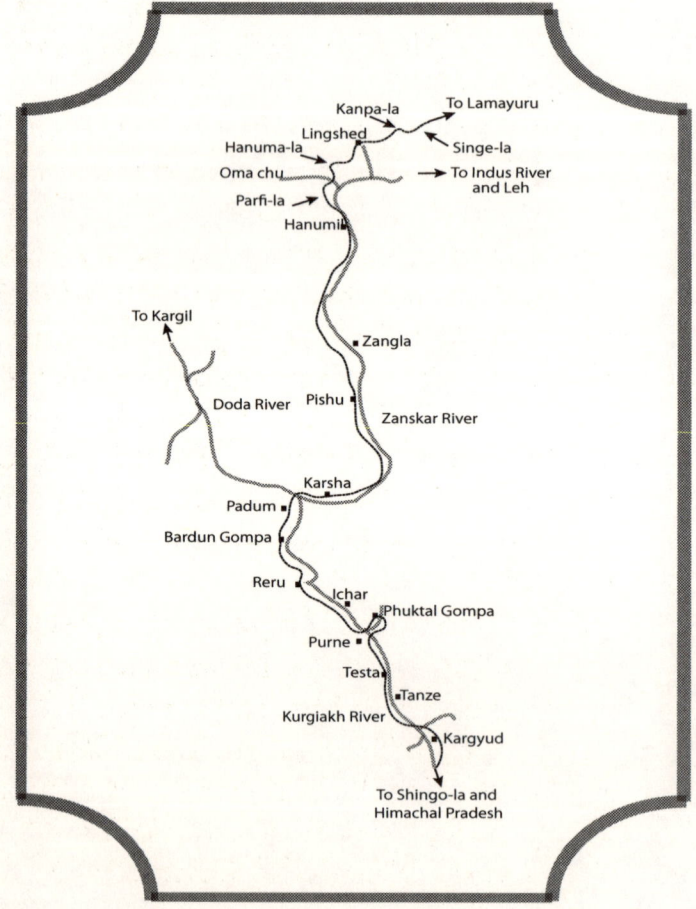

ZANSKAR, JAMMU AND KASHMIR, INDIA

CHAPTER 4
Dreams and Truth

September 8

It was a freezing night. I had difficulty sleeping because a chill had worked inside my sleeping bag. I woke and had to put on more clothes. At 5:30 a.m. my friends good-naturedly shook my tent and shouted goodbye as they started off. I unzipped my bag and put more clothes on while still lying down. Inside and out everything was frozen: boots, toothpaste, the pegs holding the tent down. I rushed my packing. Breakfast was cold biscuits and juice crystal slush.

The Zanskaris were long gone. I could see them far up the slope, ants on the horizon. Faint words and melodies from Hindi film songs trickled down to me; Padma was reliving his New Delhi summer.

The surface of the snow was firm, and a dusting of hoar frost made for good walking, but by 7:30 a.m. the temperature was rising and the crust was fracturing with each step. It was heavy work, and every fifteen minutes I stopped to catch my breath. Once again I found myself following the tracks of a yak. My oxygen-starved mind became absorbed in the trail of prints. I began to interpret the mechanics of its motion. Each hoof-mark lay almost exactly the same distance apart; its gait was slow and methodical. The hoofs were lifted with precision, dragged through the snow and placed, slightly angled backwards, with metronomic consistency. The stride length varied little and the depth of the impression related more to the amount of snow than the angle of slope. The yak had created an imprint that stood uncannily at ninety degrees from the vertical and I used the tracks as a single-laned stairway.

Morning wore on. I moved, literally, at a yak's pace. It felt natural; the yak is probably the mammal most adapted to that landscape. As the steps wore on the economical, unhurried disposition of the yak permeated me. I realized the only rhythm that agrees with high altitude is slow and contemplative. I was drifting into the true nature of walking: the absolute focus on each step, a subconscious awareness of my physiology. The physical mantra of walking was evolving in the steps of the yak.

I don't know what came first, my fascination with the Himalayas or my love of walking. About the same time I was reading Chris Bonington's *Everest South West Face* my mother decided in a fit of maternal dictatorship that the family (minus my dad since he was beyond dictatorial edicts) should be out walking after dinner. We four kids and Mum would set out in the long summer evenings along lanes and pathways on the outskirts of Belfast that in those days were bush-lined and cobblestoned. Little streams and untamed copses bisected the trails. I discovered a peaceful, composed and yet wild place was within walking distance of our house. That space was probably the closest I could get to the Himalayas of my dreams and therefore it was doubly attractive.

Eventually, my brothers and sister returned to watching TV after dinner but I couldn't let that wildness go, and to walk there, to be for the first time in my life in complete control of my movement, made those places doubly precious.

When Gareth died my Himalayan dreams were resurrected, so in a way it was only natural that I would venture to those mountains to walk. Walking over the years has become a medium for me, a way to interpret the world. Walking is what human beings were designed to do. I think our natural speed of thought is four kilometres an hour, a pace in time with our moving feet. For me the motion – the drop of the heel, the roll onto the ball of the foot, the flex of toes and the push off with a bend of the knee – is so embedded that there is home deep within the movement.

By ten o'clock I could see the stupas marking the top of the pass. As I moved towards them they came at me like a half-speed, overexposed film. I reached the summit in an altitude-induced dream-state. Prayer flags snapped in the wind. The sky's azure brilliance faded to pastel at the horizon and there melted into the ice of the peaks guarding the pass. The snow that drifted to one side of the stupa was as fine as baker's flour. I leaned against the mud-brick monument. My rucksack dug into my spine. I unslung it and dropped onto the bottom step of the stupa's foundation.

I liked that stupa. It was not neat or clean like city stupas in Kathmandu or Lhasa. It was off-kilter, unwashed, earthen, its steeple bent. There was nothing perfect there, just a homeliness that encouraged you to sit, a roughness that reminded me of the stupa's role as intermediary between Buddhist philosphy and the simple beliefs of the local people. For lay people, stupas are not just repositories of the Buddha's teachings but, because of the power they symbolize, guardians past which evil spirits cannot proceed. Without those stone spires gracing every major Himalayan pass, Buddhists believe that negative forces would congregate in a particular valley and tip the scales of good and evil towards the side of immorality.

A few hundred metres below the pass on its southern slope the snow petered out. By 4,000 metres the trail had dried and the footing was solid. The sun warmed me. I heard the chirping whistle of marmots and here and there in the shallow soils violet gentians bloomed. At one point a snow cock exploded from behind a patch of prickly sea buckthorn, and I shouted in surprise then laughed at my panic.

The Kanpa-la and Murgam-la, mere bumps compared to the morning's climb, floated past and by six o'clock I was looking down on Lingshed Gompa.

The monastery was quiet in the hour before sunset. Lingshed is a jumble of mud-brick buildings, perhaps thirty in all, built into a fifteen-degree slope. The complex is crumbling and yet has remained solid in that position for centuries. The gompa looks to be pulled by gravity; architecturally dense at the top of the slope, it is centred on the large prayer hall and shrine rooms, then the buildings thin downwards until the hillside levels and fields of barley take over. There is no road to Lingshed, no electricity, no flush toilets, no bottled gas to cook on. The village looks much as it would have two or three hundred years ago.

Legend has it that Lingshed was founded in the eleventh century by the great Tibetan translator and monastery builder Lotsawa Rinchen Zangpo. At age seventeen Rinchen Zangpo had been sent from the western Tibetan kingdom of Guge to Kashmir to develop a written Tibetan language, and then translate Buddhist texts into that language. He returned to Guge seventeen years later with his translations in hand and on his homecoming was responsible, under the patronage of the local king, for building 108 monasteries in West Tibet and what is now northwestern India.

Lingshed's positioning on the main trade route from Ladakh to Zanskar made it an important stopover for traders and travellers. But now, with a road pushed into the Zanskar Valley from the north via Kargil, Lingshed has become a backwater. Merchants and ascetics have been replaced by foreign trekkers, the new pilgrims attracted by the village's distance from highways and electric grids. Lingshed is a Luddite Shangri-la.

By the time I reached the gompa night had fallen. From the last pass I had seen the monastery in golden, late afternoon light and the buildings had looked intriguing, but with sunset they turned ominous; narrow alleys were dark and littered, guard dogs barked close by and the acid smell of urine clung to walls. Eventually, a young monk led me inside the gompa and in the firelight of the monastery kitchen I found my old friend Lama Karma.

We had met a couple of years before when I had been in Lingshed on a previous trek. He had been more than generous with his time, guiding me around his village and introducing me to his family. Since then we had met again in Leh. There was always something to talk about as the lama was interested in not just his religion but also in the history, agriculture and economic development of the community. When we met in the kitchen, he embraced me and almost immediately took me off to his room.

"Come, come," he said. "You are tired and hungry, my friend."

The room was a three-metre by three-metre mud-brick cell with one roughly glazed, wooden framed window. The lama's bed was pushed against one wall, while against the other were low tables stacked with books, a pair of candles, a Walkman-style cassette player, an open tin of biscuits and a plastic bag of dried Zanskari cheese. Almost immediately from beneath his bed Lama Karma pulled out a single burner kerosene stove and by candlelight busied himself preparing a thukpa that put Tenzin's fare to shame. We talked, ate, laughed and drank cup after cup of hot, salty, butter tea.

Lama Karma was in his late twenties and had been a monk for nearly two decades. For Buddhist families it is auspicious for at least one child to join the monastery, traditionally the youngest son. The tradition creates a blood connection between every clan and the community's spiritual and administrative centre, the monastery.

Lingshed Gompa belongs to the Geluk-pa school of Tibetan Buddhism. Tibetan Buddhism is split into four main schools of thought, the largest and arguably the most influential being the Geluk-pa tradition of which the Dalai Lama is the head. It was founded in the fourteenth century by the philosopher Je Tsongkhapa. The second largest school is the Kagyu who trace their lineage to Tilopa (the teacher of Naropa) in the eleventh century. The Sakya tradition was founded by Khon Konchog Gyalpo in the eleventh century and the Nyingma, which literally means "ancient ones," is the original school of Tibetan Buddhism created in the eighth century by Padmasambhava.

The monastery's central purpose is the same as that of all Buddhism – the elimination of suffering for all sentient beings. To achieve this the community must produce enlightened teachers or bodhisattvas who will guide the population to a higher state of consciousness through the teachings of the Buddha. Everyone in Lingshed Gompa, from the cooks to the Abbott, to artists and farmers, is engaged directly or indirectly in that goal.

But like every aspect of Himalayan culture the brotherhood is in transition. There is an awareness within the sangha – the order of monks and nuns – that the villagers have material needs. Strong steps on the spiritual path can only be taken when the belly is full. So a new variety of monk is evolving in India, Nepal and Tibet to address the questions of development in the twenty-first century. The Dalai Lama is at the forefront of the movement, as he has said, "In Tibet we paid little attention to technology and the environment. Today we realize that this was a mistake."

Lama Karma is a remote example of this new wave. Interested in language, agriculture and science, he is trying to promote growth in Lingshed through instruction in Western subjects and an emphasis on Ladakhi values. As he said, "Knowledge, not money, is the key to contentment."

When I asked how he was applying this, he chuckled and said, "Well, I must start with the children. I tell them that instead of begging for rupees or candy they should rush up to trekkers and shout, 'We need a new school, we need a new school.'"

I stayed that night on the floor of Lama Karma's room. I laid my sleeping bag on top of a thick handmade woolen carpet, which featured a pattern of interconnected dragons. In Tibetan mythology the ubiquitous dragon represents gentle power. The dragon thunders out of the heavens trumpeting the sound of compassion, a deafening roar that cannot be ignored. Between Lama Karma's snoring and the howling wind that ripped at the tiny window I too was deafened, but after climbing the Singe-la, Kanpa-la and Murgam-la, not even dragons could keep me from sleep.

September 9

The following day was spent with the monastery's painter, Lama Padma Stanzin, a man whose smooth face and easy smile implied a sense of contentment from his life's work. He wore the high-peaked yellow hat of the Geluk-pa Buddhist school, but it was forever off-kilter and with every third or fourth brush stroke he would nudge it. I liked that; brush, brush, brush, adjust the hat, refocus on the work, brush, brush, brush.

Lama Padma was decorating a new prayer room, a project that had taken him and two senior painters almost ten years to complete. On my last visit to Lingshed three years before, the room had been a colourful construction zone. Back then half-painted Buddhas and bodhisattvas, deities and mythic creatures evolved from what looked like roughly sketched, paint-by-number murals over the four walls. Colour-splattered floors appeared beyond repair and rickety waste-wood scaffolding had been draped in tattered tarpaulins.

Now the room was nearing completion. The space was about ten metres long, ten metres wide and three and a half metres high; two walls exhibited the major deities of the Geluk-pa school, a third was dedicated to the life stories of the Buddha and the fourth bore hundreds and hundreds of identical, thinly outlined, uncoloured Buddhas, a representation of the many manifestations of the one being. The fourth wall interested me the most because it was for the viewer to mentally fill in, to generate the Buddha in their own minds.

By the rear wall was the temple's focus, a two-storey, cast-metal statue of Maitreya. It was an amazing piece of religious art mainly because of its scale. The statue must have been cast in a workshop hundreds or even thousands of kilometres away and then transported piece by piece on trucks and then on the backs of yaks or donkeys over the high passes. In Lingshed it would have been reassembled, appliquéd with gold leaf and then had the details of its face and hands painted on. The figure was a brass jigsaw puzzle on a massive scale. Yet I found the statue disconcerting because it felt too large for the space. The temple roof had been heightened and the head was above the ceiling, its eyes staring through windows to the outside, not back in blessing to its devotees. There was a coolness about the image; it was aloof, removed from Lingshed's amicable dust and clutter.

To the local people, though, as Lama Karma explained to me, the immensity of the figure was moving. In a land where anything not made of wood or earth had to be imported on the backs of humans or animals, the statue's scale held power. To the villagers its size spoke of the teachings' authority.

I sat with Lama Stanzin. He was painting Buddhist imagery, dragons, snow lions and wheels of law on the cabinets that would hold the monastery's ritual objects. His concentration was unshakable. Tibetan Buddhist art is antithetical to modern styles because it shies away from spontaneity. The work is produced in strict accordance with thousand-year-old manuals. The lama had sketched the images in charcoal on the cabinet surfaces and was now painstakingly colouring the designs section by section. What moved the work from rote painting to spiritual practice was the lama's focus and understanding of the symbolism; his work was a meditation. Whereas critics can speak for hours on the possible meanings of modern art, the Tibetan style is formulaic, but within it is a millennium-old set of keys that opens the way to higher states of consciousness.

The deities the lama had painted on the walls were abstract representations of particular states of mind; many of the images symbolize the emotional impediments for individuals striving to achieve a higher state of consciousness. Tibetans believe that if a devotee meditates intently on the deity chosen for them by their teacher, they can connect with it, understand it and then the "problem" that the image characterizes will disappear. With the obstruction then out of the way the practitioner can move closer to a reality beyond the cycle of birth, suffering and death – the state known as nirvana.

The Swiss psychologist Carl Jung had a great interest in Tibetan Buddhism, and the formulation of his dream theory, where the content of a person's dreams are analyzed and discussed, can be attributed partly to his readings in Tibetan religion (Jung wrote the introduction to one of the first major works of translation from Tibetan to English, W.Y. Evans-Wentz's *Tibetan Book of the Dead*).

But for the villagers of Lingshed the high philosophy of Buddhism is something best left for the monks on the hill. For them, Lama Stanzin's paintings are a source of security, evidence that the Dharma is alive in their village and that the power of Buddhism will keep the gentle balance that generations have lived with.

September 10

Lingshed in September is a busy place. From dawn until dusk families work their land. There are no internal combustion engines or power tools to distract you from the harvest work, just people moving at a slightly quickened pace in fields and on pathways. Everything is done by hand or with livestock. It is the season that demands the most of the village, but the pace is sane and I loved that people made time to sing and that the children – babies, toddlers, schoolkids of all ages – were out in the fields helping or observing. The harvest is a necessary labour but its importance for the community also makes it a social undertaking. For me, a person to whom groceries are acquired in an air-conditioned supermarket, my time there was a lesson in how not to take food for granted.

Barley is the main crop in Lingshed simply because it is the only cereal that will grow with any vigor at 3,800 metres and the harvesting of it at that altitude is time-consuming, backbreaking work. First the barley is cut and loosely baled using home-forged scythes. Then the spiny bales are transported from the fields by humans, donkeys or yaks to the threshing grounds outside every home. At the grounds the stalks are threshed to separate the seed from the stalk; then a bed of grain is laid on the threshing ground's hard-floored circular space. The family's draft animals are tethered to a central pole and walk the circle. The pressure of their hooves cracks the barley, separating the hard shell from the nutritious core. Finally, the grain is winnowed using wooden pitchforks, the chaff taken by the wind, the kernels falling to the earth. The seed is now edible, but Himalayan barley takes a final step.

The grain is cleaned in a nearby stream and then roasted on metal plates over open fires. The roasting decreases the water content, producing a durable cereal called tsampa. The grain can be stored for years and ground into flour at any time. Tsampa is the taste of the Himalayas, and its smoky, nutty flavor can be found in everything from unleavened bread to home-brewed beer. Tsampa is the Himalayan staff of life, a fact you appreciate when you realize that every major occasion in the Tibetan calendar, from new years, to weddings, to the birth of a new child is celebrated by the tossing of tsampa to the wind.

I joined Lama Karma's family in transporting the crop from the fields to the threshing circle. The travesty of my attempts to coerce a fully loaded, irritable mule down a narrow trail sent the relatives into fits of laughter. The teasing wasn't cutting, but more an expression of surprise at my inability to manage the animals that Lingshedites grow up with. My comic management of the rowdy mule was quickly followed by a crash course in muleteering, patiently taught by the lama's uncle. He was a stern, smiling man who had a tendency when the mules would go their own way to grab the animal's ears with both his hands and wring them as if they were towels. It looked painful, but seemed to work.

Outside the family house we had lunch. The sunshine worked its way into everyone; chatter mingled with work songs, braying mules, crying babies and far-off chanting from the monastery. The meal was tsampa mixed with a flour of ground, dried peas and then kneaded with butter into a doughy lump. It was surprisingly tasty but required many swigs of steaming butter tea to wash it down.

In the afternoon I spent hours with Lama Karma's cousins winnowing the grain, throwing shovelfuls of the broken barley into the air and letting the wind take the rough husks. It's a skill that requires a deft touch, and by the end of the day itchy chaff had permeated every part of my body. The tickle in my clothes persisted for weeks.

At the upper end of village, inside the gompa, the late summer meditation retreat was underway. For the advanced monks prayer services were being held three times a day. The sound of drums, horns and chanting reverberated through the buildings and the sandstone cliff behind the monastery amplified them, delivering blessings to riverside fields at the far edge of the community.

In the evening I spent time in the monastery kitchen. I came to think of it as the warm, cluttered guts of the gompa. The low-ceilinged, dark and smoky room was a throwback to another age. Huge copper and brass urns glinted in the dim light produced by a single slit window. Fires burned constantly in the central stove, their amber light flickering on the glossy black walls. Shadowy men moved briskly through the shadows in silent woolen-soled boots. The kitchen staff's robes were the gompa's patchworked remains, stained with yak butter, soot and clouds of flour. In a poor, remote monastery like Lingshed the young monks inherit the robes of their recently deceased elders.

The older kitchen monks' hands were rough and scarred like rock, their skulls shaved clean. They were the monks whose practice is serving their more spiritually inclined brethren and yet they appear the happiest of the sangha.

The kitchen supplies meals and butter tea, not only to the monks, but to the families who labour in the fields owned by the gompa, so a stream of kettle-carrying novices flowed in and out of the fragrant darkness, all shouting and joking and spilling tea on the way. The tiny monks, some as young as seven, are constantly underfoot; for them the space must be a reminder of the mothers they left behind. For the older brothers it is a worldly sanctuary, a place removed from the rituality of the prayer hall. It's easy to see why that subterranean kitchen was the gompa's social centre.

Lingshed in those few days was magical. Time had shifted onto a different plane – it pooled in the silences between activity and rushed along during the haste of the harvest's work. I was happy eating thukpa made by compassionate hands and helping people who had no need for my ineptitude. Elements fell into place; the community and the land they were working on functioned symbiotically. I thought of the Vietnamese monk

Thich Nath Han's words: "If there is harmony and awareness the Dharma is there."

The Dharma is a cornerstone of Buddhism, simultaneously the natural law that underlies life and the actual teachings of the Buddha. I had read about the Dharma before I started on the trek, but was confused about its true meaning. To say that now I have an understanding of Dharma would be a lie, but in Lingshed for the first time I had a feeling of what Dharma might be. In Lingshed I felt I understood how a community works together, how individuals apply themselves in the process of assuring their village's survival. The practice of local wisdom, the selflessness displayed by everyone and their absorption in working for the greater good resonated with me as something integral to what the Buddha had taught. Thinking about the Dharma and the stability it creates has in some way helped me with Gareth's death. Yes, he's gone, yes, the Gareth I knew will never be here with me again, but although I don't completely understand it, I feel that Dharma in some universal sense must have compensated for the void he left behind.

September 11

In the morning, somewhat reluctantly, I pulled my sleeping bag from Lama Karma's floor and stuffed it in my pack with the clothes and books and maps I had scattered around the little room. Lama Karma had invited me to stay as long as I wanted, but because of the length of the trek I had to think months ahead. There were high passes hundreds of kilometres away that could be covered in fresh snow anytime in the next months. I had to leave. On the way out of the village I stopped dozens of times to shake hands and say goodbye. Everyone was asking when I would return, but all I could say was, "Soon, I hope."

From Lingshed it was south again to the Hanuma-la, a tiring set of switchbacks ending in a snow-covered summit. A pair of magpies escorted me up the start of the pass, the sun flashing on their iridescent plumage. They jousted back and forth, cackling and eyeing me suspiciously – talking behind my back.

On the stupa, at the divide, prayer flags had been worn to threads by the wind. I looked back to see the monastery, a collection of white matchboxes set against sandy cliffs. They looked so small, so impermanent against the crumbling massif behind them and yet for the village the monastery was the unwavering axis upon which the universe spun. Barley fields fanned out below the gompa – layers and layers of history. I thought of the work that had created those hundreds of hand-built paddies. My time there had been so rewarding, but Lingshed was distant from my history; I was not a barley farmer or a monk. Had the magic I had experienced there been merely the result of synchronicity and environment? I hoped there was something in me that could incorporate the goodness I had been part of.

From the base of the Hanuma-la into Zanskar the trail is lined with a procession of cliffs. The rock walls are the sedimentary remnants of the 250-million-year-old Tethys Ocean, evidence of the incredible forces involved in the creation and continual growth of the Himalayas, forces that have pushed what had been an ocean floor centimetre by centimetre five kilometres high.

Four hours into the day's walk I came across one cliff that stood out. Almost a kilometre long and 150 metres tall, it rose from a turquoise creek and dissolved on its upper lip into emerald pasture. The wall's geologic tattoo was coloured in golds and ferric red, dusty micas and jet-black slate. The colours were muted but subtly distinguishable. From every angle the pattern was hypnotic in its asymmetry.

The trail skirted the opposite embankment atop a hundred-metre-high precipice. This was disconcerting because when I took my eyes from the path I was drawn to the cliff wall, something disturbing on such a precipitous track. When I focused on the rock there was no scale; the wall was so immense and complicated that it could only be viewed as a whole. The cliff was new every time I looked at it. It was a million years captured in a line of stone.

The Parfi-la is the last major pass before Zanskar. Like the Hanuma it is a long slow set of switchbacks, but on the slope occasional springs released dark trickles and in the hollows greenery flourished; briery clouds of sea buckthorn stood beside tall patches of *Cirsium falconeri* thistle, purple and gold beds of milk vetch and potentilla. Red robins and brown accentors chirped and in the dry underbrush I heard the rustle of mice. Farther up the slope I saw plump marmots basking on flat stones in the sun, always with one eye to the sky, alert to circling hawks. Their whistled warnings rattled around the hillside.

Once again I was dropping into the clear world of walking. The beauty of the hill lay in its consistency – one step I would inhale, the next exhale – simple, symbiotic and yet in its detail complex. My world became focused on the relationship between the steps and the breath, yet birdsong and the plant's green sway reached me as complements to the movement. On the summit the ever-present stupa greeted me, the prayer flags snapped in the breeze and overhead a golden eagle circled slowly.

The first thing I saw on the far side of the pass was the Zanskar River flowing fast and dark. On the drier south side of the crossing there was no sign of plant life, only a khaki desert. This was the northern end of the Zanskar Valley, the farthest western outpost of Tibetan Buddhism.

I camped at the base of the pass, pitching my tent on a stony plateau not far from the river. I cooked my dinner, now back to my standard fare of rice and dal, and for the first time in days listened as the steam-engine rumble of my little kerosene stove was drowned out by the roar of whitewater.

September 12

The first village on the northeastern route into Zanskar is Hanumil, two homes set along a limpid creek that feeds half a dozen, grey-soil fields on a level below the houses. When I arrived the villagers were predictably busy with harvest business, but I lingered on the far side of the stream remembering my last visit.

Two years before, I'd joined three friends and walked into the valley during winter on the frozen Zanskar River. I had always wanted to visit Zanskar during the cold season because, with snows blocking the high passes, the area is completely cut off from the rest of India. People had told me the feeling in the valley during winter is like Tibet before the upheavals of the Chinese Communist invasion in 1949.

The winter walk can only be done after an extended cold snap – ten days of minus-fifteen-degree Celsius temperatures, then the river freezes, not solidly, but thick enough for groups to take advantage of the ice shelves that form along the riverbanks. For a few weeks in mid-winter Zanskaris can walk the flat ice to Leh in only six days, as opposed to the two weeks it takes to cross the high passes in summer. Groups undertaking the winter traverse sleep in caves along the riverbanks. At Hanumil, for the first time in almost a week, we could have slept indoors, out of the extreme cold, but the guides arranged for us to spend yet another night in an open cave on the opposite bank. They would not venture into the village because the district's most powerful shaman was in the midst of his winter retreat. The superstitious Zanskaris had no desire to disturb such a formidable power.

Zanskar is devoutly Buddhist and yet shamans and oracles, the men and women who harness the energy of local animistic forces, abound. Tibetan Buddhism has a multi-layered recognition of shamans and local deities; they consider them removed from the high religion of the monasteries and yet are certain these indigenous protectors have been "pacified" and turned for the good of the community by Buddhism. Today many monasteries and even the Tibetan government-in-exile consult oracles on topics ranging from crop yields to foreign policy. The relationship harks back to Padmasambhava. In his mission to rid Tibet of demons and bring Buddhism to the people, he converted many local deities to the cause of Buddhism. Guru Rinpoche proved to Tibetans the power of Indian Buddhism while simultaneously incorporating many of Tibet's old ways into what would become the Tibetan form of Buddhism.

The shamans of Zanskar generally act as healers, channelling local spirits for the benefit of paying clients. The Zanskari approach to treating illness is an example of the intercourse between ancient animistic forces, Buddhism and contemporary medicine. When I asked my Zanskari friend Namgyal about what he and his wife Dolma did when their children were sick, he said their first course of action was to take the child to a local monk who would perform a prayer ceremony or puja and arrange traditional, specially consecrated herbal medicine. If this had no effect, then they would seek the services of a shaman who would attempt to exorcise the afflicting demon. If the shaman's ceremony had no effect, their last option was to take the child to the district medical post in the main town of Padum. There, if the local medical officer was on duty, they would spend much of their meagre savings on prescribed allopathic injections and pills.

The valley between Hanumil and Pishu is a rolling landscape. On either side of the river rose disintegrating rock walls animated by late afternoon's fragile light. I moved past Pidmo, another village in the throes of harvest. Zang-la, on the opposite, eastern side of the Zanskar River, moved into view. Man-made entities almost indistinguishable from the landscape, its castle and monastery were just visible on their hilltops. Eventually, I saw Pishu off in the distance, a cluster of earthen houses huddled together against the gritty wind.

In the village I went in search of my friend Namgyal Dorje only to discover he was off in the pastures tending to his yaks. His wife Dolma invited me into their house and was only too happy to ply me with butter tea and flatbread. She catered to me while watching over her four children, all of whom were grappling for attention. She looked different than the last time I had seen her. Swaddled in five layers of felted wool shirts and jackets it was difficult to discern her shape, but after fifteen minutes of sideways glances I realized Dolma was pregnant. When I inquired in Hindi, she indicated with her fingers that she was in her eighth month. While I was in Dolma's house she never stopped working. Dolma was three weeks from giving birth and doing the work of a small army with only a light sheen on her forehead to betray the strain.

That afternoon while I relaxed and drank my tea I became absorbed in watching her feed the fire with jagged sticks and cow dung, placing the fuel expertly and blowing on it only enough to ignite the kindling; both wood and breath are precious commodities at that altitude. There was an artistry to the way she made a task I laboured at for hours appear elementary.

Namgyal arrived just after sunset; his eyes widened when he saw me. Namgyal and his father Aba-lay had been the guides on my walk into the valley on the frozen river. We shared good memories of that trip and had met in Leh and Manali since then. As he gave me a hug, I smelled yaks, his homemade cigarettes and the dry grass he fed his animals. Namgyal declared it was time for chang. Dolma poured us each a measure in chipped teacups and then one for herself.

On our first cup I congratulated Namgyal on the pregnancy. He shook his head saying it was not a good time for a child; his wife was needed to help with the autumn fieldwork. I was surprised. I interpreted his comment as a laying of blame on Dolma for an unwanted pregnancy, but he quickly took responsibility. The conception had occurred in deep winter, and as Namgyal said, "It was my fault. I had no patience. I was too quick." Whether his haste was in the actual event or the seasonal timing I didn't pursue.

It turned into a long evening of barley beer and tsampa thukpa with Namgyal narrating the problems of the Himalayan farmer under the glare of a kerosene lamp. The winters were too cold, the river was not the right level in the spring for good irrigation, one yak had died from an undiagnosed disease that summer and his wife's vegetable patch was producing less than usual. He had thought of moving away, south to Manali or east to Ladakh. Namgyal worked occasionally as a trekking guide and pony man, and had travelled throughout Northwestern India. To him life beyond the mountains appeared easy. He had seen hundreds of Westerners on holiday, but admitted to knowing little of the intricacies of life on the other side of the Himalayas and in his heart he was afraid to leave the barren security of his fields.

Dolma left us to put the children to bed. Our conversation slurred when my friend substituted distilled rice wine, arak, for the brewed chang. We were talking in contented circles touching everything from local politics to the insemination of yaks. Then out of the darkness Dolma returned with one baby awake but quiet in her arms. She sat at the edge of the arc of silver light and out of nowhere began to sing. In a voice that fluctuated from monastic chanting to the high-pitched call of a shepherdess, she sang local songs, accompanying herself with a hand-held, metre-wide, single-skinned drum. Her voice was ambrosia. Almost imperceptibly her voice altered between a crooning ballad and an adult lullaby.

I lay back amongst the rugs and sheepskins, the alcohol and altitude working through me. The kerosene lamp sputtered out and in the leftover flickering candlelight Dolma transformed into a fur-clad shaman. She smiled, her many layers heaving with her long breath. She caressed the drum, her hair shimmered – night black flecked with gold – the baby dozed angelically in her lap. She had come to lead her followers into that state where dreams and truth are irresistibly mixed.

September 13

It was a late groggy start, but with only five hours of walking to make the monastery village of Karsha there was no rush. The way follows the course of the Zanskar River past villages and shrines, along narrow ledges and through spartan fields. Sporadic canyons lead down from the cliffs. I could see trails winding up the muscular scarps to the east. The valley is wide but curves gently southwest. Down the path the wind blew steadily against me, warm like a desert scirocco. A gauzy layer of glittering sand coated everything.

By mid-afternoon I was within sight of Karsha Gompa. The monastery buildings, dozens of them, drop down a steep hillside. It was a chaotic assembly of mud-brick cubes in every size, from a single room to gymnasium-size prayer halls and shrine rooms. Parts of the complex looked to be forgotten, the adobe walls falling apart, door frames hanging without doors, faded curtains blowing through tiny openings, while other buildings were freshly whitewashed with new glass in the windows.

I moved along the base of the escarpment below the main gompa. An old man shouted greetings. I turned to wave and in that split-second a flock of snow pigeons, fifty or sixty, erupted behind him in a slate grey thunderhead. The sudden whoosh of their action caught me off guard. I released a concentrated breath. The similarity of the sounds, my breath and the autumn land exhaling through the pigeons' flight, impressed me. The earth and I were both drained from summer's efforts.

I struggled up the hill opposite the main monastery and reached the Karsha nunnery. There my friends, the nuns, Ani-Garskyid and Ani-Pema (Ani means nun in Tibetan), chatted busily between themselves at my unexpected arrival. I had met them when I had come to Zanskar a few summers before. My friend the anthropologist Dr. Kim Gutschow had lived in the nunnery on and off for many years and introduced me to the nuns. Kim spoke perfect Zanskari, but I had to communicate with them in a combination of Hindi, sign language and a smattering of mutually understood Tibetan and English words. Quickly, with great slaps on my back and lots of laughter, they ushered me out of the wind and into the warmth of their kitchen.

Ani-Garskyid and Ani-Pema were tiny women who barely reached my chest. It seemed their smooth, sun-darkened faces were forever struck with smiles. They had just returned from twelve hours of fieldwork, cutting and carrying loads of barley and clover, helping the families who were working the monastery's land. Their patched burgundy robes were permeated with the smell of smoke and goats. I thought they must be tired and so sank down on a cushion expecting us all to relax. But as soon as I sat they rose and moved to the miniscule kitchen where they began to prepare dinner. They would not accept my offers of help.

With a man in the house Ani-Garskyid went to see their neighbours and somehow procured chang. I complained of being uncomfortable drinking alcohol in the nunnery, but they would have none of my protests and never let my glass get more than half empty. In the kitchen I heard the sound of chopping and boiling and the metallic clang of pots and pans. Thirty minutes later they emerged with a small miracle, the most delicious Zanskari thukpa I have ever tasted. The soup was thick and buttery, laden with chunks of local cheese, tsampa gnocchi, spinach, potatoes and turnips, all fresh from the nunnery's garden. They had created a dish that brought out the flavours of the valley: dairy produce, seasonal vegetables, the gamey taste of roasted barley.

The two of them chatted in Zanskari, seriously and excitedly. Every once in a while they posed questions to me in the free-form combination of languages and signs we were using to communicate. They asked about nuns in my country, how many Buddhists there were, what did Christians think of the Buddha, what did women do if they didn't work in the fields? They were genuinely excited to have a visitor. The meal wound down, the chang bottle emptied. I sat back, replete in that atmosphere of affection, and when they considered their duty with me complete, they proceeded on to their responsibilities to the Buddha. Side by side, in unorthodox harmony they sang mantras before the tiny Buddhist statues and photos on their altar. I thought of my Nana singing hymns, not in church but around her house. She had such a beautiful voice, I could have listened for hours. An Irishman, drunk on Himalayan barley brew, lullabied by smiling Buddhist nuns. I dropped my head in thanks.

September 14

The night before the anis had almost carried me to a room removed off to one side of the nuns' living quarters. There on a raised shelf of mud bricks they had made up a bed for me. They had even spread my sleeping bag out. I lay down and almost before they had left the room I was asleep.

In the morning they brought me sweet milky tea and from the courtyard in front of the nunnery showed me, far down the hillside, where they would be working and then they left me on my own. After a slow breakfast I walked down to the fields and spent the morning with them carrying loads of wiry barley stalks to the threshing grounds near people's homes.

In the afternoon I joined the nuns in their small hall for the daily prayer ceremony, sitting quietly off to one side as they chanted mantras, lit incense and waved ritual objects before the paintings and objects on the main altar.

In the evening I was invited to dinner with the Karsha Lon-po in his house next to the convent. The Lon-po is the last in a long familial line of advisors to the King of Zanskar. He was a tall, straight man in his sixties and wore long burgundy, monastic robes and the golden hat of Tibetan Buddhism's Geluk-pa school. His thin face, relaxed eyes and long-fingered, unscarred hands implied a life of attentive thought. The Lon-po exudes nobility.

He is a man of many experiences – a father, husband, politician, chief minister, doctor, teacher and finally, when his wife had passed away, he took religious vows and became a monk. He still teaches at the village high school in Karsha and every summer walks in the mountains collecting the herbs he needs for his Tibetan medicine consultations. Nowadays, though, most of his time is spent in religious practice. The Lon-po even has a mischievous side, a half-smile here, a twinkle of the eye there and with that rascally undercurrent he leads a conversation to new questions and more complete answers.

The Lon-po has seen his valley through independence from Britain, invasion from Pakistan, the implementation of a Muslim bureaucracy from Kashmir, the building of roads and now, a new incursion, tourists seeking the last Shangri-la. When I asked him if all these changes in such a short time had been difficult, he said that for some in the valley it had been trying but for him it was not so hard because he understood his history and religion: "Change is what we deal with every day."

We talked for hours on Buddhism, education, modernization and at the end I had to ask how he stayed so vigorous at an age well past the lifespan of the average Himalayan. For the first time in our talk he laughed out loud, an infectious rumble that had me chuckling. His eyes glimmering, he said, "Well, yes, this is easy – I just stay happy."

September 15

The five kilometres from Karsha to the Zanskari capital, Padum, is a transition zone; it is a movement from an ancient Buddhist culture with its roots in religion and the landscape to a community wrangling with the idea of what the future could be. The dusty plain that stretches between the two is where the Doda River from the northwest and the Tsarap River flowing from the south meet and form the Zanskar River. Across the Zanskar hangs a neglected, wooden-planked, steel-cable suspension bridge. When I arrived, a caravan of two dozen pack horses were at a standstill on the north side. The wind was blowing the bridge back and forth and the horses refused to move on to it. They dug in their hooves and bucked their loads almost as if they feared crossing the cleft between Karsha and Padum. I made my way around the crowd, the pony men pulled back the horses blocking the entrance and I crossed the river with both hands clutching the frayed cables.

From the river it's a gentle climb to the main town. Along the route a bare concrete mosque with a tin-roofed minaret sits two hundred metres from a derelict gompa. Farther up the hill a bus stand with a single broken-down vehicle off to one side made an effort to be the town's centre. Around that widening in the road the up-valley smells of dung fires, aromatic ground cover and fresh-cut barley were replaced by those of diesel fumes and human excrement. The few hole-in-the-wall shops lining the turnaround were filled with packaged foods, milk powder, butter, freeze-dried soups, minute noodles, jars of Nescafé coffee and White Rabbit brand chewy candy from China. I couldn't help but notice that most of the boxes and bags were long past their date of expiry. It seemed Padum was the last place on earth for merchants to offload their merchandise.

I stayed that night in a concrete-block guest house a hundred metres from the bus park. My bed's metal frame screeched every time I took a deep breath. The window was set with a warped wooden frame that looked like something out of *Alice in Wonderland*, and through it the wind moaned and whistled. But in the evening men came to the café for tea and chang and thukpa, and over dinner I met with one of the organizers of the summer's anti-government protests, Tsewang Chosdor.

Mr. Chosdor, a local politician, is rich by Zanskari standards. He has an impressive house ten kilometres from Padum, drives a red jeep and spends his winters south of the mountains in the state capital, Jammu. He is a big man with a large head that hints at the personality he affects, that of a bull yak. Quiet, but inclined to outbursts, he had a slightly bellicose air that I had not detected from anybody else in Zanskar. As our talk wore on I couldn't help but think that he was a caricature of the Indian politicians he undoubtably chummed around with in Jammu.

Mr. Chosdor explained that Zanskar was being abused by the state government. The war in Kashmir and the ensuing collapse of the region's thriving tourist industry made Zanskar, a valley untouched by the insurgency and increasingly attractive to foreigners, an appreciable part of the regional economy for the first time in its history. It was Zanskari culture that was drawing tourists and generating hundreds of thousands of rupees in tax revenue and yet little of that money was being reinvested in the valley. The Zanskaris wanted more say in the decisions affecting their home, but after years of ineffectively lobbying the government the activists had to play the only card big enough to make the state politicians take notice. By shutting their borders, the Zanskaris attracted attention from the central government in Delhi and within a month state officials were visiting Padum on fact-finding missions.

However, to their credit the style of the protest was decidedly peaceful. According to Mr. Chosdor, the tourists had only been barred from the area around Padum and those who were already there were invited to dinner at local homes, told about the situation, and offered transportation to Kargil on the main Srinagar-Leh road.

In Leh the story had been reported quite differently. There, tour operators peddled rumours of trekkers being stoned, guides being beaten to a pulp, and even the possibility of kidnappings. Mr. Chosdor said there was only one "minor" confrontation (he didn't explain what the incident was or what had sparked it) but swore that foreigners were not involved. The tour guides in Leh had taken the rumours for truth because in India, where violence frequently explodes for lesser reasons, all rumours are believable.

I went to bed as the crowd emptied from the restaurant. I climbed the outside steps to my room and above the wind heard two happily inebriated Zanskari men singing Bollywood hit songs from five years before.

September 17

I left Padum early, following a track that, with the recent storms, had lost its gravelled surface and been returned to mud. I marched beside trains of yaks and goats on a greasy surface that brought frequent hilariously uncontrolled collisions between me and the animals.

Bardun Gompa, ten kilometres south on the Tsarap River, is renowned for its prayer wheel, the largest in the region. The vertical wooden drum is over five metres tall and encased in brass and silver. Inside are 108,000 handwritten prayers. One hundred and eight is the most auspicious number in Buddhism as it is the number of impediments in the way of individuals reaching a higher state of consciousness. I was looking forward to pushing the cylinder round and round. There is something satisfying about walking in circles while pressed against 108,000 mantras. Tibetans believe that with each rotation every individual prayer is sent off on the wind to help whoever is in need of them. But my arrival at the building was dampened by a seemingly rabid Tibetan mastiff guard dog chained at the entrance to the monastery. I retreated after the snarling beast lunged at me repeatedly. There were no monks or a caretaker in sight, so there was no point in waiting and I moved on. It was a frustrating start to the day.

However, the situation was explained to me that afternoon five kilometres farther on in the village of Mune. A man at the tea shop said since most of the monks were at home helping with the harvest, the lone caretaker, who was also involved in his own harvest preparations, was concerned about icon thieves and had left his dog to guard the monastery while he went about his business. It was sobering to think that people were willing to steal religious artifacts from such a poor area, but unfortunately there is a booming market for Tibetan Buddhist artwork and the statues and paintings in monasteries are often unprotected. They are easy pickings for criminals in need of something more than a cultural identity.

Ten kilometres farther up the river I reached the fields below Ichar village. It was late in the day and from the stretch of hand-built paddies that stepped down from the village I could see the harvest was almost complete. Neatly laid sheaves of barley were spread atop the plateaus like golden fans against the battleship grey soil. On other fields pea vines were rolled into tidy rings and arranged in interlocking circles.

I sat down on a flat rock above the terraces and watched as two hundred metres away a trickle of people headed home after the day's work; children sang while their mothers hummed, baby-toting fathers whistled out of tune and grandparents wheezed along in time. It was a symphony of laboured wind.

Ichar is separated from its fields by a fifty-metre-deep canyon, at the bottom of which flows a small stream. The path winds down into the chasm and then up the other bank. Topping each side of the trail are protective stupas. High above those monuments I could see the work that had brought the community into existence – a narrow channel sliced and built into the cliff wall to deliver water through an irrigation system to the fields below. Before the canal had been dug the plateau would have been an arid hillside. I could see five hundred metres or so into the canyon but the start of the canal was still farther back.

It was an impressive piece of engineering completed centuries before the advent of power tools. The work had been the product of many families and generations, a true community effort. In a way, the channel was evidence of the population's faith in the landscape. Before they started the work they would have to had trusted that snow-melt water would continue to flow. They needed confidence that earthquakes would not destroy their work. They had to believe that the soils of the new paddies would stay fertile for generations.

I descended the divide between the fields and the village in the last hour of evening. A flock of sheep, half of them black, half white, appeared from farther up the canyon. They moved in a single dense mass, a checker-patterned carpet, their oily wool glinting in the late light. Noiselessly they entered my line of vision. The shepherd, absorbed in their movement, ignored me, and just as silently they flowed out.

September 18

Out of Ichar I was followed by a dog, a scruffy, grey-brown mongrel with black patches dotting its flanks. He was a runt, shunned I assumed, by the mastiff guard dogs who dominate every village. He skipped along at my feet, staring up, tongue lolling to one side. He tagged along for kilometres. I was of two minds about my new friend. I was lonely, and it would be nice to have a partner by the stove, a sentinel outside my tent, but what would I do when the trek finally came to an end? It would be impossible to bring my new friend home. I was torn. I wanted him to join me but knew any relationship was doomed.

I picked up a rock, deciding I would give him three chances. I threw the stone near his paws. He tucked his tail between his legs and scampered away, looking back with true puppy dog eyes. That was it, I thought, but five hundred metres farther on and he was back, clambering up the rocks close to my left, eyes still on me, paws lightly padding along the scree. I took another rock and aimed. He shot off again. But another five hundred metres and he was back, shadowing me through the boulder fields. I chucked my last stone, praying he would understand my tough love, hoping he would ignore my callousness one more time. He leaped away. I moved on. When I looked back after five minutes there was no sign of him.

It was difficult for me not to think of Gareth, how as a teenager I had ignored him. He was my little brother and little brothers don't have much to tell an older sibling in those trying years. It's easy to regret in retrospect, but that is part of growing up. It's best to dwell on the shared laughs and mutual discoveries.

In the watered draws along the path sparse birch and poplars grew, while on the open hillsides thyme, sage and saxifrage poked through the stones and sand. The trail kept to an even grade along the banks above the river. In winter that stretch is one of the most hazardous on the river-ice walk from the upper Tsarap Valley down to Padum. The hillside's grade, the lack of trees and the even, shaly surface make it extremely prone to avalanches. A Zanskari once told me that some men prefer to navigate that section under the drunken influence of chang. They sing, shout and laugh their way through the danger zone hoping, as he explained, that the antics would make the vengeful earth spirits happy and thus let them pass without mishap.

After lunch I moved through the prosperous village of Cha, situated on a plateau up the east bank of the river. Its fields were spread across the lower tableland in a seamless patchwork. The little gompa at the centre of the village was freshly painted and draped with colourful banners in blue, white, red and gold. The village was in a festive mood, ready for the arrival of Dagom Rinpoche, a renowned Buddhist master who makes annual teaching visits to the upper valley.

In Purne, across the river, the villagers were also in the throes of organizing for the teacher's visit. They were whitewashing stupas, sweeping the areas between houses and grooming horses tied to the walls by the fields.

I stopped for tea at a roadside chai shop and chatted with the woman who owned the local guest house. Drolma was a square-jawed mother of four and a shopkeeping entrepreneur. Before I was halfway through my cup she was bemoaning the lack of tourists in the area that season. She estimated the protests in Padum had cut the number of trekkers by more than half. Drolma had spent a considerable amount of money on stock for her little store and most of it would now sit unsold over winter. She was in the process of scratching out the packages' date of expiry markings, saying, "I don't know why they put these on the boxes. In Zanskar we eat tsampa that has been in the granary for two or three years."

I tried to explain the significance of the dates, but Drolma had invested hard-earned money and she needed a return; if tourists bought the products next season without checking the dates, it was their own fault – *caveat emptor*. I thought about the stock on the shelves of the little shops in Padum and wondered if it too would sit there until some unsuspecting travellers bought it.

At Purne the Tsarap River, which flows from the east, is joined by the Kurgiakh River from the south. The main trail now followed the Kurgiakh, but I wanted to make a detour up the Tsarap to see Phuktal Gompa. It was late in the day and I knew I would have to hurry to reach the monastery before dark.

I moved fast but the pace didn't bother me. I was absorbed in the scenery. The trail wound through a terra cotta gorge where the Tsarap River flowed aquamarine. In midstream, spray-shined ochre boulders glimmered. The scene reminded me of the coral and turquoise birthstones every Tibetan child wears as protection from evil spirits. Those colours in the landscape lent it a sense of security. I felt the closeness of the land around me. In the cliffs, the water, the sky, semi-precious stones were mirroring the environment. In those colours there was a connection between children and the landscape. I felt safe and strong and as the sun's last rays illuminated the path I rounded a bend to see the gompa, carved into the cliffside.

Phuktal monastery wraps around a spring-bearing cave set into a hundred-metre-high cliff above the Tsarap River. Over time its buildings have spilled out of the grotto and down the hillside. Centuries of what looks like impulsive construction have produced a series of buildings and rooms that have been built to fit the rock they are attached to. The result is a labyrinth of nooks and crannies, secret passageways and hidden rooms.

The gompa dates from the fifteenth century. It is far removed from Lhasa, the intellectual heart of Tibetan Buddhism, and possibly its remoteness made it a favourite destination for meditators and mystics. Its most famous resident, however, was the Hungarian explorer and linguist Alexander Csoma de Koros. In the 1820s and 1830s he walked, with only his rucksack and a knowledge of twenty-seven languages, from Europe to Central Asia in search of the ethnographic roots of the Hungarian people. Arriving in the Himalayas he wrote, at Phuktal and Zang-la, the first Tibetan-English dictionary. From Zanskar he eventually made his way to Calcutta where he worked for the British government as a linguist. He never returned to his homeland and never fully accomplished his goal of discovering the background of the Magyars. He died young in 1842 of an undiagnosed fever in Darjeeling, Bengal, the summer capital of the British Raj.

In the monastery I was shown a room for the night by one of the older monks. It was a Spartan cell without even a window – strange, I thought, since its positioning above the river meant it must have a great view back towards Purne. The monk left me, closing the door. He had given me a small kerosene lamp made from an old tin can of sweetened condensed milk. Amber shadows wavered on the walls. After the spacious, colour-shot walk up the Tsarap the room felt claustrophobic.

September 19

The next day I spent in the fields below the gompa doing something I enjoyed, helping with the harvest. Seeing four young monks, two boys and two teenagers, heading out to the fields that morning I asked in Hindi and sign language if they were working on the harvest and whether I could give them a hand. They nodded and waved for me to follow them. Tenzin, Tinley, Karma and Thondup were excited as it was a chance for them to interrogate me on the ways of Westerners. The questions were the result of personal experiences with trekkers and what the boys had heard on the radio or read in magazines. Only the oldest boy, Tenzin, knew much Hindi so he translated.

"Why do your people always wear so many clothes?"

"Why are Western ladies never with their children?"

"Why do your people only want to eat rice and not tsampa?"

We went to the other side of the river. I had a tingle of pride in my understanding of the mechanics of the harvest. When we arrived at the cut barley I immediately got the smallest monk, Tinley, who looked no more than eight or nine years old, to stack the sheaves on my back. The little monk giggled, intentionally rubbing the barley around my shoulders to make sure that the itchy stalks worked well into my clothes. I followed the older monks towards a family's home and dumped the barley in a neat pile on the threshing ground. Four days in the fields and I was an expert!

We spent the morning weaving back and forth between the fields and the threshing grounds where the family's yaks and donkeys were breaking down the grain. By the house the grandfather of the family laughed every time I returned with a load, shouting at me in Zanskari and pretending to whip my backside with the rope he was using to keep the livestock circling. I asked Tenzin what the old man was saying, and the monk laughed, "He is saying hurry up, white yak, hurry up."

Late in the afternoon we made our way back to the gompa and after an hour of trying to extract prickly barley stalks from my shirt and jacket I joined the monks for dinner in the granite cavern that serves as the monastery's kitchen. The boys sat on either side of me, smiling. Tenzin told me the senior monks were impressed that I had helped in the fields. On the other side of the kitchen sat the elders, ancient, gap-toothed men in handsewn robes. The room smelled of bitter fresh-churned butter tea, juniper smoke and thukpa. There was no electricity, no gas, not even a glass window. Looking at the old men slurping soup from wooden bowls with handmade wooden spoons it was hard to believe we were not in another era. But thoughts of those possibly simpler times were snapped back to the twenty-first century when the head cook extracted a bread-box size battery-powered radio from a cloth sack and, setting it gently on the stone wall by the stove, tuned the crackling receiver to a cricket game between India and England happening somewhere thousands of kilometres to the south. The younger monks gathered around the set. The older men finished their meal and left the kitchen.

September 20

I was up early. Tenzin was brushing his teeth on the edge of the monastery courtyard, which looked south over the river. In the background was a ragged line of 5,500-metre peaks freshly dusted with snow. When he spat out his foaming toothpaste it fell for seconds before silently staining the rocks far below.

I returned to Purne and crossed the Kurgiakh River back to the main trail. There I met a caravan of six men and thirty horses heavily laden with government-supplied rations – rice, wheat, sugar and kerosene. These were their winter stocks, subsidized by the Kashmiri government and trucked in from Srinagar and Kargil to Padum. Those staples would be added to the hundreds of kilos of tsampa, dried cheese, goat meat, dried apricots and preserved vegetables the mens' families would consume during the long cold season.

The pony men were smiling, holding hands, joking between themselves. The company was almost home. It was only five kilometres to their village of Testa. In the short time I was with them the group repeatedly erupted into a sing-song uproar, a musical wail that careened off the steep walls lining the river. When I asked the lead man, Samdup, why they made so much noise, he told me they were excited to see their families and wanted to insure their people knew they were coming.

Near the village their families, many of whom were working in the fields, ran to greet them and joined the caravan. By the time we reached Testa there were dozens of women, children and grand-parents all singing, dancing, whistling and telling jokes.

The Kurgiakh Valley widens after Testa and meanders along a narrow plateau to Kuru. There the harvest was complete. The fields were barren and leathery, and pigeons and horses rummaged through the stubble, salvaging what little the humans had left. Along irrigation ditches and between fields neatly stacked loads of fresh-cut grass lay weighted down by flat stones. These would be fodder for the animals. Nothing was wasted; everything was needed to survive the seven-month winter.

Another five kilometres on, to the far side of Tanze village, a procession of a dozen people emerged from behind a house. The lead pair of figures held high two burgundy and gold banners. Following them, four monks and two laymen, all in silk brocade and the high-peaked golden caps of the Geluk-pa school, rode powerful horses, bronze and smoky greys. Two of the men held flags, which snapped in the breeze. It looked like a scene out of an Akira Kurosawa samurai film.

As I drew closer I saw the village people were all in their best attire, men in clean one-piece, neck-to-foot woolen robes in navy blue or brown. Some of the older women wore their heirloom, turquoise-studded peraks, the broad, flat, felted-wool headdresses that stretched from their foreheads to their backs and were sewn with semi-precious stones. The monks sparkled in their vestments. Their horses' bridlery was polished to glittering. I knew it had to be Dagom Rinpoche departing for the next village.

I had been wanting to meet him and so hurried up the small rise to catch the parade, but by the time I crested the hill the horses had disappeared in a cloud of dust. Making their way back home through the powdery mist the villagers came towards me. They were surprised to see a single white man and seemed ecstatic about their recent audience with the Rinpoche. They crowded around, patting me on the back, chatting in broken English. They assumed I must have been there to meet the teacher and, as if in consolation for a missed opportunity, one of the families invited me for tea.

The cup of tea turned into a meal of steamed dumplings, momos, in the kitchen of the Dorje family. The room was amazing. It was centred around a woodstove that reminded me more of a lady's brooch than a kitchen appliance, with its sides and front door covered in hammered brass Buddhist symbols. The walls were lined with shelves stacked with steel plates, cups, saucers, bowls, hand-carved wooden spoons and ladles and sparkling pots and pans in brass, copper and aluminum. It was cluttered but organized and very clean. It was a space that spoke of the family's pride in their home. The father, Phuntsok, was a teacher in the local school and spoke some English. He invited me to stay the night and when I agreed he translated my answer to the three small children. Modup, Tsering and Tashi all cheered and climbed onto my lap.

September 21

I woke in the Dorjes' kitchen with Tara, Phuntsok's wife, lighting the fire to make the day's first tea. She smiled and indicated for me to stay sleeping, but I couldn't and instead watched from my sleeping bag as she made the tea. Then she went and fetched her youngest child, Tsering, who nestled into his mother's lap as she mixed dark tsampa flour and water, kneaded the dough and made fresh chapatis. There was a beautiful economy to the way she worked. I remembered Dolma working in her kitchen in Pishu and was reminded again of how impressive Himalayan women are. By the time Phuntsok and the other children had woken, the breakfast of fresh bread, home-churned butter and steaming tea was ready.

After a week of tracking him, I finally met Dagom Rinpoche in Kargyud. It's only a seven-kilometre walk from Tanze to Kargyud but as soon as the village came into view it was apparent some kind of festival was underway. Many horses were hitched to buildings on the outskirts of the village. Houses were freshly whitewashed and small crowds dressed in their Sunday best mingled in the dusty spaces between houses. When I asked an old man if the Rinpoche was in the village, he nodded seriously and pointed in the direction of the largest house.

In front of the home I joined a queue of people by the main door waiting to meet the teacher. After fifteen minutes a young monk ushered me through a pair of low archways into a simple, five-metre by five-metre wood-panelled room. One wall was lined with windows looking out over the stark, rugged mountains that dominate the village, and another was stacked with shelves of the Kangyur and Tangyur, the canonical texts of Tibetan Buddhism.

In the midst of this knowledge and beauty, sitting in cross-legged lotus position, was the teacher. He was a large man with a soft face and inquisitive eyes. He stared at me but it was more investigative than invasive, a part of the confidence he exuded. There were two other monks in the room but he dominated the space. I bowed and presented him with a kathak, a silk blessing scarf. He accepted it and placed it around my neck, conferring his benediction. He motioned me to sit beside him on a stool just below and off to one side of his dais. He introduced himself and asked my name, nodded and smiled, then continued on with his audience.

I enjoyed watching the interaction between the master and his students. Each of the villagers prostrated, offered their kathak, received blessings, and then presented the teacher with an offering which an attendant monk then added to a pile of gifts off to the left. The Rinpoche accepted, keeping his eyes completely focused on the devotee until the next entered his vision. Cotton bags of dried cheese, balls of aged butter, slabs of fresh cheese – dairy products, the specialty of Zanskar, spilled off the small mountain of gifts.

The Zanskaris venerate Dagom Rinpoche, not so much for what he is as for what he embodies. The Rinpoche represents one of Tibetan Buddhism's key concepts, that of the reincarnate master. He is the latest in a line of teachers who trace their lineage back to the eighteenth century. Rinpoche literally means "precious one" and to Tibetans that is what their teachers are: jewels of knowledge capable of lightening the lives of all who come in contact with them. Rinpoches are the repository of the Buddha's wisdom and living examples of the Dharma.

I had been anxious to meet the Rinpoche. I had a fantasy that by being in his presence I would refind the faith I had had as a child saying my prayers every night by the side of my bed.

In Belfast I had spent every Sabbath morning at Sunday school. It wasn't that my family were devout; it was more a community event in 1960s Northern Ireland. I enjoyed learning about Jesus, absorbing myself in the mythology, and with a childlike trust believed in the miracles he had performed. It was so beautifully simple – one God, one messenger, one saviour, it was all there. I took seriously my commitment to Jesus and every night I would kneel by my bed and repeat the Lord's Prayer, adding my own flourish at the end by asking God for special protection for everyone in my extended family. The groundwork had been laid and sometimes I wonder why I didn't hold on to that, why I couldn't sustain my own Christianity.

In retrospect, I know it was Belfast and the unconscious loathing of its sectarian violence that planted the seeds of my disillusion. The move to Canada, a place at least geographically removed from the tribalism of competing faiths, nurtured the idea and it was reading and self-determination that brought about my separation from those early beliefs. Simple faith, I know now, is empowering but one-dimensional while the considered faith, one derived from personal exploration, is a belief you can call your own, something that will survive the storms of everyday life.

I was impressed with Dagom Rinpoche. He was a compassionate, wise man but still I was hesitant. Unlike the Rinpoche's Zanskari devotees I had not prostrated in front of him. When I had bowed before the statue of the Buddha in A-Tisey I had felt the power of being absorbed, but I was a step away from laying myself bare before another human being. After an hour of watching person after person putting their forehead to the floor I excused myself, shook the Rinpoche's hand and left the room feeling empty. I was worried I had missed something.

Kargyud was full of people. The local families, friends and relatives, those who had come from other villages to meet the Rinpoche, were sitting everywhere chatting, smiling and drinking tea. I had no desire to impose myself on those gatherings, so I walked another kilometre farther up the valley and found a meadow on which to pitch my tent. After the press of the crowds in the reception room it was good to be back out in the open. I made my dinner, washed the dishes and lay down in the open to watch the stars. My body was buzzing, but still I was concerned I had lost an opportunity.

September 22

I rose early and continued up the Kurgiakh Valley. Two hours into the day's walk, while caught in the rhythm of my footsteps, a flicker of movement on the scree slope above me caught my attention. I stopped, heard the river and the wind and between them the beating of my own heart, then I saw them, nine bharal, Himalayan blue sheep. Just a shade greyer than the surroundings, only their motion betrayed them, skipping from stone to stone one hundred metres up the hill. They must have gotten my scent because they were moving fast in a tight group over rough ground. It was magnificent to watch. They were effortlessly agile. I kept my eyes on them, unblinking, scared they would dissolve into the landscape. They topped a small ridge and disappeared.

It was barren ground beyond Kargyud; the cultivated paddies stopped not long after the village. The valley narrowed and the land looked only fertile enough for grazing. The slopes were a mixture of scree and patches of low scrubby juniper. Even the golden-leaved poplars I had seen in the watered draws lower down the valley had petered out.

The sky, which had been bright and sunny for weeks, clouded over in the afternoon and with the loss of the sun the temperature dropped. It was strange how the landscape I was so used to seeing in full sunlight from dawn until dusk was now grey and shadowy. It was a more threatening place. For the first time I saw how the mountains stared down on the valley, how they penned the people in.

I halted at the base of the Shingo-la, the 5,000-metre pass that would take me out of Zanskar and into Himachal Pradesh. My plan was the same as on the Singe-la – start early on ice-crusted snow and not stop until I reached bare ground on the far side.

My camp that night was a desolate grey-green meadow in the process of receding to winter. Sheep and goats had sheared the grass to stubble. There were loose rock walls built at strange angles around the clearing, remnants of shepherds' camps. I cooked dinner on my chugging stove but the noise brought out neighbours, a family of mouse hares, chubby, guinea pig-like animals with long, spiky ears and wide observing eyes.

They monitored me intently from twenty metres away, their long ears turning, listening for danger, their noses twitching, trying to catch the smell of my rice and dal dinner. They ventured no closer and I fell asleep to a chorus of their high-pitched whistles circulating around the scree slopes.

CHAPTER 5
Dangerous Places

September 23

I rose at five a.m. It would be a long day to make it over the pass. As I packed my sleeping bag I saw mouse hare paw prints close by. They had waited for me to fall asleep and then crept to within inches of my head and taken the few scraps of rice I had intentionally left by my pack.

The sun was still behind the horizon, the temperature well below zero. I was anxious to move, to warm up, but as I started to walk activity in the rockfall to the left caught my attention. I imagined it to be the mouse family and went to investigate. I peeked behind a chest-high, loose stone wall a hundred metres from where I had camped and there found a dozen men huddled and shivering around an infant dung fire. All of them were cloaked in rough wool blankets and smelled of hard work and woodsmoke. They were dark and mustachioed; all of them had towels wrapped turban-like around their heads. The group turned and stared with bleary eyes.

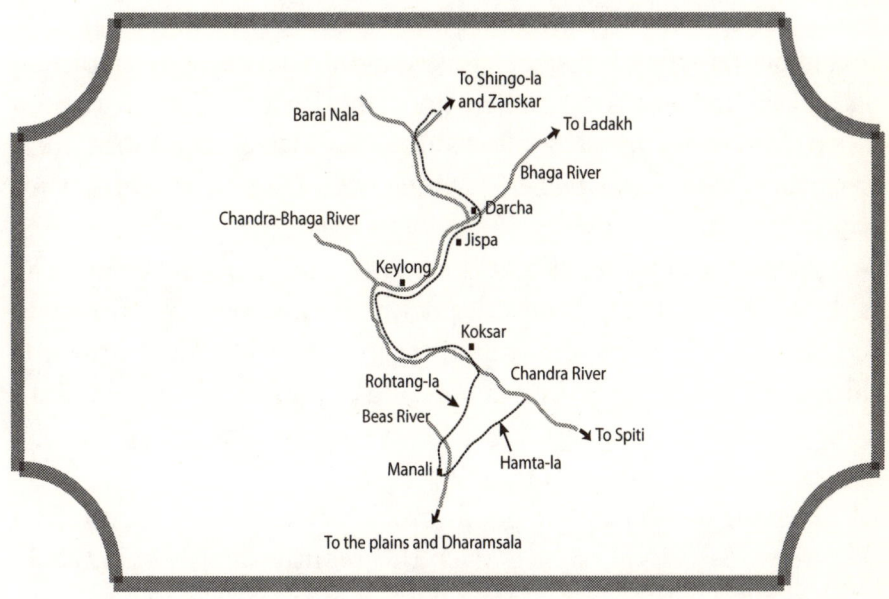

LAHAUL, MANALI, HIMACHAL PRADESH, INDIA

One man stood up, shook my hand and offered a jolly invitation for breakfast tea. I declined his offer as I was anxious to get moving. Then the man confirmed what I had guessed from their thin clothes, sockless feet and dark complexions. They were Nepali road workers who had finished their annual contract and were heading for the trailhead at Darcha to start the long journey back to their country. I went around the circle and shook each man's hand as he offered it. We bid our farewells, saying that maybe we would all share chai at Darcha.

I felt sorry for those men. They were part of the immense, transitory Nepali workforce in India. Over one million labourers find work south of the border, taking jobs that even the lowest caste Indians decline: hazardous factory work, back-breaking road construction, kitchen labouring, street sweeping and toilet cleaning. That they leave home to find such menial labour is a comment on the destitute state of their own nation. The economic refugees I'd seen shivering by the fire that morning had all smiled but they looked used and hollow. They had been beaten down by months of second-class citizenship. With their wheezing breath and frozen plastic shoes I wondered how they would ever make it over a 5,000-metre pass.

Snow cover started not long after the climb began. The surface was hard and I moved quickly. At just over 5,000 metres the Shingo-la is snow covered all year round. I walked upwards through a world of white as incandescent snow slipped into a bleached sky. A spectral fog hung close to the ice. Pale mist floated on the slopes around me.

Pushing upwards felt good, every stride solid. I focused on the steps. My body, which over the months had rebuilt itself, had adapted well to its new environment. I had a stronger, harder body. To walk hard at that altitude, to feel my muscles and mind moving smoothly, sliding together as well-oiled elements, was meditative, something simultaneously physically challenging and mentally relaxing.

But four hours into the walk the smell of death broke my contemplation. The thick, festering odour grew stronger. I smelled it for ten minutes before I saw it, half-buried in the snow, half-devoured by crows, the molding carcass of a horse. Shredded skin hung from its architecture of bones. The animal stared at me from behind hollow eyes. Its mouth was stretched wide, a full set of teeth smiled from a lipless maw. It was the first of four horse corpses I saw that day. The skeletons were a morbid reminder of how, in the violent storms of two weeks before, a pair of local men had lost their lives on the Shingo-la.

When I heard the news I had had difficulty believing it. I had seen Zanskaris sleep outside at minus-thirty degrees Celsius covered only by a tattered blanket. It was inconceivable that two of these examples of local adaptation should perish in a freak late summer storm, while the middle-aged French couple they were guiding had survived. But the more I thought about it, the more I realized those men were victims of their own forgetfulness. In tennis shoes, cotton clothes and with the attitude of being on a fair weather stroll, the pair had been overconfident and ill-prepared. The two pony men had walked the Shingo-la dozens of times and, in this case, familiarity breeds not contempt but complacency.

In the blizzard, which developed with brutal speed, the older guide had become confused and separated from the group. The number-two man, a teenager, had then lost his nerve and walked into the storm without explaining to his clients what his plan was. He never returned. The two tourists, who had come equipped for whatever the Himalayas might unleash, struggled down to Kargyud. There the story was pieced together and search parties were dispatched, to no avail. The bodies were never recovered. Two men were dead because they had forgotten what Zanskaris have understood for millenniums – respect for the mountains that dominate their lives.

For the Buddha Shakyamuni, it was a vision of death that brought him to renounce his coddled princehood in the ancient Nepali city of Kapilvastu and strike out in pursuit of a way of life beyond death. The Buddha, then known as Prince Siddhartha Gautama, led an extremely protected life and it was not until he was twenty-nine years old that he left his palace for the first time. Outside, over a series of three trips, he met an old man, a diseased man and a decaying corpse. The prince was shocked by these visions and became distraught when Channa, his charioteer, explained that everyone must die. On another trip outside the palace he met a Hindu ascetic and after discussing religion with him decided to join the order of monks and find a way to overcome old age, illness and death.

Eventually, through much experimentation, he discovered his way to a state of higher consciousness by forging what became known as the Middle Way, a path between the extreme depravations of the ascetics and his own previously indulgent princely lifestyle. Gareth's death had given me the jolt to begin my own exploration. I don't expect to defy death, but I have a wish to explore the way. I have no doubt that this will be an investigation of many lifetimes; I am no Buddha.

At the col I stopped to tie a prayer flag I had bought in Padum to the summit stupa. I gave thanks for my safe arrival and remembered the two lost souls. I turned south, out of the Shingo-la's shimmering whiteness, in search of the southern valley's greenery. After the hard slog of the climb I felt as if I was flying on the downhill. The creak of my boots was music to my ears. I felt the rush of air in and out of my lungs; it was weightless, and with the pull of gravity, so was I. In the moments between steps I felt the magical synchronicity of my body's parts. Strangely, the thrill was heightened by the thought of the two men on the Shingo-la because in the wilderness of the pass I had glimpsed death's inevitability. Impermanence is reality. Death was there, not as the Grim Reaper, but as a catalyst.

Far down the pass I reached a narrow, thin-grassed pasture and with a cloudless sky didn't bother to pitch my tent. I lay down in my sleeping bag. A cream-coloured butterfly landed on the hazy blue nylon shell, its wings pulsing slower than the fall of the sun. I lay back. Darkness was overtaking light. I stared at the Milky Way, its stars thick as fog. I breathed, expecting the air to be sprinkled with diamond dust. Sleep is a small death – dreams a new life.

September 24

I woke to find my sleeping bag surrounded by bleating goats. They stared at me, golden slit eyes inquisitive, nuzzling their snouts into my nylon cocoon, assuming the best grass lay beneath my mattress. They were a curious gang that took great pleasure in huddling around as I prepared my tsampa porridge breakfast.

The trail started steeply downhill but by early afternoon the path had levelled and transformed to a gravel road that followed the Barai Nala (nala in Hindi means stream). As it descended the land became more populated. I had crossed a border and was now in Lahaul district of Himachal Pradesh State. Mud-brick mansions were replaced by concrete block bungalows. Electric wires, the umbilical cords of modernization, connected the villages. A four-wheel-drive, battered and spewing black exhaust, lurched along the track. Near the village of Palamao I saw a schoolyard filled with students loudly repeating Hindi lessons. A hiss like a deflating tire spread through the group as they recognized a foreigner was close by and the entire class turned their backs on the teacher and rushed to the edge of the compound, shouting at me in grammarless English, "You, Now, Go, How, Out, Goodbye, Top notch, Brother, Man."

Ten kilometres farther on I reached Darcha, the trailhead village at the confluence of the Bhaga River and the Barai Nala. It was not what I had expected. From the path above the village I saw a line of temporary cafés roofed with army surplus parachutes. A kilometre-long traffic jam of stationary buses, trucks and jeeps snaked around a ridge to the north. Along the double-laned gravel road hundreds of people milled around, talking, smoking, playing cards on the ground and drinking chai. Over rice and dal in one of the cafés a pair of stranded truck drivers, Pradip and Sunny, told me, in English, how the rains had destroyed roads throughout the Himalaya.

"Bloody, fucking crazy, man," said Sunny. "One day we are making our way from Chandigarh to Leh and the next we're almost washed into the bloody river."

Both men were from the same village in Uttar Pradesh state. Pradip, the older one, had worked as a driver's helper for eight years from the age of ten before he got a chance to drive a truck and when he finally secured a driver's position he had brought Sunny, a relative, on to learn the trade. Both men's hands were permanently etched with spidery black lines of grease. Both of them chain-smoked. They were excited to tell their story.

They had been transporting rice for the army, from Chandigarh, the capital of Punjab state, to Leh. They had been driving a day and a half when the storm first hit and they had camped that night twenty kilometres south of Darcha when rain and darkness combined to make it impossible for them see what was on the road ahead. They laid out their sleeping bags on the bench seats in the cab of the truck and hoped the storm would break by morning.

But they were woken abruptly around three o'clock. The rear of the truck was moving sideways. Sunny threw off his sleeping bag and scrambled outside. The hillside was flowing with water – "like a waterfall, man" – eating away at the road. What had been solid ground was turning to quicksand. Behind him he could see a truck they had travelled with over the Rohtang-la was already halfway off the road. He ran back and pleaded with the drivers to abandon the truck and join them but they wouldn't come.

Back in their truck Pradip had fired up the diesel and driven a few hundred metres to higher ground. Sunny jumped in and they drove an hour or so along the disintegrating road until they were stopped in Darcha by the police. As Sunny said, "It was just like a movie, man. Pradip the driving hero and me his right-hand man." Pradip was more pragmatic: "The roads ahead and behind us are washed away. How long are we going to be stuck here? No driving, no pay."

After lunch they invited me to join them for some whiskey back at their truck. I politely declined, knowing that Indian truck drivers have a reputation for drinking hard and long and I wanted to find a decent campsite for the night.

The route I wanted to follow, down the Bhaga River and over the Rohtang-la to Manali, had been badly damaged.

Early morning moon over a stupa in the Indus Valley.

A Zanskari monk, during the barley harvest.

Above A Drokpa woman near Kargil, India.

Above right A weaver on a traditional loom in Leh, Ladakh.

Right A small boy takes a break from helping his family working in their fields.

Monks near Lamayuru monastery.

Left Monks blow ceremonial copper and brass horns on the parapets of Thiksey monastery.

Right A monk caretaker of the Buddha Maitreya statue at Thiksey monastery in the Indus Valley.

A storm passes over the small monastery above Leh Palace in Ladakh.

The author relaxing on the saddle of a high pass between the Indus and Zanskar valleys.

Photoskar village.

Lingshed monastery from above.

An elderly monk at Lingshed monastery.

A small family farm irrigated by the local stream on the route from Lingshed to Zanskar.

A stack of barley on the threshing grounds above Lingshed village.

An Indian girl prepares to make a cow dung patty, which will be dried and used for fuel.

Moreover, the Leh-Srinagar road, the main route into Ladakh from the railhead at Jammu farther to the west, had been closed for even longer and much of the traffic that would normally use that road had opted to try to reach Leh using the Manali route. Hundreds of drivers had no choice but to wait. The army engineers in charge of reconstruction didn't expect the road to be open for two weeks.

It was boom-time for the food tents in Darcha. I doubted the restaurants had enough supplies to keep such a crowd fed for a fortnight and was glad I was not a hotel owner trying to obtain payment from irate truckers.

In one respect the ruined road was a blessing. Walking with no traffic, I could enjoy the scenery and hear the river without the background din of head-splitting air horns.

I found a nice campsite that night, a small, close-cropped pasture surrounded by golden-leafed poplars within sight of the Bhaga River.

September 25

My first stop on the quiet road to Manali was Jispa, a tiny, four-house village best known as the site where the Dalai Lama performed a Kalachakra initiation in 1994. The Kalachakra, or Wheel of Time ritual, is the most public of the Tibetan tantric ceremonies. The Dalai Lama has performed the initiation around the world, from hundred-thousand-seat sports stadiums in Europe to monastery courtyards in the Himalayas.

Tantric practices are part of the Tibetan Buddhist or Vajrayana (diamond) path. The Kalachakra Tantra deals with time and revolving cycles, from the birth and death of universes to the cycle of human breath in and out of the body, and through those connections attempts to relate the individual with the universal.

The ceremony in Jispa had attracted 30,000 people from all over India, Nepal and Tibet. According to the anthropologist Kim Gutschow, who had travelled over the Shingo-la with the nuns of Karsha for the ceremony, it had been a "Himalayan Woodstock." A tent city had been set up around the grounds, and nomads from the western plains of Tibet, the Changtang, rubbed shoulders with New Delhi businessmen, reclusive Buddhist meditators came down from their cave retreats and aspiring local politicians preached to the assembled crowds about how good the district would be if they were elected. It was a beehive of activity as monks, nuns, lay practitioners, healers, shamans, oracles, even weather makers, all assembled to partake in Buddhism's biggest spectacle. (The Dalai Lama was known to travel to large outdoor initiations with a man who could change the weather through his meditation, thus always ensuring a sunny day for the event.)

When I passed through Jispa, however, all that remained of the event was a beautiful temple and a wide gravel field. The temple was a two-storey concrete structure. Interestingly, the concrete had been formed to imitate the traditional Tibetan mud-brick and wood temple construction style. The technique could have looked cheap and overdone, but the building had been painted with the same precision that Lama Stanzin applied to his murals in Lingshed and the effect was of a newer building that would age well.

The field in front of the temple was broad and long. It stretched for a few hundred metres from the river to the road, but it was a skeleton ground, grey and bony; it needed people to make it attractive. The field was adorned with only four wind-whitened poles, delimbed poplar trees, and from them, yellow, green, red, white and blue prayer flags snapped in the breeze.

The woodblock printed flags feature Tibetan prayers and images of tigers, dragons, snow lions and the mythical reptilian bird Garuda. In the centre of each piece of cloth was a picture of the wind horse from which the flags draw their Tibetan name, Lung-ti. It is believed that when the wind catches the prayers they ride off as horses on the wind. The flags' colours represent the five elements: green – earth, yellow – wind, red – fire, blue – water, and white – air. The wind horses carry the blessings through the elements to where they are needed most.

A massive change in wind, a freak, unpredictable surge of air off the Pacific Ocean, is what created the colossal waves on Elk Lake that led to Gareth's death. Thinking about wind as something positive, something that delivers goodness, helps me comprehend the loss. Transforming something with terrible power into an obliging entity is a comfort.

On the initiation ground a single monk wandered in the distance. He waved at me, seemingly unconcerned with a visitor. His robes billowed around him in the breeze and he continued on to the river.

From Jispa I moved towards Keylong, the district capital of Lahaul. For the first time in weeks I passed thick groves of trees, small man-made forests of poplar. The golden woods rustled nervously, and their fall colours of saffron, rust and cherry red were shocking against the sandy barrenness of the hills. I stopped by the river. A hoopoe bird, red with black and white stripes, bobbed past, its eyes to the ground, searching for autumn seed. I sat for an hour in the shade of the poplars going through the ritual of making tea – collecting water, boiling it on my chugging stove, dipping the tea bag until the perfect colour was achieved, adding milk powder, sugar, cardamom pods, ground cinnamon and dried ginger, simmering it again and then leaning back, sipping the sweetness of India and listening to the leaves' whisper. The bubbling brew, the rumble of the stove, the thump and wallop of the river, the tickle of the leaves were a chaos of gentle sound that only added to my quietude.

I reached Keylong as darkness overtook the valley. The town is near the junction of the Bhaga and Chandra rivers. Buildings stretch up the hillsides in an unordered mix. Along the streets hundreds of young trees planted to stabilize the hillside created a boulevard effect. Keylong was the first major Himalayan town since Leh that had the potential to be beautiful in the midst of the mountains.

I stayed the night in a guest house. When I spread my sleeping bag out that night it was dark, and after a long day's walk I had only one desire – sleep. The next morning, I discovered a fantastic view over the fields of Khardong village and the mountains south of the Bhaga River.

September 26

The next morning a throbbing pain in my lower right jaw woke me. My mouth felt as if it was crawling with stinging insects. I spat, expecting blood, but produced only milky saliva. A week before I had broken a lower molar in Zanskar, fittingly by biting into a frozen chocolate bar. Now I was worried the stumpy remains were getting infected. The inevitable trip to the dentist could be postponed no longer.

Visiting the dentist in India is an unappealing prospect. In every major town on the subcontinent, you find men who hang big-toothed signboards marked Dentist outside their hole-in-the-wall shops. I have talked to Indian "dentists" who claim they can perform everything from extractions and fillings to root canals and jaw reconstructions. One practitioner I came across in a Delhi backstreet had arranged his patients' extracted teeth, like a row of tiny ivory trophies, on a shelf facing his current client. With that in mind, I decided to catch a bus from the north side of Rohtang-la to Manali and then another overnight ride to Dharamsala, the seat of the Tibetan government-in-exile. There I knew a proficient dentist associated with the Tibetan government's Delek hospital. After the dental work I would return to Manali and continue the trek.

Koksar, at the northern base of Rohtang-la, is a fifty-kilometre walk from Keylong. I started the day with sorry expectations but within a few kilometres the ache hissing in my jaw dissipated. Villages passed by with the people shouting questions from balconies and fields: "Where are you going, friend?" "Why don't you stop and have a tea?" Friendly shopkeepers and the gentle roar of the chai-wallahs' stoves are what I remember of that stretch of road.

Five kilometres past Keylong the Bhaga River joins the Chandra. The valley broadens and the vegetation becomes greener. Although I was technically still on the arid, monsoon-free north side of the Himalayas, the extreme dryness in the air that characterizes Ladakh and Zanskar was being replaced by a more temperate subcontinental Indian humidity.

I was fortunate to have lunch in a café whose owner was a veritable mine of local information. Lobsang Dawa was a short, chubby man with a big smile and broad hands. For twenty-five years he had worked as an inspector of roads for the government and had seen his valley move from the eighteenth to the twentieth century in the two dozen years he had been employed.

"When I started we had no motorable roads here. Now we have trucks moving day and night," he told me.

The speed of development, he admitted, had created problems regarding economic expectations and challenges to traditional culture, but he pointed out there had been difficulties with the old ways too – shorter life spans, lack of schooling, scarcity of government services. The balance between the old and new is what he said was important. He didn't want his grandchildren to not understand what it is to be Lahauli. "You've got to have a sense of who you are," he said, holding his grandson on his lap. Sometimes, he admitted, he wished for the old days because he thought they were simpler times, but as he said, "I quickly get over that, because in the old days, at my age, I'd be dead."

Koksar, on the bare northern slope of the Rohtang-la, was a motley collection of roadside cafés and stranded vehicles. From the cafés, a few hundred metres away on the north bank of the Chandra River I could see a few houses but in Koksar there were no actual homes; it existed only to service truck drivers and waylaid travellers. The cafés smelled of whiskey and piss. Their concrete block walls were stained with betel nut juice and dog shit. Inside one of the buildings I could hear drivers hooting and hollering at a television game show broadcast from Delhi.

There was nothing there to encourage me to stay, but whole sections of the road up the pass had been washed out in the recent storm and there were only unscheduled buses now crossing the pass. I was too late to catch a bus or truck that day and had no desire to overnight in the midst of a crowd of drunken truck drivers. So I tramped another fifteen minutes downriver and on a patch of grass that overlooked bands of bright poplars on the river's far bank I pitched my tent.

Brown accentors and grey wagtails hopped around my stove as I made dinner. Two magpies cackled and stared at me from boulders in the distance. A wild rose bush, long gone from bloom, twitched in the breeze off to one side of my tent. The wind that channelled down the valley kept up through the night. It caught the loose edges of my flysheet and slapped a constant reminder of its presence.

September 27

The next morning back at Koksar I joined the mass of impatient travellers. Rumour had it that a bus bound for Manali would arrive sometime in the morning. It was starting from Keylong but would proceed only as far as the first rock slide up the pass. There we would have to walk over mud and rocks to meet another bus, which would deliver us to the next break in the road. Again we would walk; again we would be met by another bus. The process would be repeated four times over the Rohtang to the village of Nehru Kund at the western base of the pass. From there the last five kilometres of road into Manali had literally disappeared in a flash flood of the Beas River and our journey would be completed on foot.

The crowd was abuzz with a new word, "shuttling." To my companions "shuttling," running from one decrepit bus to another, seemed like a grand adventure.

Around eleven a.m. we spotted the bus a kilometre away. It was silver and blue and from that distance bore an uncanny resemblance to a biscuit box on wheels. A buzz ran through the crowd. It swayed towards us and pulled to a halt, the interior already bursting with passengers. The mob on the road stormed the vehicle, and inertia pulled me with them. I was catapulted upwards and found myself competing for roof space with two dozen Nepali labourers. Things calmed as the seating politics settled. However, I was a poor politician. There was no room on the luggage rack for me and I was squeezed to the edge of the aluminum roof. I held onto the frame's steel bars while my feet dangled over the side panels.

The engine roared to life. The conductor made his rounds swinging a bamboo cane. Unfortunate souls hanging from the open windows were beaten to the ground.

The coach laboured out of the village. With that kind of a load it would be a small miracle if we made it to the first slide. However, I've learned the Indian bus is an ugly, hardy breed. It wasn't fast or elegant, but moved sluggishly and with a great conviction over a surface that had ceased to be a road.

From the rooftop, fantastic panoramas evolved. My feet outlined 300-metre abysses as the bus crawled along inches from their edge. To avoid vertigo I frequently glanced over my shoulder at the passengers stretched out beside me. The Nepalis were grouped in huddles, chatting, smoking and playing cards in the wind. My most interesting companion, however, was a Tibetan lama seated at the peak of the roof's mound of baggage.

He was old, and though I find it impossible to accurately estimate the age of Buddhist monks, he looked to be well into his seventies. His grey-white hair was tied in a bun, samurai style, his face veiled in a beard that fell from his chin in a wispy spike. Since most Buddhist monks I had met wore the close-cropped hair of the Geluk-pa school, I reckoned that his beard must make him a member of the older Nyingmapa order. He wore burgundy robes and had a thick wool blanket wrapped around his shoulders. He sat cross-legged, facing into the wind, while his fingers gripped the jute rope holding down the hillock of trunks and suitcases. Occasionally, he would turn and smile but generally appeared lost in contemplation.

At the first slide shouts and clapping erupted. The adventure had begun – we were about to shuttle. I decided to help the lama with his gear, an assortment of rice sacks and tarpaulin bags, more possessions than I thought a monk would need. We scurried through the rocks, loaded down like mules, and on the far side regained our rooftop space. The cycle continued: the slow rumble over disintegrated roads, the feverish dash across the slide and the sailboat sway of the new vehicle's movement.

Three-quarters of the way up the pass we entered a band of clouds and a cold damp began to work under my clothes. With the temperature barely above zero I was debating whether my infected tooth was worth the trip. My hands felt to be locked in a cadaverous grip on the railings. The road workers seemed impervious, their composure unchanged. Huddled tight together, their backs to the wind, they shared cigarettes and spoke quietly. On his hill of baggage the lama was savouring the weather's change, as moisture clung to his face and his beard splayed back on both sides of his neck. I swear the man was smiling.

The wheezing tin bus arrived at the summit and without so much as a second breath careened down the western slope at speeds that made me nervous. With the increased wind chill I shivered uncontrollably, my hands frozen to the rack. Again my roof-mates let the weather pass them by; the speed seemed to do nothing more than ruffle their hair. They had lived in worse conditions while building roads such as this one and nothing could now destroy the fact they were going home.

After what seemed like a lifetime of hairpin turns we came to a line of ramshackle cafés, known as dhabas in India, just above the treeline. They were temporary, corrugated tin huts in the avalanche shadow of a line of two-storey, house-size boulders.

Some form of primary rigor mortis had set into my joints. It took me a minute of pure concentration to unclench my fists. I staggered from the roof and through numb lips ordered hot coffee at the closest table. I guess because I had helped him with his luggage I was joined by the monk and we shared a silent meal of greasy omelets and stale bread.

By the time we rejoined our bus the clouds had risen and the drizzly rain had petered out. It felt as if the worst was over. Around me the Nepalis started to sing, faint, tuneless Hindi pop songs. Another two hours, I thought, and I would be in a hotel room in Manali, immersed under a hot shower for the first time since Leh.

We reached the treeline. It was the first time I had been below the Himalayas' 3,200-metre treeline since the start of the trek. There the pavement was in better shape. With the greenery the view disappeared but I was glad not to see the road switchbacking beneath my feet. However, in the forest's shade the temperature dropped and the road became iced over. Just as I was starting to recall some of the advantages of mechanized transport, the driver lost control. The old bus careened off the ashphalt, lurched drunkenly down the bank and slammed square into a towering deodar cedar.

The crash threw me cleanly off the roof. I landed spread-eagled on the mossy forest floor with my back to the vehicle. I turned reflexively. The bus, with its eighty passengers staring out the windows, was tipping up onto two wheels. I was directly beneath it. In that split-second animal instincts overran me. Muscles I'd never encountered contracted and in one clean, physically impossible movement I leaped two metres from my prostrate position and out of the danger zone.

Throughout the dive my eyes were fixed on the bus, as it rose, reached a point of equilibrium, hung on that axis and then, just as gracefully, dropped back onto four wheels. It was vehicular ballet. For a split-second, the inanimate object had been bestowed with an elegance reserved for animals.

The quietude of the moment broke instantly. With four wheels back on the ground a communal howl rose from the passengers, windows popped from the fuselage and a human cascade rolled down the flanks of the bus.

I stood, shaking uncontrollably. I leaned over, reached for the ground and felt solid earth. I sat down and looked up. The lama, still on his hill of baggage, still gripping the jute ropes, was laughing.

Eventually, I retrieved my pack. I didn't wait for another bus; I thought it better to walk the last kilometres to Manali.

Three days later in Dharamsala a gentle-fingered British dentist did what she could for my rotting tooth. "That must hurt," she commented, seeing the broken molar. "Not much," I replied. She touched it with a steel instrument and I jerked uncontrollably from the chair.

I had been able to contact some old friends. For the first time in months I had a real conversation in English. It had been a relaxing time, but it was October. Soon the first snows would come to the high passes, so I booked a seat on the night bus for Manali.

October 3

The bus from Dharamsala back to Manali left at eleven p.m. It was almost empty and after the mishap on the Rohtang-la I was glad to be inside the vehicle. The driver continued at a leisurely pace, stopping at every village. The ambling ride put me at ease. At 3:30 a.m. we pulled up at a chai stall in the middle of nowhere. Its two incandescent light bulbs were the only illumination I had seen for kilometres. On a string bed outside the building the driver fell asleep. The passengers were left to fend for themselves.

I ordered tea and began talking to the passenger who had silently appeared by my side. He was a short, compactly built man with a rounding of his words that made you think he was comfortable with an audience. Prakash Anoop was the public prosecutor from Mandi, the district just south of Manali. I enjoyed talking to him. He spoke perfect English and projected competence. He was an autodidact who surprised me with what he knew: "Oh, you are from Vancouver Island. Beautiful place, I have heard, with mountains and beaches and flowers while the rest of Canada is under snow." He believed a broad knowledge base was important for his law practice.

We ordered more chai, sweet and thick in sticky glasses. My friend made a conversational leap and began to address the emergence of the "New India," the India being driven by the country's recent economic boom. It was four a.m. and I was tired, but the barrister was just starting to hit his stride. He did not get many chances to talk to foreigners and wanted an external opinion on the changes in his country.

"Just look at advertising," he said, raising his hands. "Companies telling everyone, not just the people with money, that they need newer things, they need more things.

"... Twenty years ago my education was enough to gain respect. Now I am a lawyer without a car or a laptop computer, so people think I am a failure." Prakash was not happy with this New India.

His diatribe continued. He was a good man caught in the rush of transition. The New India, according to him, was rolling headlong into a world of superficiality. It was five o'clock and even the constant flow of chai could not keep my eyes open. He asked my opinion but all I could offer was that Indians needed to manage the change themselves. It was a nothing statement and he knew it. His mouth dropped; he had wanted more from someone who lived in a place that represented the potential future of his country. He wanted to say something but didn't. He looked sad and our conversation petered out.

The driver woke with a start not long after and immediately stumbled without a word back to the bus. The engine roared to life and with that, the alarm we were waiting for, the group shuffled back to our seats.

I stayed that night in a nondescript concrete hotel in Manali. It would be my last night with a shower and the potential for a nice meal so I took advantage. I showered before and after dinner and treated myself to a meal at the best South Indian restaurant in town. But I was anxious to get back on the trail. I was restless in bed that night, like a child on the night before Christmas.

October 4

From Manali I walked south five kilometres on the main road along the Beas River, then where the small Alaini River meets the Beas I turned northeast and followed the creek up past Prini village towards the Hamta-la.

By late morning the houses of Prini had disappeared below me. The trail wound through steep paddies divided by stone walls. With the increase in altitude the view grew more spectacular. To the west Manali looked like a Matchbox toy set placed in the forest. Far up the valley I saw the grey and white face of the Rai Ghar glacier, source of the Beas River. I followed the path of the river downwards and along its course could see the open sores of the flood's recent destruction. Against the swathe of the river's ruinous path, the main road and the tiny cars moving along it looked trivial.

I stopped outside a lone house far above the village. Below it was a jigsaw puzzle of geometrical paddies, and not far above it the forest began. Drenched in sweat and breathing heavily I unslung my pack and sat on a rock. I took a bandana from my pocket, wiped my forehead and from over the balcony of the house came a voice asking if I'd like a glass of water. I looked up to see a beautiful, raven-haired woman leaning over the banister. She looked South Asian but spoke English with a London accent.

I nodded – there must have been an amusing look of shock on my face – then left my pack on the balcony and followed her inside. In the sun-stroked, pine-panelled living room she sat on a low stool, cross-legged, facing the valley. She turned and smiled, her focus caught between me and the fresh leaves she was pulling from an aluminum basin on the floor. Her skin was a transparent olive tone, her almond eyes framed by long lashes. In the split second before we submitted to the conventions of etiquette I saw her twin in my mind's eye, a miniature painting I had recently seen in the Indian National Museum, a pen and watercolour portrait of Radha, the consort of the Hindu god Krishna.

I dropped onto a worn stool by the window. She handed me a stainless steel tumbler of water and, after placing the bunch of leaves she was holding back into the bowl, she held out her hand and introduced herself as Sheraz Khan. She was an Anglo-Pakistani on her annual "retreat" in the Himalayas. She rented the house for four months a year and used it to read and relax. The cabin was simple, with a single wooden room, a narrow bed against one wall, two wash basins, a chair, a few stools and an unvarnished pine table scattered with cooking equipment.

I was surprised Sheraz was alone and asked if she felt safe five kilometres from the nearest village. She gave me a scorching look. "Well, it seems you're on your own!"

I finished the water and realized the leaves, which I now saw strewn everywhere, were marijuana, *Cannabis indica*. I recognized the thick resinous scent hanging over everything. She saw my roaming eyes and said simply, "It's harvest time."

Sheraz was rubbing the leaves between her hands, extracting the resin to make hashish. When I asked if she was doing it for sale or personal use, she grinned, "Personal consumption. If I'm going to smoke, I'm going to make sure the stuff is good."

It seemed like a lot of plants for a single woman.

The presence of the hash made me nervous. Manali is the drug capital of India. Marijuana grows wild in the Himalayas, but in recent years it has become a highly lucrative, illegal cash crop. Gone are the indigenous, feral weeds talked of and smoked by overlanding hippies in the '60s. Now genetic technology developed in Holland and industrial herbicides insure the quality of the mind-altering tetrahydrocannabinol in the plants.

Police estimate that over 20,000 hectares in the Kulu Valley are planted with marijuana. The huge amount of money involved has attracted organized crime; Israeli, German, Irish, British and Italian gangs compete with the Indian mafia. The turf wars have become violent. Since 1992 fifteen foreigners have officially gone missing in the valley, but unofficial estimates by the non-governmental organization Fair Trials Abroad put that number at fifty internationals. Few bodies have been found and the bulk of these disappearances are attributed to gang infighting and unpaid drug debts.

Sheraz gave me some plants, showed me how to remove the superfluous parts and gently roll the leaves between my palms until a heavy paste dislodged. With her melodic instructions my apprehension disappeared. The grey, molasses-like substance grew blacker as the layer on my hands became thicker until eventually it could be rolled into a ball. The technique was simple and measured. Maybe it was the resin in the air, maybe the rhythm of the repetition, but I found the process immensely soothing.

For a few hours we sat making the substance Hindus call charas. Charas is closely associated with Lord Shiva, the creator-destroyer of the Hindu pantheon. Many of his followers, Shaivite saddhus, smoke hashish, using its hallucinatory qualities to connect themselves with the god. Smoking for them is a complex set of offerings that transforms the consumption into a religious practice.

Once during the great Shivaratri festival in Kathmandu, the largest annual celebration of Shiva in Nepal, I smoked with the saddhus. The ritual started with the preparation of the hash and tobacco mixture. First they muttered mantras beneath their breath and used their left thumbs to massage the mix held tightly in their right palms. Then, in time with another set of mantras, they stuffed the sticky shreds into their vertically held, clay chillum pipes. Using steel tongs they took embers from the nearest fire. In a religion obsessed with purity, fire and water are the elements of ultimate cleanliness. Then, holding the ember tight to the pipe's bowl and with mighty puffs, they worked the hash into a pulsing red orb. With the smoke rising the ascetics exhaled, held their pipes to the heavens and into the cloud offered Lord Shiva the first taste of the charas, shouting, "Bom, Shiva."

Sheraz invited me for lunch. We had a simple meal of rice and lentils on her balcony. The view stretched up and down the Beas Valley, from the glaciers to the jungle. The paddies, which started a hundred metres below the house, were green with a late season crop of rice and other more secretive crops. The fields stepped down three hundred metres almost to the river. The air was crisp and I could smell sandalwood soap on Sheraz's skin. The thought of staying flashed in my head. But companionship was not why I had started the walk, and besides, the goddess had not requested my presence. When I left, we shook hands and then on second thoughts gave each other small kisses, cheek to cheek, in the French way.

Where the fields ended the forest began. For a North American that seems logical, but in South Asia where overpopulation has created intense pressure for wood, such a transition is rare. Virgin forest is scarce, but on the Hamta-la I found myself for the first time since Pakistan in woods thick enough to block the view to the valley. For a forest-dweller such as myself it was a small homecoming. I was at ease surrounded by deodar cedars and chir pines. Above me I watched the curves of their limbs undulate in the breeze while my feet tripped over labyrinthine roots. Their sharp scent was everywhere. The forest floor was mossy, and in the hummocks and depressions the season's last flowers, *scullteria* and *swertia*, held to their colours of violet, pink and eggshell white.

I stopped well before sunset, not wanting to leave the intimacy of the forest. I built a fire, a wood-fed blaze of crackling sticks, furious and clean after the dozens of smoldering yak dung fires I had nurtured above the treeline. It was a fire to lie beside and dream.

When Gareth was seventeen and eighteen he spent two summers working with me in the forests of northern British Columbia. We, along with thousands of other young people across the country, were replanting areas that had recently been logged. Treeplanting was good, hard work, the kind of job that brought out the best in people. In the tent camps we lived in, sometimes a hundred kilometres from the nearest town, almost every night someone would light a campfire and tired people would emerge from the darkness seeking company. The golden circle around the fire was a place to relax, to have a few beers and talk bullshit before you wandered off, exhausted, to bed. The campfire was a space between night and day, a place removed from work, somewhere for relationships to blossom and rivalries to be brought into the open. There, from the edge of darkness, I could observe the people I supervised.

Gareth, I was happy to see, was the kind of person who fit in easily, a gentle, easygoing guy. A young man you could rely on. Deep down, he was shy, the baby of the family. Around camp he didn't readily accept the approaches of the girls who were interested in him. He had been sheltered by older brothers and a sister. He needed re-inforcement, the kind of thing I should have given, but I was too busy with my own life. Now I see it as selfishness, too absorbed in myself, too concerned with what others would think. At the time I thought I was making Gareth tougher, stronger, bringing him to find his own way. In retrospect I regret not shouldering into him, letting him know I was there and that we were brothers, together, in the bush.

The flames leaped and crackled, oily cedar boughs popped and fizzed, pine needles snapped in contained blue bursts of gas. The moss beneath me was as thick and soft as a mattress.

October 5

I passed through the conifers, beyond a stratum of rhododendron, birch and matted juniper, and back into the alpine. Flocks of sheep grazed in the parched meadows. The shepherds were on their way home from the pastures along the Tibetan border to Kulu and farther east another fifty kilometers to the Brahmour Valley. In undyed Nehru jackets and woolen pillbox hats and the loose, sunbeaten complexions of those who live outdoors, they had a frayed, comfortable look. Two things about them were constant. Lit or unlit, a *bedi* – the small Indian cheroot – always hung from their mouths. Their other steadfast appendage was their dogs, broad-faced, muscular black-brown beasts. They were intelligent animals that sat unaffected until their masters gave a command, prefaced by the dog's name, which brought them leaping into action, rounding up lambs and keeping track of bears and wolves. The intensity of their gaze was disconcerting.

One group invited me to dinner. They had no shelter beyond their blankets, so we sat in the open. A fresh wind blew from the pass. Over the fire they cooked rice and fleshy shanks of mutton, the blistering fat spitting off the circle of stones containing the blaze. When I told them in Hindi and sign language that I was a vegetarian, they laughed. I had made a great joke and I laughed too because not to eat meat was to undermine their existence.

Around the fire the men told stories, but the dialect was beyond me. I concentrated on their body language. Their hands moved with the drama. One man told of a tussle with a bear, holding up a three-fingered hand to prove his courage (and luck). Another related the dangers of crossing an engorged stream, one arm moving in a dryland breaststroke while the other held an imaginary lamb tight to his chest. A third man recalled the comedy of travelling to Delhi. He bellowed impersonations of the rickshaws' horns and goose-stepped haughtily around the fire in imitation of the city folk's arrogance.

Then there was silence, one of those regular conversational lulls, and they all gazed at me. It was my turn. So I launched into a tale, part English, part broken Hindi, part hand motions of how once I'd been surrounded by a pack of wolves in the Yukon Territory. I had been trapped by a dozen pairs of glinting wolf eyes on a geological seismic line, a three-metre-wide clearing slashed, straight as an arrow, for tens or even hundreds of kilometres through the sub-boreal forest. It was a story the shepherds could relate to and, although my yarn was in a mix of languages, I could see in the flickering light how their eyes tracked me. I slashed the air with my hands to make clear the futility of the predicament. I howled at the moon like the lead wolf and rustled loose sticks to underscore my retreat through the bush. I dropped to crouching, holding my hands wide to show how the wolves dissolved into the forest. With my escape the audience exhaled and then erupted in applause and laughter.

October 6

My friends sent me packing after breakfast with a few strong slaps on the back and half a dozen lentil-filled chapatis wrapped in greasy newsprint.

I walked hard but there was no defined trail. I connected meadows and scree slopes and was on the Hamta-la by noon. The breeze on the summit was dry and dusty. The pass is a watershed – to the north lay the desert valleys of the Tibetan Himalayas, to my back fell away the forests and meadows of the mountains' subcontinental slope. Below me again was the Chandra River, a source stream of the Chenab, the main river of Kashmir, which itself joins the Indus in Pakistan and outlets in the Arabian Sea.

On the way down from the pass I was sure I'd lost my way. The path followed a fifteen-centimetre granite ledge above a sixteen-metre drop, a line better suited to goats than humans. I proceeded cautiously, moving with awareness, one foot in front of the other, gently, carefully, feeling my twenty-kilogram pack evenly balanced on the curve of my spine. I was fully aware of my own mortality because if I fell no one was there to pick me up; no one but the mountain goats would even know I had fallen. Each step was a meditation, a focused connection between my body and the stone. All else was peripheral. I thought of Michel in Skardu, climbing to be with God, moving closer to the infinite and of my own brushes with the divine in motion.

When I had been a ski racer I had on a few occasions, in great races, functioned in what athletes call the zone; any analysis of my body, my competitors, the snow, my skis, the people cheering along the trail – all that disappeared. I became part of the movement: body, mind, skis and snow all moving together. It was symbiosis. In those times, even though I was pushing myself to the limit, there was no pain. Pain has no place when you are moving perfectly. Those moments were flawless because they were without time in a sport that classifies itself by the clock. I know now that one of the reasons I enjoy walking so much is because when I'm moving on my own two feet for hour after hour, day after day, time itself loses its significance.

Years after the trek, while editing this book, I wondered whether Gareth had had such an epiphany the night of the accident. A moment or moments when all the rowers moved in unison, blades clipping into and out of the ruffled water. The shell moving, accelerating under the combined effort of eight men's muscle. The V wake of the boat spreading out behind the team. Faster and faster, moving against the inevitable. I hope he had that, a glimpse of infinity before the void.

I camped on scree by the Chandra River. The water ran clear and fast over great broken slabs of granite. Green moss, *thylacospermum caespitosum* and woolly-haired, yellow-flowered *tanacetum* eked an existence from between marble-veined and mica-chipped boulders. On the bank I felt the knock of stones tossed by the current, the tremors carried through earth and water. The sun set and the moon climbed around the Pir Panjal range. It lit the valley in ashen light and stirred its namesake river; chandra in Hindi means moon.

I made dinner and revelled in its simplicity. My life had been pared to essentials. I drew water, cooked rice. I looked at the stars. There was contentment in doing one thing at a time. It was a life of perpetual meditation.

In a more formal sense I had learned to meditate in a Thai Buddhist monastery five years before with a charismatically humble septuagenarian monk named Buddhadasa Bhikku. The first time meditation had affected me I was ten days into a two-week silent retreat, forty minutes into the sitting and I felt my mind separating from my body. I was scared. I found myself looking down at my cross-legged corpse, thinking, "*Shit*, how do I get back in there?" I wanted out of the meditation, but not while my being was disconnected. Then, for no other reason than that I wanted it, my spirit dropped back into the lotus-positioned body. No noise, no fanfare, just movement – up and down – an elevator of consciousness. I realized, for the first time in my life, how I had authority over my scattered thoughts.

But the meditation I found on the Himalayan trail was different. It was a steady contentment, a knowledge that I was in the right place at the right time. I was walking when I should walk and sleeping when I should sleep. Beyond that I needed nothing.

CHAPTER 6
Finding Gods

October 7

Late in the morning in Chatra Bharu, farther east up the Chandra River, I stopped for tea and chatted in Hindi with the Tibetan man who ran the chai shop on the side of a very dusty road. The hamlet is a single unoccupied government house and a tea stall, itself no more than a ragged army surplus tarp attached to the building's mud-brick wall. Not much reason to linger. The man, maybe ten years older than I, was a scruffy fellow in dusty jeans and a loose, well-patched woolen shirt. He had just finished shaving but the job was erratic. He had only a broken shard of mirror to work with, and dark hair sprouted in knotted patches along his jaw. Across his cheeks he had applied a thick layer of glistening coconut oil. His face shone as if he'd just finished running a marathon.

We talked slowly in Hindi. His name was Pema, Tibetan for lotus, the flower that rises blooming out of the swamp's decomposing muck. He told me he had lived in Dharamsala for almost ten years and had worked as a cook, even preparing

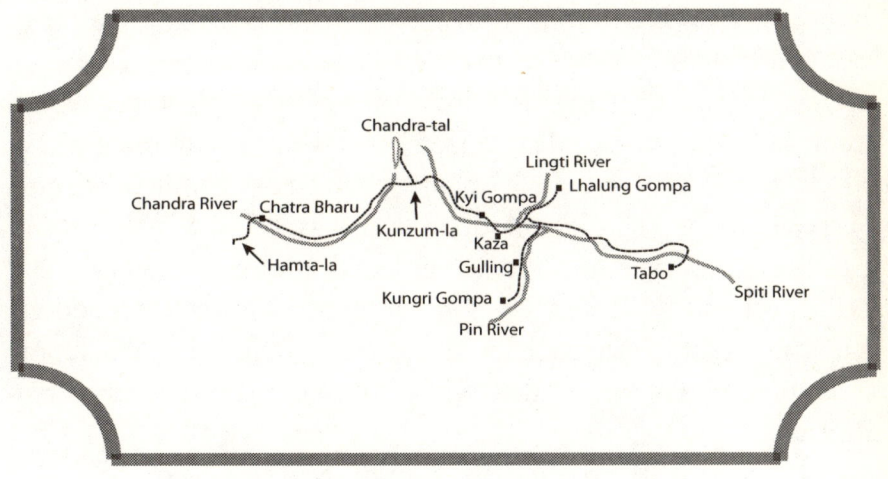

Lahaul and Spiti, Himachal Pradesh, India

food for the Dalai Lama. I asked what the great master enjoyed eating,

"Everything!" he said with a huge grin.

His Holiness has a healthy appetite but according to Pema he particularly enjoys momo, the half-moon shaped meat and vegetable stuffed dumplings that are relished throughout the Himalayas.

Maybe sensing my interest, Pema leaped from the bench where we were enjoying a cup of sweet chai and declared in English, "I make you Dalai Lama momo!"

I protested but he wouldn't listen and strode off to his kitchen, a tiny building to one side of the tea stall that I had assumed was the outhouse. I followed him into the room's kerosene reek and watched the man transform from a dishevelled chai-wallah to a self-assured cook. He beamed in the light of the one sooty window. Spices, vegetables, grains and oils were milled, mixed, sieved and pounded. He was so caught up in the cooking that he completely ignored me. I returned outside and lay in the shimmering heat of the noon sun until, an hour later, he emerged from the darkness bearing a platter of momo artwork.

He placed the tray delicately on an unsteady three-legged stool in front of me. The dozen, translucent dumplings gave off an aroma that would have made the most fulfilled salivate. Through their pale skin of flour and water I saw a matrix of green, gold, orange and red: chilies and coriander, tumeric and garlic, carrots and spinach. I could have wolfed them down, but they were arranged in such perfect symmetry, each momo a ray of steaming sun radiating from a mound of saffron carrot chutney.

I stared at them for half a minute. They were beautiful. Pema was silent, rubbing his hands against his greasy apron. I placed one in my mouth. I bit the juicy pocket and the contents melted on my tongue. I exhaled the vapour and smiled. My friend's face lit up.

Pema had put his entire effort into producing food for someone he had only just met and would probably never see again. He presented his creation in the same spirit he had cooked for the man who embodied his beliefs. His momos were an offering not just to me but to the workings of dharma; they were a pure gift that would return to him in some future life. For twenty minutes in the dazzling midday sun I savoured his offering.

Near the bridge at Batal I happened upon two men laid out on top of a pile of fifty, overstuffed burlap sacks. It was twenty-five kilometres in either direction to the nearest house. I stopped, we shook hands, they offered me some of the flat tsampa bread they were eating and I asked them why, in the middle of nowhere, they had so many bags and what was inside. The younger of the two pulled himself up from his relaxed position, thrust his hand inside the nearest sack, pulled out a dozen dark brown pellets and exclaimed, "*Sheet!*"

I took the handful of hard balls, rolled them around in my hand and realized that the men were straddling fifty sacks of sheep shit. The dung would be transported by the next available open truck back to their village and there it would be sold as fertilizer and fuel. To me this collection was nothing short of a miracle. Ovine excrement varies in size from that of a pea to that of a marble; to load fifty large bags in an area where I could see neither sheep nor grass was something exceptional. I asked the older man how they'd done it. With a ratty fur cap of goat or maybe marmot hide perched on one side of his bald head, he said, "Chutsu mangpo," a long time.

The tattered gravel road between Lahaul and Spiti links two of India's most remote districts. The band of mountains along the Tibetan border is India's least inhabited region. It was hard to believe I was in the world's second most populous nation, a country that boasts over a billion people and two million kilometres of roads. There had been no traffic at all that day. But as I wound my way up the nineteen switchbacks that lead to the Kunzum-la, a metallic clatter and grind cut the silence. Around a bend towards me, inching cautiously along a path that barely accommodated their breadth, came four sturdy, snout-nosed trucks. They were the ubiquitous Tata 1210 lorries, a utilitarian, '60s-design Mercedes successfully transplanted to the subcontinent. With over a million of these carriers on the road, the 1210 has replaced the buffalo and the horse as India's primary goods hauler. Painted in saffron, green, blue, purple, pink and yellow, their air horns blaring, sparkling mylar film tassels fluttering from their mirrors, the chain of vehicles making their way down the sixth highest road pass in the world resembled more a carnival than a convoy.

In India truck bodies are delivered as bare-bones chassis: wheels, frame, engine, a roofless, seatless cab and a standard, bulbous, saffron orange hood. The buyer finishes the vehicle and, other than the standard colour of the hood – orange being the colour of Hindu India – every aspect of the truck is customized by the purchaser. What left the factory as stock issue becomes as individual as the owner. The box, fabricated undoubtedly by a local sheet metal workshop, will be painted with flowers and animals, pictures of beaches and harvest-rich fields, images to soothe the ride. Other drivers have race cars or jet fighters fashioned on their cabs; these are the top guns of the road, the trucks you want to steer clear of. The swing gate at the rear of the box will be lettered, in Hindi, Urdu and English, with admonishments for any vehicles following behind.

"Horn Please"

"Dip Lights"

"40 Km/h Max Speed"

"Ride With Shiva"

To enter the cab of a Tata truck is to enter the driver's home. In the area between the front seat and the rear bulkhead lies a narrow, vinyl-covered bench. In this one-metre by two-metre space the driver and his assistant, usually a preadolescent boy from a poor family, will sleep, cook, eat, play cards and tell stories. The dark panelled rear wall is decorated with posters of favourite Bollywood stars. Each night, in whatever far-flung area of India the team finds itself, they drift off to sleep mutely serenaded by the well-endowed maidens of the Hindi silver screen. The dashboard, on the opposite side of the moving home, positioned above the instrument panel and overlooking the road ahead, is reserved for framed photos and glued-down statuettes of gods and gurus. Sometimes these icons, no more than the size of an outstretched hand, are complete dioramas: plastic, golden-coloured gods and goddesses in intricate bas-relief temples, circumscribed by angels and elephants and lit by haloes of blinking red LED lights. Nighttime is for dreaming. Daytime is steered by faith in the gods.

Through the dusty windshields I could see the drivers were as surprised to see me as I was them. The entire convoy came to a shuddering, air-brake hissing halt. Out jumped the drivers and their helpers, surrounding me in a cloud of diesel and bedi smoke. The men, surprisingly thin for truckers, smiled through three-day beards and bombarded me with questions.

"My God, brother, are you alone?"

"Are you O.K.?"

"You must be crazy."

They wanted to make tea in celebration of our meeting. I thought that four trucks stopped in the middle of a one-lane road on a 4,550-metre pass was not such a good idea, but they insisted no more traffic was due that day. They were the experts and we all climbed into the cab of the lead driver's truck.

Choti, the vehicle's assistant, got the kerosene stove burning in a burst of gold and blue flame. He was a Lilliputian boy with a spine so bent he had to twist his head sideways to look up at me. On the burner he placed an aluminum pressure cooker. Dilip, another driver, pointed his exquisitely long fingers at the stove and explained that without a pressurized pot at that altitude the water would not boil hot enough to make a good cup of tea. Another assistant, a feral-looking boy called Devinder, offered a stainless steel plate with a broken assortment of coconut biscuits.

All of them, including the preadolescent assistants, smoked cheroots. The cab was hot and sweaty, smelled of wet tobacco, coriander, fennel seed, unwashed clothes and the background reek of diesel. The wind whistled through the poorly sealed edges around windows and doors. Everyone was talking at once. I had expected to be jovially interrogated by the truckers, but instead everyone was asking everyone else questions in Hindi about me. I was a living, breathing, tea-drinking museum piece.

Chai in an assortment of glasses, steel mugs and chipped tumblers was passed around. Being the guest I got a dramatically stirred extra spoonful of sugar. The brew was sweet enough for the spoon to stand up in. The tea went down fast. The rate of conversation increased with the downing of the drinks and when everyone was finished I saw Kumar swiping his finger around his glass to get the last taste of sugar and with that motion, the crew, in a display of wordless synchronicity, evacuated the cab. I followed.

Outside we all shook hands, pummelled each other on the backs and shouted our farewells. The truckers climbed into their juggernauts, fired up their altitude-choked diesel engines, revved clouds of jet-black exhaust and zig-zagged like a saffron snake down the mountainside. The noise and smell followed them, drifting farther and farther away until eventually diesel was replaced again by dust.

October 8

From a cold and windy camp on the Kunzum-la I turned north and followed a good trail towards Chandra-tal, the largest lake in Lahaul and Spiti district. In summer it is bordered by green meadows and is one of the Himalayan shepherds' favourite pastures, but by October the flocks had dispersed and the hills were brown and stony. The odd thorny shrub stands out only for its offsetting verticality. Chandra-tal's broad finger of water, a kilometre long and five hundred metres wide, is unexpected in such high arid country.

I pitched my tent in a brisk wind that continued through dinner and subsided only when the sun set. I rested outside, leaning against my pack and relishing the silence. In the darkness I was very much alone. The black-billed magpies that had stood inquisitively on the crest of my nylon house and observed me eating my rice and dal had left with the sun. Even the marmots ceased their whistling.

On the hills opposite my camp I saw the moon's first sign, its chromium rim edging over the black line of the earth. The pale light illuminated the bony slopes behind me. Two slivers had been cut from the disk's perfect symmetry. Light crept down the hillside and across the lake's surface, as if incandescent lava was crossing the water. Gradually, the moon's reflection floated to the lake's centre and hung there, framed in black light. My breath was deep and even, my eyes unblinking. I was too drawn to the subtle movement to let go, and then from the south a gust rattled the fabric of my tent, brushed my cheek, rippled the surface and shattered the mirror. The moon was replaced with a thousand glinting lights.

The lake that haunts me is Elk Lake. Every time I drive by it I mutter mantras in remembrance of Gareth.

That night in January when I arrived home from Europe after crossing eight time zones and having been hit with the knee-buckling shock of Gareth being gone I couldn't sleep. It was raining but I had to see the lake, so at two a.m. I pulled on my shoes, threw on a waterproof jacket and waded into the wet, black night. I can remember the smudgey glare of the streetlamps and the little splash each footfall made on the soaking pavement. It took half an hour to walk to the lake.

The place was deserted. The odd car whooshed by on the highway that borders its eastern edge, but other than that it was quiet. No wind. I walked out onto the dock of the national rowing centre at the lake's southern end. The pontoons swayed back and forth with my movement and made sucking sounds as if they were trying to release themselves from the water. At the end of the dock I could barely make out the far shore. Black water, black land, black sky only differentiated by shades of their darkness. It was a lonely place. Out there in the blackness there was nothing to hang onto, nothing solid visually, physically, psychologically. Gareth was still there in that lake, alone. God, that was sad. The poor boy, so cold, so all alone. I repeated his name over and over, just letting it run from my lips, letting it disappear into the darkness, "Gareth, Gareth, Gareth." What a beautiful name. I repeated it loudly and softly until the words mixed with tears and eventually the tears took over. I returned wet and cold to the house where everyone still slept.

October 9

From Chandra-tal it was back on the same trail to the Kunzum-la and then east downhill to the Spiti River. The valley is dry, drier even than Ladakh, and bordered north and south by the same sedimentary and metamorphic mountains. The Precambrian rock is stratified in a thousand shades of ochre and terra cotta, umber and sienna. Golden autumn willows illuminated the erosion-scarred draws. The only water is the glacial-fed river, flowing clear and fast, pure snowmelt.

The Spiti Valley is the eastern half of Himachal Pradesh's Lahaul and Spiti district. Like Zanskar and Ladakh it is part of the Tibetan diaspora. Its residents follow the same forms of Tibetan Buddhism and their language is derived from pure Tibetan.

In the afternoon I dropped into an easy rhythm, stopping only to drink water or appreciate the odd skeletal, knee-high bush of *caragana* or *lonicera*, tough alpine survivors, long out of flower. At one point I heard the clack, clack of slipping rocks and looked up to see a pack of wolves two hundred metres above me. Two silver backs and a trio of golds scampered away, unhurried.

I spent the night at Gyumu-thang, a 200-metre by 400-metre plateau of undulating grass hills in the crook of a bend in the Spiti River. I camped near a huge fin of rock chiselled with carvings similar to the Buddhist petroglyphs I'd seen in Ladakh and Baltistan. The Gyumu-thang boulder's design concentrated on stupas and monasteries. It was primitive work, rough and shallow, the artistry of dedicated amateurs. But in it was a spontaneity that implied deep conviction. The images held devotional power that more polished efforts could not express.

Alongside the ten-metre-high stone was a cliff twice its height. I pitched my tent at its base. Mice burrows and the last silver shocks of caper blossoms showed amongst the rocky debris. The cliff acted as an echo wall for every noise within a kilometre and as the afternoon light crept down its surface, I listened to myself talk and heard the chuffing repeat of my kerosene stove.

Darkness came and with it a wind that funnelled along the escarpment, ripping past my tent, sending the loose nylon into fits so loud it was hard to think. The pitch kept up for an hour until the pale glow of moonrise filtered past the rock and then it suddenly ceased. But the crescendo was replaced by subtle chinks and whirs, gentle banshee wails that made me strain to hear more. Sternly I told myself that the echo wall was playing tricks on me, amplifying the carousing of marmots and mice, but in reality I was scared. I was alone. There was no one for twenty kilometres and in my fear solace lay with the chiselled stone ten metres away.

I found myself dwelling on the carvings. Fear had brought me to connect with a boulder sculpted centuries ago by men in similar circumstances. Far from home while herding sheep or goats, unsure of the power of their surroundings, doubtful of their ability to alter the negative events that hover in the background of everyday life, they had linked themselves to the land by working trusted symbols into it: the stupa, the architectural representation of the Buddha, and the monastery, the repository of the tradition's wisdom.

That night I joined the shepherds I'd seen for years prostrating and chanting mantras on the high passes. I understood now it was not superstition or high religion that compelled them to show that respect. It was the need to connect with the environment, because the land is the undercurrent of the dharma, the most obvious place where people connect with the Buddha. By repeating their religious practice until it was part of them and in the process understanding the land on a multitude of levels, they integrated themselves with it. The land became family and there was protection in its fold.

October 10

For a mountain river the Spiti is surprisingly wide. Here and there bony plateaus cut from the cliffs to the waterside. On those flats ragged sheep graze. There was no need for fencing as the flocks were hemmed in on all sides by precipices. From river to ridge it is a landscape of layers. Often the tablelands are riven by creeks, some flowing, many dry. Seasonal waters have carved deep fissures through the loose earth and along the miniature canyons wind and water have shaped files of pockmarked hoodoos, medieval-like steeples that look to be the refuge of gargoyles.

Not that I saw any of those mythical creatures, but the Spiti Valley is a land of mirages. In the morning the river's long straight lines enabled me to see three or four villages ahead. From the village of Hal I could see the regional capital, Kaza, more than twenty kilometres downriver to the east, but in the rarefied high altitude air I swore it was a quarter of the distance. Strangely, those depth misperceptions invert themselves after midday, as the temperature increases and features ahead disappear in waves of heat or dust kicked up by late-afternoon squalls. Distance in that environment is nebulous. You can interpret space infinitely; your mind knows a kilometre is a thousand metres, but a tired body wants those metres to pass swiftly and an occupied mind lets space move through it like water over sand. In such a realm of mirages distance is best measured one step at a time.

Following the rough road down a hoodoo-sided draw late in the morning I saw, across the narrow stream, a trailer-size, boxy, yellow air compressor and around it a huddle of construction workers lightly waving their hands in conversation and smoking bedis. They were upgrading the road, making it passable for Tata trucks and creaking buses. They were five hundred metres away by the circuitous road but only one hundred metres directly across the creek. They seemed to be ignoring me, so I ignored them and enjoyed the sense of my footfalls on the stony trail, always uneven yet consistently solid, each step a drop and gathering of my self, a movement forward ...

Then ...

BOOM!

One hundred metres away the cliff exploded and jagged rock spewed in a 180-degree arc. I cringed, threw my hands over my head and dropped headfirst to the ground. My pack rode over my shoulders and drove my face into the gravel. My senses were wrenched. Flight or fight. The aftershock rolled up and down the canyon, beating against my chest. The ringing in my ears was deafening. For a second I was newborn, without knowledge of past or present. I hovered.

The shock waves receded and slowly I rose. I dropped my hands to my hips and felt my legs. Everything still there? The explosion had coated me in a skin of powdery dust. As I stood pebbles fell from the folds in my clothes. The closest major debris, a shattered orb of pink-flecked river stone twenty centimetres in diameter, lay mockingly two metres away. Fear turned to anger. I strode down the road towards the crew who were now wide-eyed and talking agitatedly amongst themselves. They were gathered close to the compressor, as though there was refuge in its modernity. The hot bite of rage was climbing from the base of my spine.

"Who's in charge here?" I shouted in Hindi.

No one stepped forward. Their faces dropped to the ground, but one man guiltily caught my eye. I stepped up to him.

"Why were there no signs about the blasting? Why didn't anyone shout a warning when you saw me over there?" I demanded, pointing to the other side of the gorge.

The foreman endured my attack, his canvas-shoed feet scuffing stones, hands deep in his pockets. When I ran out of steam he waited, one, two seconds – he had experience with apoplectic interrogators – then looked up. His face had three days' growth and his eyes were criss-crossed with a matrix of blood-red vessels. There was alcohol on his breath.

"Most sorry, sir," he said. "We were not seeing you. We were not expecting anyone from that direction. No one is *ever* coming from that direction."

He offered a weak, yellow-toothed smile.

The crew was not local. They had the thin, dark faces of northwestern plains Indians: Punjabis, Uttar Pradeshis, Biharis. His assumption was based on a few days or a few weeks of observation. It was his release from almost killing me.

But what could I do? I raised my hands in surrender, let out an exasperated groan, and stomped off.

From years in India I knew I had no recourse. The bosses were far away in Shimla or Delhi and any complaint to the police would be shuffled, with effusive smiles and handshaking, under the table. Foreigners involve reams of paperwork. There was nothing to do but put distance between me and them. I strode off, trying to remember the feeling of my feet on the ground.

In retrospect the confrontation rather than the explosion or the sound that rang in my ears for hours afterwards was what disturbed me most. The anger, something I hadn't experienced in months, wrenched me from my contemplation; it brought me back to the daily grind of accusations and the laying of blame. In the end I knew I was right to walk away, to let the incident drift and recover the composure I had found in those mountains. Focusing on my steps was the best way to reconnect with the reason why I was walking alone through the greatest mountains on earth.

October 11

Ten kilometres farther down the valley from my campsite was Spiti's regional capital, Kaza. From the west the village looks to be an orderly set of prefabricated tin buildings, a collection of squared-off soup cans in silver, red, and green set amidst a stony valley. From a distance, in the sun, they shimmer as if they don't exist in this reality. After the mud-brick mansions of the upper valley, with their familial air and warm dark interiors, these were blatant imports. Strange, in such a land of extreme weather, that the Indian government uses steep-roofed monsoon designs and paper-thin sheets of corrugated iron from Uttar Pradesh and Bengal rather than indigenous techniques and local craftsmen.

After securing a room in a sheet metal guest house I went for a stroll and was relieved to discover, close to the river and far below the road, an old section to the town. I followed a maze of alleys down to a small bazaar. I needed supplies and at the first shop the young owner, Lobsang Phuntsok, invited me in.

My seat was surrounded by tea chests full of lentils, rice and sugar; dented metal bins on sagging wooden shelves brimmed with nuts and dried fruit. We sat behind a line of poorly cast aluminum pots and pans hanging from the ceiling, and looked out through the open, wooden-shuttered front doors. The place was comfortable, dim and dusty. It had the archaic, cluttered smell of gathered dry goods. Bundles of polyester rope in yellow, blue, green and orange hung theatrically from the ceiling. Colour prints of Hindu gods and moisture-eaten calendar photos of Swiss mountains wilted on the walls.

Lobsang offered tea. We drank and chatted. We munched on the almond-like kernels of apricot pits and shared pieces of heavy soda bread made from barley.

Lobsang was dressed in jeans and a jean jacket. His black woolen watch cap was embroidered with a New York Yankees logo. He was curious about the outside world. Our chat steered from nuclear bombs on the subcontinent to sitcom television, Bollywood, Hollywood and the rise of Hindu and Muslim religious fanatics. But we were constantly interrupted by the most interesting aspect of Lobsang's shop, his customers.

Gangs of women, young and old, trooped in and out of the store testing my friend's shop-keeping skill. Mostly they came from out-lying communities ten to fifty kilometres away. Lobsang said they ventured into Kaza only once every month or two. For them the trip was a major shopping expedition. They came in clusters of five or six, their shopping lists in hand, and from their shoulders hung battered nylon bags emblazoned with the logos of distant airlines and Delhi department stores. The bargaining was never aggressive but the women were persistent, returning four or five times over an hour to drop the price, rupee by rupee, of a kettle or a sack of beans. The negotiating was as much to gain face as about saving money. The talented bargainers had a revered place in the campaign and were consulted in chattering huddles between exchanges.

After each purchase Lobsang gave me a sideways glance and told me how much he had made on the transaction: five rupees on a pot, three rupees on a few kilos of sugar, fifty paise on a half-dozen stainless steel spoons. The women always left smiling. Hands were shaken and greetings were exchanged on behalf of shared relatives in distant villages.

When one of the groups left Lobsang shook his head. "They all know my costs. It's the bargaining they enjoy."

I asked if he ever made any big profits. He laughed and nudged me in the ribs. "Only when tourists come shopping."

October 12

From Kaza I walked back up the Spiti Valley to Kyi Gompa, the largest monastery in the area. I had passed it the day before but it was too late in the afternoon to visit. The monastery sits atop a hill on the north side of the valley. The buildings are a tighter, more compact version of Karsha. When I was there it was in the throes of construction activity. A bamboo exoskeleton wrapped the 500-year-old prayer room and the screech of compressed-air tools drowned out chanting monks.

A young lama was designated to show me around. I followed him through a series of musty meditation cells and unlit alcoves crammed with statues and scroll paintings of fierce-looking deities. The monk offered little commentary. He had been press-ganged into being my escort and his heart wasn't in it.

But in one of the smaller prayer rooms I happened upon a sepia-toned, black and white photo of the Kyi Rinpoche, the head of the monastery. It must have been taken soon after his enthronement as the boy in the picture looks to be four or five years old. In it he is seated in a cross-legged lotus position on the roof of the gompa. He sits straight-backed on silk cushions. His little body is draped in elaborate brocade, dragons and stylized clouds are embroidered on the cloth around his shoulders, snow lions and eight-spoked wheels of dharma encircle his chest. He wears the high pointed hat of the Geluk-pa school. It is an accessory that transports him centuries back in time. His torso is framed by two-metre-high rooftop tantric tridents and in the background are the thinly snowed peaks of late spring.

It is a staged shot, expertly exposed, an image you would remember for anthropological rather than artistic merits. But I was absorbed by it. What held me was the boy's face. He has the cherubic features of a child, yet his eyes and mouth are of another person. Pursed and serious, his lips are those of a scholar trapped in debate. His eyes have a gaze that transcends time; in them is the glare of prophets. They are eyes you feel will never blink. The intelligence and confidence of one who understands his calling dwells inside the tiny body.

I never met the rinpoche but the image is etched in my memory; it returns to me when I wrestle with the concept of reincarnation.

Reincarnation is a bedrock concept of Buddhism. For Buddhists, the inevitability of life after death eliminates the fear of an end to this life, and in the openness of that individuals are free to concentrate on living the best they can. It is the accumulation of good deeds based around wisdom and compassion that leads Buddhists higher and higher up the ladder of rebirth until eventually, after many lives of struggle, they are reborn in a state of higher consciousness: nirvana.

For me the photo of the rinpoche is an icon in the orthodox Christian sense, a two-dimensional image that carries with it the power to make you believe. There is a child, a tiny body only recently released from his mother's bosom, his little mouth now ready with answers, his clear, unwrinkled eyes penetrating, hard as diamonds. They are features beyond time, almost as if an accumulation of lives had concentrated in that being.

Reincarnaton is one of the reasons I was attracted to Buddhism. In the years after Gareth's death, it had been impossible for me to believe that all the great and powerful energy that had constituted my brother could just disappear. Poof! How could that be? How could the teenage vitality of someone so loved vanish?

A Christian interpretation of his death told me that he must have gone to heaven, up there with the good men and women of my life, my Nana and Papa, my Gran and Granpa. But that still didn't explain how all his positivity could just evaporate into thin air. In the years after his death I read widely about religion and death, and reincarnation seemed to offer some explanation.

From my readings Buddhism postulated the most complete portrayal of reincarnation. The mind of a deceased individual does not transfer directly into that of a newborn. Instead, the five aggregates of a person (form, sensation, perception, mental formations and consciousness) break down at death and these components reform with the aggregates of other deceased individuals and create a new being. Gareth was not existing as Gareth in some tiny body, but his spirit, the components of his being, were continuing in another form. There was solace in this for me, in the thought that all his great smiling, humorous, hard-working inquisitiveness was out there blessing others.

I walked back to Kaza through sunset. As night fell the stars, one by one, pricked through the enveloping darkness until by 7:30 p.m. the sky resembled a phosphorescence-riddled sea. On the horizon silhouetted mountains transformed into black-light vacuums, so dark they drew weight from the moonless heavens. Through it all wound the Milky Way, a trail of crystal smoke rising and falling in an infinite arc.

October 13

I followed the Spiti River twenty kilometres west and then cut north on the smaller Lingti River towards the village of Lhalung. The valley was desolate. Rain there is a rare occurrence and yet the river flowed thick and fast, nurtured by the glaciers hanging from the snow peaks on the border with Tibet. The village sits five hundred metres above the river, and its fields descend step by step to the water. The few people I saw in the paddies and around their houses gave me that shy smile Tibetans reserve for the unexpected. I asked an old lady for directions to the gompa and she pointed to the only dense patch of trees on the hillside.

In the midst of the copse was a pair of two-storied, flat-roofed buildings, whitewashed with red accents around the doors and up against the roofline. The compound was small, twenty metres by twenty metres, more of a lha-kang, or temple, than a monastery. Spreading over them was an ancient willow, its branches stroking and connecting the roofs of the two shrines. The tree was moving from blazing colour to hibernation and my footsteps kicked up clouds of golden leaves.

Tenzin, the twenty-something monk who had appeared within minutes of my arrival, unlocked the weathered main door, its jambs shone black from centuries of touch from sweaty hands. The lha-kang, he explained in halting Hindi, was more than seven hundred years old. I was taken aback. There are only a handful of Buddhist temples in India that old and I had never heard of this one.

From the midday light we entered the dusk of the sanctum. The central temple is a low, rounded structure completely surrounded by a narrow, enclosed passageway that devotees use to circle the inner shrine. In the walkway shards of frescoes peeked out from behind layers of adobe. It appeared that the hall had once been entirely decorated. Seven hundred years of history had been plastered over with mud.

We circled the shrine room using the outer hallway and returning to the front door entered the inner sanctum. In the half-light I saw life-size, three-dimensional statues pushing out from the walls. The central altar was dominated by weathered statues of the Nyingma triumvirate: Padmasambhava, the tantric missionary who founded the school and brought Buddhism to Tibet; Chenrezig, known in Sanskrit as Avalokiteshvara, the thousand-armed embodiment of compassion; and Lon Chenpo, the fourteenth-century philosopher monk who codified much of the Nyingma liturgy.

Tenzin sat on a cushion to one side of the statues and began a ceremony, or puja, reciting prayers and accompanying them with a hand drum and cymbals. I had not expected this. Outside he had materialized beside me still eating his lunch, but now I saw the bits of rice that had been stuck to his hands were washed away.

I sat cross-legged beside him. The only light was the refracted sun flushed through the open door. In the shadows I could just make out the monk's face, and the statues were blurry phantoms. The space rippled with the *thunk* and *ding* of Tenzin's music and the bass tone of his chanting. The vibrations shivered in the air around us. Tenzin continued and syllable by syllable, minute by minute I forgot my own hunger. I lost track. Time moved on until all of a sudden the music stopped. Tenzin cleared his throat, tucked his drum and cymbals into silk coverings and slipped them under the low table in front of his seat. He stood and left without a word or a wave goodbye.

I moved my hands from my lap, my fingers tingling. Slowly I twitched my toes, shook my feet, my legs and then my arms. I rose and made my way outside. Tenzin had gone back to his cell. From the doorway of his hut he waved and smiled, but turned and went inside before I got there. I walked on by. He wanted to be alone. So did I.

As I retraced my steps back down to the Spiti River I kept coming back to Lhalung, back to the feeling in my bones that that building was more than bricks and mortar. That night, camped on the banks of the Spiti's southerly tributary, the Pin River, I began to make sense of it. I was able to step back and in my mind's eye view it from far above. With that perspective I was able to imagine it for what it could be: an architectural mandala.

In Tibetan Buddhism practitioners use the mandala, generally a series of circular images, to visualize in meditation the steps along the path to higher consciousness. The best known images of Tibetan mandalas are drawn by monks on flat surfaces using coloured sand. These two-dimensional mandalas are layered in decreasing sized circles from their outside to the centre. In the Kalachakra mandala, for example, 722 deities, or manifestations of Kalachakra, are portrayed within a twelve-layered circle about two metres in diametre. But the mandala is more a psychological construct than a physical one, and could just as easily be a piece of landscape or architecture viewed with the correct mindset. At their core mandalas are universal maps, cryptographs that outline a way of understanding the universe and the individual's place in it.

That evening, lying in my green-roofed tent, I visualized Lhalung as such a map. The exterior of the compound with its mellow light and gold-leafed fringe was everyday life, the place you need to move beyond to begin the process of understanding. The enclosed passageway, with its ancient wall paintings surrounding the inner shrine room, was where the search begins with those initial glimpses and realizations of powers greater than the self. The tiny pilgrimage that devotees make through the tunnel is a process of coming to terms with the power that the central deities represent. The inner sanctum, the area you move to after the journey around the passageway, is the home of gurus and gods. It represents the place all Buddhists want to reach. Being there, in a psychological sense, implies a realization of what the deities represent and how they relate to higher consciousness.

I lay in my tent for hours piecing this together, until finally sleep surprised me and my overactive imagination surrendered to my bone-tired body.

I woke in the middle of the night to the whisper of snowfall. It is the gentlest sound imaginable – the footsteps of a sleepy mouse or the exhalation of forgotten breath. I opened the tent flap to see the Pin River framed in lunar white; the snow-covered boulders on its shores looked to be downy spheres bracketing the river's quick blackness.

October 14

Morning came with the sound of birds – "dzchit ... dzcheet." It was a pair of brown dippers close by my tent. I unzipped the door and saw them hopping on riverside rocks, their tiny talons wrapped in snow. The world outside was white, the perspective flattened by the dull light. I sat in my vestibule and made coffee and tsampa porridge as the river, black against the snowy borders, rushed by. I packed my tent in a hurry and trudged into swirling clouds of spindrift snow.

Five kilometres up the valley I reached Gulling village. I was drained from walking through calf-deep snow on the unplowed road. I arrived at the same time as the local bus from Kaza; the passengers stepped down unsteady and pale-faced. The ride up from the Spiti River through deepening snow must have been harrowing. But three men got out in a state of glee. Dark-skinned and mustachioed, wearing balaclavas, multiple scarves and heavy tweed jackets, they were a breed apart from the woolen-robe-wearing locals.

Once off the bus the three leaped up and down, clapped their hands, slapped each other on the back and threw snowballs in the air. It was grand to see such staidly dressed grown men acting like excited children. Following the calisthenics they came breathlessly into the dhaba where I had gone in search of chai. They ordered tea and in the tiny space sat down beside me on a bench by the window. The man to my left smiled, showing a line of huge, sparkling white teeth, and inquired in English what I was doing there. I told them about the walk and they nodded their heads gravely, muttering, "My God" under their breaths.

I asked them what they were doing in Gulling, and they said they were government servants auditing the accounts of the village council. All three – Sunny, Hari and Mukesh – were originally from Kolkata but for many years had been working for the central government in Delhi. I had to ask what they had been so excited about when they had gotten off the bus. Mukesh pointed outside, his face breaking again into a huge smile. "The snow, my friend, the snow." None of the three had ever seen snow before.

It was another ten kilometres up the valley before I came to Kungri Gompa in late afternoon. The clouds that had brought the snow still hung close to the earth and the three large mud-brick buildings that make up the monastery seemed to float towards me out of the mist. Kungri was built in 1331 and is the only monastery in the Spiti Valley associated with the Nyingma Buddhist school.

As with Kyi Gompa new construction was underway; bags of cement, wooden concrete forms, stacks of iron rebar and piles of gravel, sand and dirt all lay as if abandoned around the buildings. The gompa was a mess. I was disappointed; it was not my image of a Buddhist monastery. The Karshas and Lamayurus were my archetypes – monolithic, unchanging architectural relics. I wanted the monasteries to be as timeless as the teachings. But it was selfish grumbling.

Buddhism teaches that all constructs, human or otherwise, are impermanent. For me to think that a building could be as eternal as the dharma was naïve. Everything changes, even the appearance of a religion. Concrete gompas, fibreglass sculptures of the Buddha, gaudy mass-produced posters, plastic gods glued to plastic dashboards – these are not what is important. At the heart of any religion is what the icons represent and to perceive that you must strip back personal ideas and encounter the imagery in the pure state out of which it was created. Mukesh, Hari and Sunny seeing snow for the first time – that was the state in which to view religious iconography.

Past the rubble I reached the main dukhang. I wanted to find someone to ask about a room in which to stay, and it was only when I was outside the main door that I heard the sound of a single standing drum beating away. I removed my shoes, unslung my pack and stepped from damp flagstones into a twilight-dark, gymnasium-sized hall. At the opposite end of the room, his back to me, facing a triumvirate of statues, was a single lama performing a prayer ceremony. He was draped in a thick burgundy cape of homespun wool, fuzzy with age. Butter lamps sputtered on the altar, illuminating his silhouette and lighting a golden aura around him.

I moved off to one side and sat on a woolen rug close to the back corner of the room. I felt voyeuristic but said nothing and let myself be taken by the drum and prayers. The old man's instrument quivered with each strike of the bentwood stick. The sound hung in the chilly air. We were together for at least half an hour before the lama stopped his chanting.

He wiped his face with his hands, placed a burgundy and gold silk cover on his loose-leaf prayer book and inserted the drumstick into the instrument's frame. He rose unsteadily, wavered in the vertical and shuffled his feet into a pair of thick, worsted wool slippers. He put his hands together in prayer and lifted his head to the statue of Guru Rinpoche on the altar. Then, finishing his prayer, he lowered his head, turned and pushed off across the polished timber floor. His woolen slippers glided easily on the floorboards. With a few pumps of his legs he skated past me, silent, like a ghost. His momentum stopped as he hit the doorsill and he converted his momentum into a couple of quick steps. With that he was gone.

I stood, a little dazed from the thirty minutes of silent sitting and from what I had just seen. Slowly I stood and went outside. It was pitch black. I still didn't have a room and it was too late to set up my tent. I made for the first light I could see and was led to the monastery's kitchen.

Tenzin, the man inside, was the lone caretaker of the monastery; his wife and son stayed at the family home in Kaza where he returned a few days a week. In Hindi he told me there were only a handful of lamas at the gompa and no official rooms for rent, but he offered to let me bed down in the storeroom behind the kitchen. He then generously offered me some of his rice and dal. We ate in silence and soon after I slipped into my sleeping bag on the flagstone floor of the storeroom. My stomach was full, my sleeping bag was laid in the corner of a warm room, I had seen things I would remember forever. I was blessed that night.

October 15

At sunrise I returned down the Pin River and followed the Spiti River east. My goal that day was thirty kilometres away, the monastery of Tabo. I was walking on a paved road with almost no traffic so I moved quickly, happy in the consistency of my steps. At one point in the morning I watched a golden eagle turning and turning above and wondered why it would choose this valley, a place of such meagre fertility. Why not fly south across the mountains to the harvest-thick paddies of Punjab or Uttar Pradesh? I looked around; stony ridges cut sharp lines on the horizon. The sky was a cloudless aquamarine. The river was unceasing, the colour of precious stone. The air was crisp, even in the piercing sunlight. There was openness and simplicity in that landscape.

It was almost dark when I arrived in the village by the monastery. I quickly found a room at the monastery hostel and shared a meal of rice, dal and fresh chilies in the smoky kitchen with the family managing the rooms. I was the only guest.

Tabo was established in 996 by Lotsawa Rinchen Zangpo, the same great translator who founded Lingshed Gompa and 108 other monasteries and temples in the western Himalayas. Tabo is particularly important for Tibetan Buddhists because the complex's nine temples and the artwork inside them have been built, renovated and reworked again and again over the past 1,100 years. The result is that the Tabo temples are the most complete chronology of the development of Himalayan Buddhist art in the world.

It is a small miracle that Tabo survives. All but a half dozen of the 108 temples and monasteries that Rinchen Zangpo founded have been destroyed, but Tabo is untouched. This is surprising because Spiti, which had traditionally been ruled by Tibet and then Ladakh, from the late seventeenth century onwards suffered a series of invasions from warring Hindu states south of the Himalayas, first from the Kulu Valley and then from the Dogra people of Punjab state. Even in the past fifty years, only the quirk of an arbitrary political boundary that makes Spiti part of India rather than Tibet has spared it the destruction of the Chinese Cultural Revolution. Tabo Gompa now stands dignified but alone.

I had heard much about the artwork at Tabo, but detailed descriptions can lead to great expectations and I wanted to see the gompa with the eyes of a child. My first glimpse late that afternoon assisted in the process because from the main road, the original temples are a set of nine low, unornamented earthen mounds – primitive sandcastles – not what one would expect of one of the world's great treasure houses of religious art.

That night after dinner I listened with the family in their kitchen to crackling news reports from the BBC World Service on the radio. It was the first time in weeks I had heard an extended conversation in English. I found I was having difficulty keeping pace with the words of the announcers. My mind was slowing down, something I was not unhappy about.

October 16

Early the next morning I walked to the compound. Tabo is known as the Ajanta of the Himalayas, in reference to the great Buddhist cave temples in Maharastra state near

Mumbai. When arriving at Ajanta, in the tradition of Indian salesmanship, you are inundated with amateur guides harassing you to hire them for exorbitant rates. At Tabo I had expected some kind of official entranceway with written instructions and guides waiting by the gate. There was nothing of the sort. I wandered unobstructed into the temple area. There was no one there, but that also meant there would be no keys to enter the locked temples. I decided to circumambulate the complex, hoping someone would notice and take pity on me.

The buildings were smooth tan squares with curved edges and walls that tapered gently inwards as they climbed – so different to the jagged verticality of the surrounding mountains. Most were two-storey, mud-brick constructions freshly replastered with fine-grained golden adobe. In places the façade had contracted and cracked; spider-webbed lines flowed across the surfaces, translating unseen patterns from the submerged millennium-old superstructures. The entire compound was floored with the same unblemished mud. No trees or plants grew there. No garbage or leaves bucked in the breeze.

I continued circling the buildings in a clockwise direction. Tibetans call this a kora. The circumambulation of any shrine is considered auspicious. To round a religious object, and the sacred entity could as easily be a mountain or lake as a statue or temple, to view it from every angle and sense your relationship to it, and ultimately to absorb some of the power the object possesses, this is the essence of these pilgrimages in miniature.

Eventually a monk, only a boy, maybe sixteen or seventeen years old, approached me. He asked in broken English if I wanted to visit the main shrine room. I nodded and in response he jangled the keys hidden beneath his burgundy robes. The boy spoke only when spoken to. He had a recently shaved head and the razor had left small puckered nicks criss-crossing his scalp.

He unlocked the door to the largest hall, the Sug Lhakang, the Temple of the Enlightened Gods. I untied the laces on my boots and left them on the porch. He kicked off a pair of blue and white rubber thongs. We entered a dim alcove, then a passageway flanked by a pair of life-sized, sword-wielding terra cotta guardians. At their feet, before the closed double doors of the assembly hall, I shut my eyes. I was excited; I had read so much about this place and now I was here. I could smell the dust reeling in the ancient air and the cheap rose-water soap on the monk's skin.

Deliberately I opened my eyes as the boy pushed through the inner door. Before me was a large cave-like room, cool and very, very dry. A shaft of light beat down from the single slit in the roof and, with the breeze from the open door, sun-shot dust motes flickered in the beam. I stepped in.

At the rear of the room was an altar, a metre high and covered in white and gold silk. This is where the Dalai Lama performs prayer ceremonies when he is at the gompa. On the altar was a framed photo of His Holiness. To either side of the dais were vertical, pigeon hole-like cases holding loose-leaf books wrapped in saffron brocade. This was the Tabo library: 40,000 handwritten, rice paper pages that reputedly predate the temple itself.

On the far side of the altar sat a four-bodied statue in silver and gold, each figure looking off in one of the four cardinal directions. It was a human-sized representation of Vairocana, the embodiment of the continuum of reality. He is the primordial Buddha, the Buddha that is with us life after life after life.

In horizontal file, partway up the four walls, shadowy three-dimensional images emerged from the darkness; statues of deities and bodhisattvas floated against a painted background. Above and below them the walls were covered with frescoes depiciting Buddhas, saints, teachers, monks, nuns, angels, kings, queens, mythical beasts, palaces, stupas, gompas, merchants and everyday people, men, women, children. The place quivered with stories but in the cold and silent half-light I couldn't make the connection I wanted to. To compensate I moved closer to the wall. The images were smooth but not glossy, painted with ancient stone-ground colours, still grainy and colour-charged a millennium after their application.

I put my face breathing distance from the Buddhas and bodhisattvas and smelled the earth of a thousand years before: bricks and mud, pure water, bright air, a landscape full of gods.

I tried to listen. I put my ear close to the surface. I heard my own breath, felt my own heart thumping steady against mud bricks.

The space was neither alive nor dead but it throbbed with energy. With strange bodies evolving out of nothingness, fear would have been the simplest emotion but the thin air was weighted with something else, something I couldn't quite identify – maybe it was compassion. I looked to the teenage monk. The beads on his roasary clicked as they slipped through his fingers.

I rounded the temple, circling the central shrine, enjoying the soft tread of my sock feet on the mud floor, a surface worn smooth by the passing of devoted millions. I felt the gentle bounce of my body adjusting foot to foot. A small dance caught me each time my heel rolled up and onto my toes. Blood flowing, temples pulsing, cool air leeching under my collar. I circled and circled the room. The statues tracked me. My thoughts slowed, my mind cleared. Experience was being let go of, and the faith of a millennium was rolling over me.

As I left the temple I offered my hand to the young monk; Namgyal was his name. We shook and it was a strange gesture, insignificant in relation to the gravity of where we had just been, but I needed something physical, something tactile to offset what I had felt inside the room. Namgyal's fingers were talcum-powder soft.

In the hostel after lunch I debated if I should return to the temple. Would going back destroy what I'd experienced there? Maybe it was greed, but I went.

The temple, in the five hours since morning, had transformed. The sun was high and what had previously been a twilight grotto was now fully lit. In the light of day the statues on the walls had taken on personalities. The early morning light had created a uniform feeling in the temple but now the statues on the wall, the frescoes behind them and the figures on the altar were all emanations of the energy I had had so much difficulty identifying earlier on.

With the benefit of sunlight I studied the paintings behind the statuary. The murals were so detailed it took minutes to appreciate parts of single figures. From an artistic sense the walls were cluttered. Images were piled upon images and yet each piece was somehow balanced and connected: there was a harmony in the imagery, a pattern to the chaos. They made me want to learn more, want to understand what had motivated hundreds of artists to create that place. I thought of Lhalung, of how my neophyte mind had been moved and of how, for the initiated, Tabo, its larger, more intricate cousin, must hold exponential power.

That night I lay in my guest house bed staring at the concrete ceiling and thinking. Throughout my journey I had felt a spirit, a compassion in the landscape, and now I was experiencing that energy in human constructions. Lhalung and Tabo were not architecture holding religion; they were architecture being religion. It was all a very long step from my Presbyterian childhood.

Every Sunday morning we attended church in Belfast. Mass was a dour affair, everyone sitting ramrod straight on oak benches, women in hats, men in dark suits, the smell of old cigarettes, wet wool and the sour aftersmell of grandparents. I couldn't stop fidgeting. I remember trying to sit on my devilish hands while my older brother poked me for a reaction. All around us were grey stone walls and the stern imagery of Scottish Protestantism – Victorian-era oil paintings of Jesus and his disciples and sober stained-glass windows backlit by a hazy sun. It was minimalist decoration constantly overshadowed by the wrath of God.

The priest on his altar was the room's focus. I remember his tight collar, wet lips and aggressive body language. The atmosphere expanded and contracted with his breath. I feared him. He expounded from an impossibly thick Bible and pointed his finger at the Beyond. He was God's representative. God in that church was a frightening old man.

But I knew another God. Every night, kneeling by my bedside, eyes clenched shut, hands clasped in prayer, I asked God to help in solving Ulster's Troubles and I asked him to keep my family safe. God and I talked. It didn't resolve the conflict – the killings went on – but we conversed. I enjoyed those nightly discourses. There was intimacy, a relationship beyond language, something that infused me with confidence.

That God receded from my consciousness when I gave up my nightly prayer. By the age of nine I had become too indoctrinated in the rational to believe in the efficacy of conversation with a nebulous old man in flowing robes. My fear of God, which in a subtle way heightened my attraction, disappeared when my family moved to Canada. Our church-going ceased. Without intimacy or fear there was no reason for me to follow that God. But a childhood in such a place leaves a mark. After Gareth died I went in search of what I had had before, the innocent discussions with the God in my bedroom. Maybe in Tabo, in the half-light of morning, with sixty-six terra cotta deities' eyes upon me and a contented feeling that I couldn't fully describe, maybe then I finally found that God again.

CHAPTER 7
Harvest

October 17

I left Tabo without visiting all nine temples. The fear that had nagged me when I returned to the Sug Lhakang in the afternoon, that of spoiling what I had already experienced, returned when I thought about the other temples. I didn't want to dilute what I had felt in the Sug Lhakang by rushing around eight other temples in a single day. Tabo is something special and I know I will return when there is time to give all the temples the respect they deserve.

I had a leisurely breakfast of tea and chapatis with the mother and youngest daughter of the guest house family before I left Tabo. The mother generously gave me the leftover bread for my lunch.

Back on the road I was surprised by the almost complete lack of traffic. The route wound gently along the Spiti River. Tightening cliffs channelled it on, pushing it faster and faster towards its meeting with the Sutlej River. At one point in the

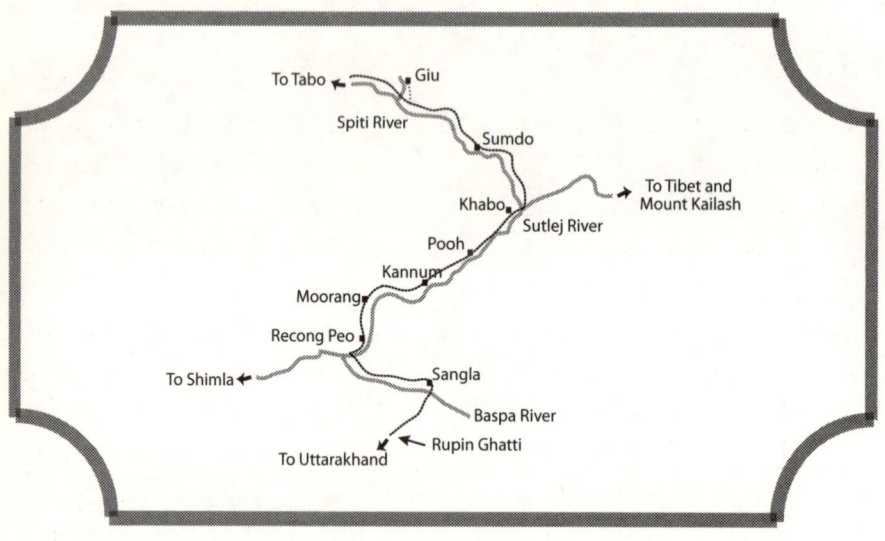

KINNAUR, HIMACHAL PRADESH, INDIA

morning a gang of goldfinches bounded by me, undulating in a single mass, their chirpy song mingling with the water's noise.

I traced the river another twenty kilometres east to where it was joined by a creek from the north and followed this upstream towards the village of Giu. The creek's passage was a narrow winding valley which widened after six kilometers, so I could see the village in the distance. In the opening the wind howled from the north. I leaned into it and was relieved when I reached the shelter of the village buildings. At one of the first houses a lady waved me over and using sign language invited me in for tea.

It was an odd cup of tea. Her house was, I think, the village post office, although I saw no sign outside. Red boxes secured with huge medieval locks lay in one corner, tossed on the dirt floor were sacks bulging with the squared-off shapes of envelopes, and cardboard boxes secured with twine created an unsteady wall near the doorway.

I sat in a wooden chair on one side of the room. She poured me sugary chai from a stainless steel thermos and took a seat behind a rickety wooden desk. Behind her on a mattress on the floor two babies cried and cried. She ignored them and after pouring the tea, ignored me, not saying a word the entire time I was inside the house.

The wind beat against the building using anything not battened down to make a noise. I drank the tea quietly while she wrote things in a hardbacked ledger. When I finished I stood to go, but I wasn't sure if she expected me to pay for the tea. I put my hand in my pocket searching for money and she stopped me with a look that would have set fire to a brick house. She stood and opened the door for me to leave.

I'd come to Giu because of rumours I'd heard, from as far back as Kaza, that the mummified body of a lama had been discovered in the vicinity. Local legend had it that the Indian Army had been digging a drainage ditch around its camp and had unearthed the body. Nobody I asked had any more details.

On her doorstep I asked the lady in Hindi where I might find the mummy and she pointed to a knoll above the fields where a white shack tottered in the gale. I thanked her and she nodded. Inside, the children were still crying.

Outside, on the right side of the front door, a huge black, roughly carved wooden phallus, a sign of protection, hung from the eaves. Its tip was painted red, its base girdled by a thick, black bush of leftover cassette tape – pubic hair. The celluloid ruffled in the breeze. It looked remarkably organic.

Clouds had rolled in and powder snow bucked in the squally air. In the pastures men were tilling cold, grey soil with wooden plows. They moved slowly, shouting at their yaks in the rhythmic singsong way that's common throughout the Himalayas. Snow pigeons hopped amongst their feet, foraging for passed over seed. As I neared them the farmers smiled and touched their foreheads in greeting.

Up on the hillock, inside the corrugated steel shack, was a low wood and glass case surrounded by a platform for circumambulation. I stooped down to look inside the display. There on a base of mud, draped with silk scarves and semi-precious stones, was a shrivelled human body. I had seen Egyptian mummies in a museum as a child, but at Giu, 3,000 metres up in the Himalayas, the perfect shrunken body seemed entirely out of place.

It was obviously the remains of a man. The body sat upright in a cross-legged position. His right hand, tight against his body, was frozen in the attitude of counting a string of prayer beads that would have disintegrated over time. His shoulders were hunched forward to frame a slight, bony chest. Even though the skin was tight and wrinkled, I could see his face was frozen in a look of weary satisfaction, the corners of his mouth tipped upwards in the slightest of smiles. I imagined the lama serenely passing from this life, counting his prayers, in the clear light of meditation.

For many dedicated Tibetan lamas that is exactly what happens, because death is the focus and culmination of their life's practice. In the Nyingma school's teaching, the *Bardo Thodol*, the *Tibetan Book of the Dead*, the transition from this life to the next is described in exhaustive detail. For those who understand and apply the teaching, death unfolds not as a tragic end but as a transition from this life to the next. By approaching the body's end with a calm and informed mind, by seeing it for what it is, a manifestation of impermanence, death becomes something not to fear but to resolutely accept. I returned to the monk's ever so slight smile. Death is a lesson.

Gareth, like the monk, passed from this life with a look on his face that spoke of a gentle exit. I will never know the fear he confronted in those awful minutes while hanging onto the shattered hull of the rowing shell or the thoughts that possessed him when his body finally gave out and slipped quietly away. I can't dwell on those images; the pain is too much.

What I hold onto is the face I saw in the cold light of the hospital morgue. It was so relaxed, no wrinkles or lines, his skin pale to the colour of snow, his mouth a thin line of blue with his lips curved ever so slightly upwards in a half-smile.

People say that in the later stages of hypothermia a feeling of warmth comes over you. I can see him remembering a warm summer's night treeplanting in northern Canada, a group of tired friends gathered around a sparking blaze, the atmosphere full of satisfaction and potential. Or even better, I think of him imagining himself as a child holding tight against the warmth of our mother's skin, her tender heat around and through him, his body attached to the one who loved him most.

That's how I imagine his last moments – warm and full of love. I saw that in the expression on his face. It's not that of someone dreading the end; it's the face of a man resigned to the unavoidable and ready for what the next stage would bring. Gareth had realized what we all know deep inside us – that death is inevitable, that this passing will come no matter how hard we pull away from it. He saw his time was now and let himself drift softly out of this life.

I left the drafty shack. Outside snowflakes blustered. I retraced my steps through the village and down the creek. The temperature was dropping rapidly and the stream was now edged in spider-webbed patterns of ice.

My campsite at the lower end of Giu Creek was a tiny island. I pitched my tent surrounded by the stream; water rushed by inches from the door. I had reached the spot by leaping a ford of ice-caked boulders and as the sun disappeared I watched from the vestibule as their glassy coating paled and thickened. Then came night and the sky was splashed with the diamond streak of the Milky Way, so dense I could have grabbed a handful. I had never seen so many stars.

That night the temperature plummeted and when I woke the little river had been reduced to a trickle encased in ice. I opened the door to see a sparkling, crystal-gilded world where everything from the swaying grasses to my tent's fly sheet was shimmering with frozen spray. It was beautiful but biting cold. I rushed to pack and warm myself with movement.

October 18

Back on the main route by the Spiti River I found the road had been freshly paved. On the even surface I didn't have to worry about twisting an ankle and moved briskly, feeling the synchronicity of legs and arms and heart and lungs, letting my mind wander. But in the hamlet of Sumdo this got me into trouble.

The little village is the checkpost where the road branches northeast to Tibet. With India and China on questionable terms the road is closed and the soldiers were edgy. As I entered the village I made the moronic blunder of taking a wrong turn and walking directly into an army camp. Suddenly I was surrounded by three gun-toting infantrymen shouting at me in Hindi. I was inside a barbed-wire fence. It was obvious that something was seriously wrong and I threw my arms up in surrender. The troops marched me off to their commander's office, their chests puffed out with the pride of having captured an "alien."

The officer was grave but congenial. Interestingly, he didn't want to give me his name. Maybe it was some kind of need-to-know security situation on the border, or maybe he was worried this tourist could cause him headaches higher up the chain of command. We talked in English and I tried to explain I had committed a dundering mistake, that I had walked into their barracks by accident and I'd be happy to excuse myself as quickly as possible.

He told me that unfortunately that was not possible because his men had "caught" me and a report would have to be written. For now the Inner Line Permit, the piece of paper issued by the local Chief of Police in Kaza entitling me to be in an area so close to the border, would have to be verified, and until then I would remain in detention.

I was going to jail. I asked how long the proceedings would take and he replied jauntily, "Not so long."

From experience I'd learned that "Not so long" in India can mean anywhere from one hour to one week. I handed him my permit and was escorted away.

This was a particularly uncomfortable situation because to insure I had enough time to walk through both Spiti and Kinnaur district to the south I had doctored the dates on my permit from the maximum allowable one week to two weeks. I was extremely nervous that the police commissioner in Kaza would verify the documents had been tampered with. With India's infatuation with paperwork, this discovery could lead to a very serious situation.

The detention room was hardly a cell. It was more lodging for visiting officers. It had a clean-sheeted bed, a side table, an unbarred window and a radio tuned to a cricket game somewhere far to the south. The only jail-like element was the guard who sat in the opposite corner, an archaic wooden-stocked rifle on his lap, khaki woolen watch cap pushed slackly back on his head. I wouldn't even have noticed him if he hadn't had the uneasy habit of staring at me for minutes on end and then loudly clearing the phlegm from his throat. These leering fits were broken every half hour or so when he would jump up from his chair, rifle dropping to his side, and inquire, "Tee, sah?"

The first time he did this it took me a moment to realize that he was offering his prisoner tea. My chai arrived in a china cup and saucer, the sugar in its own caddy. My guard drank from a chipped earthenware mug. I was being treated more as a V.I.P. than an inmate, but as the first hour led to the second and then into the third it was difficult not to imagine unpleasant scenarios. What could the commanding officer and the police commissioner be talking about?

By the fourth hour my guard had gotten over his distant inquisitiveness and had started to ask questions in simple English. "You like cricket?" "You have wife, child?" "Your work, what?"

We were actually getting along quite well. Then the captain entered, jolly and smiling. "Oh, Mr. Lineen, most sorry to take so long, but border communications are always so difficult." He handed back the permit.

He said, "Everything is most definitely in order. Thank you so much," and promptly invited me to lunch. I declined, anxious to leave the place in case they wanted to double-check my papers. I exited in a rush, issuing thank-yous and receiving a stiff salute from my tea-toting guard.

I walked out of the gates of the camp as fast as I could, not looking back, keeping my eyes to the road. I didn't stop in the village and kept on walking until dusk set in. Then, still paranoid that the authorities would discover my forging, I walked up off the road five hundred metres until I found a small copse of birch trees and there, hidden from the road, I laid my sleeping bag down.

October 19

I was up early. I was still worried about the police, but I would be walking the road most of the day, so if they really wanted to catch me it wouldn't be that difficult. I tried not to think about them and focused on walking. At Sumdo the Spiti River makes a dramatic 90-degree turn to the south. With each new tributary it grows more powerful and near Ganfa village its full force is channelled through an impressive gorge. The canyon walls are an aggregate of sandstone, feldspars, magmatites and loose granite slabs. It's an incredibly unstable backdrop to National Highway 22, which in some places is cut directly into the canyon walls.

Sumdo also marks the border between Lahaul and Spiti district and Kinnaur district. Again Kinnaur is a Tibetan-influenced region within India. It has its own dialect and most of the population are Tibetan Buddhists.

At the village of Khabo the Spiti River merges and is absorbed by the Sutlej River. The Sutlej is the farthest east and, at 1,500 kilometres, the longest of the Indus River's tributaries. It originates from Rakas Lake near the base of Mount Kailash in southwestern Tibet. From there it flows west and crosses the Shipki-la into India. Through Kinnaur the river quickly loses altitude and it is through this section that the Sutlej stakes its claim as the fastest river in the Himalayas. At Khabo it is a swirling, whitewater mass of curls and eddies, thick and grey with the earth of Tibet, completely untamed, violent in its rush to get to the Indus and the Arabian Sea.

At Khabo I had tea at a stall near the road and chatted in Hindi to the wide-eyed boy who served me. The owner had gone home for a siesta and the young boy, Choti, a nickname no doubt as it simply means small in Hindi, was excited to make me a cup of tea on his own. The boy looked to be ten or eleven years old. He was slightly built with a lean face, a thick crop of black hair and the dark skin of someone from the southern side of the mountains. He told me he was from Bihar state, his family was poor and he had come from his home with the man who owned the chai stall to work as a helper.

The owner had been on pilgrimage to Bodh Gaya, the town in Bihar where the Buddha achieved enlightment. Bodh Gaya is the most important of the four main holy sites for Buddhists (the others being Lumbini in Nepal where the Buddha was born, Sarnath near Varanasi, where he gave his first teaching, and Kushinagar, where he died). Every year hundreds of thousands of Buddhists from around the world make the journey to Bodh Gaya to circle the Bodhi tree. It was under such a tree, a long-limbed sacred fig, that the Buddha vowed to sit and meditate until he gained a higher state of consciousness and after forty-nine days of concentration he achieved his goal.

Choti told me how his father had approached the chai shop-owner and asked him to take the boy because the family was too poor to feed him. Taking an unpaid job in a village thousands of kilometres away was the only way he could survive. It seemed strange to me that Choti was so pragmatic about something that could loosely be defined as slavery. But the boy defended the chai shopowner, saying he was a fair man who had taught him to read and write and fed him as well as he did his own family. The boy could leave at any time, but had no money for bus fare or the desire to leave Khabo at present.

"I am learning to count money. This will help me in the future," he said. Choti missed his mother and brothers and sister but said that if he was with them now he would be hungry, so it would be harder for him and them.

When it was time to pay I gave him a large tip. Choti was excited at the money and said he would say a prayer for my safe return to my family. As I left I saw him lighting a stick of incense and waving it in front of the brightly coloured postcard pictures of Buddha and the Hindu god Shiva that hung side by side on the mud-brick wall behind the tea stall's stove.

Five kilometres from the village, with no houses or fields in sight, I came across three old ladies sitting by the roadside. They weren't chatting, only sitting quietly, just being together. Two were kneading bone prayer beads between their gnarled fingers, while mantras fell unconsciously from their lips. The third was spinning a wooden-shafted prayer wheel of copper and silver with two hands. She repeated her mantras so loudly they were easy to hear above the river's roar. I shouted, "Tashi Delek," which means hello and good luck in Tibetan. They looked up together and returned the greeting, with gap-toothed smiles. For no reason they set me laughing and as I moved away I could hear them too, chuckling and talking amongst themselves, their meditation happily interrupted.

Tibetan Buddhist practice amongst most lay people is very different than the rituals followed by the monks and nuns. Generally people gauge their devotion by the amount of prayers they repeat. Everywhere in the Himalayan Buddhist world you see men and women, generally older people, carrying their prayer wheels, clicking through their prayer beads or circling stupas and monasteries while reciting mantras.

I like this idea of movement and prayer. Around holy sites, Bodh Gaya or the Dalai Lama's home in Dharamsala, for instance, there is a constant stream of people. They move clockwise – the flow of life – around the particular shrine while talking in groups or just walking alone. What has struck me, especially about the older people and this practice is that they continue on with whatever conscious business they have, conversing with friends, talking on mobile phones, even reading a book, while subconsciously repeating prayers and spinning their prayer wheels. Their religious practice is something integral to their daily lives, a constant experience.

This perpetual experience is something I have found vital in my life. Gareth's death, of course, is a continual backdrop in my existence and over time it has moved from heartbreak to understanding. But similarly for me now marriage and children are constants that have taken me to depths and gifted me with sublime joy. Writing too – the truth of a story only develops through long and intense consideration. Running from something never brings comprehension. Consciously practising in the intimacy of what you want to understand is the surest path to wisdom.

I camped that evening on a small, irrigated plateau between the grey cliffs that held in the river. From above, on the road, it had looked to be a wild grove of rhododendron and willow, but when I climbed down and reached the flat ground I pressed through a curtain of young alder trees and found myself in a marijuana plantation.

Huge drooping, five-fingered leaves of *cannabis indica* waved languorously in the breeze. The air was full of their slightly sour aroma. I sat down wondering whose secret it was. I thought about maybe moving on as it would not have been good to be there if the owner decided it was time to harvest the crop. But it was almost dark. I didn't think they would come in the night and so set about making my dinner. It was another brilliantly clear evening and I laid my sleeping bag down between the almost tropical looking plants. Sleep came to me accompanied by the thick resinous scent of dope, a smell completely alien to the fragrant simplicity of the high-altitude desert.

October 20

Villages drifted by and the road seemed not quite real. Maybe it had something to do with the clouds that had rolled in, or the stomach ache I had recently developed. Maybe it was my lack of company. Mostly I attributed my uneasiness to the road itself. Dead animals where crushed and splayed across its surface, blackened motor oil pooled in its depressions and convoys of transport trucks shook its foundations. Fifty metres on either side was a different world, one shaped by nature. In that fragile high-altitude desert I came to view the line of crumbling blacktop as an unsewn tear on the landscape.

Feeling a bit sorry for myself I arrived in the town of Pooh. I had been looking forward to this visit. The explorer, mystic, and artist Lama Anagarika Govinda had described the village in his 1947 book, *The Way of the White Clouds*, as "a Shangri-la." Unfortunately, what I saw from the road did nothing to brighten my spirits. Another razor-wired army camp graced Pooh's outskirts and from there cement and corrugated steel shacks extended to a bus stand that was merely a garbage-strewn widening in the road.

Sixty years before Lama Govinda had described a verdant oasis, but all I saw were unstable slopes, a few spindly trees and diesel spills mottling asphalt and stone. I dragged myself into the chai shop for another sickly sweet milk tea and asked the owner where I could find a guest house. He wiped his greasy hands on a sweaty singlet and pointed up the hill.

"Upper village guest house. Maybe!"

The upper village lay five hundred vertical metres above the road. I had already walked thirty-five kilometres that day and was not relishing the climb, but I'd promised myself I would spend a night in Lama Govinda's Shang-ri-la and so tossed my knapsack on and pulled myself upwards. The thought of the ascent proved more painful than the climb and within forty minutes I was standing outside the public works department guest house where a few helpful locals tried to find the elusive caretaker. He came with a wide smile and quickly showed me a grubby single room with a shared toilet that had been blocked for weeks then stated a price that was five times what it was worth. He claimed the guest house was the only tourist accommodation in Pooh. It was obvious why he was smiling. I needed rest but the man was so unctuous, I knew I'd feel better walking beyond the village and putting my sleeping bag down amongst the rocks. So I said goodbye and went in search of food.

Passing a construction site on the edge of the old town I asked the foreman in Hindi if he could direct me to a restaurant. He smiled, displaying a full set of gold teeth, and put his hand on my shoulder. "Friend, it looks like you need somewhere to lie down rather than a plate of food." He gave me directions, first to a restaurant and then to the town's only private inn, a hostel that seemed to have slipped the mind of the guest house caretaker. Then in mid-sentence he smiled again and said, "You don't need directions. The ladies will escort you."

I could see nothing of these ladies until I followed his gaze downwards where a pair of dwarf twins in immaculate Kinnauri costumes – black woolen, ankle-length dresses and embroidered shawls in green and red – stood beside me. They smiled, and they too had glimmering sets of gold teeth. The foreman talked to them in what must have been Kinnauri, the ladies giggled like teenagers, then each grabbed one of my hands and hauled me off in search of the guest house. So there I was, beyond tired, a six-foot-two grown man shouldering a huge red pack, being dragged through winding village streets by a pair of chattering four-foot-six matrons.

My escorts were a local good luck charm. Everyone we met said a respectful hello and tried to touch the ladies' foreheads in blessing. The sisters recoiled and screamed in mock horror, but left each encounter laughing and smiling. They spoke no English but were constantly pointing at things along the way, chattering to me in Kinnauri, giving me, I presumed, a guided tour of the town.

We arrived at the door of a large house. The ladies knocked loudly. There was no sign indicating it was a hotel. The owner appeared, looked me up and down, smiled at the twins and motioned us inside. He led us to a large ten-bed dormitory room where the sisters began jumping up and down on the mattresses. This was their way of testing the bedding. The owner begged them to stop and after a few minutes they deemed one fit for my worn bones. Then, standing on the bed so they stared the owner in the eye, arms folded on their tiny chests, chins jutting out assertively, they haggled a price. A rate was agreed upon, ten rupees. It was twenty times less than the government guest house. With that they leaped from the bed, bowed, put their palms together in the gesture of prayer, and left.

Had it all been a dream?

I laid out my sleeping bag and was settling in when I heard the sound of drums and horns coming from a building on the far side of the village. From the window I saw thick white smoke two hundred metres away and heard shouting children. When I asked the manager, he replied there was a mela, a festival, underway at the temple. I had arrived on the day of the harvest celebrations. The thought of the festivities was like a shot of caffeine. I grabbed my sweater and rushed off through the alleys.

I had been pleasantly surprised as I'd followed the ladies to the hotel; the narrow lanes of Pooh were the antithesis to the lower town's dereliction. Many were lined with apple and apricot trees, some were cobbled, others fronted traditional wood and stone high-roofed houses. I realized that Lama Govinda had arrived on the high route from the north, through orchards and barley fields. In his day there was no drivable road to Pooh.

At the temple, a whitewashed, two-storey building with windows that looked down on the village, most of the townsfolk had assembled around the edges of an open, football pitch-size courtyard. They created a human perimeter around a single line of about eighty men and women moving in a slow, deliberate promenade. The dancers were joined by touch, right hands on the shoulder of their forward neighbour, left hands holding a scarf that linked the entire group. The crowd moved together, everyone stepping methodically in time to a drumbeat. The dancers sang in a high-pitched chant accompanied by bass drums, cymbals and horns. The line shuffled from one foot to the other, their bodies connected as one. The sum of them all undulating around the courtyard looked like an inebriated serpent.

In the centre was a small stone pillar, old and worn, carved with what looked like Sanskrit letters and guarded by two stern-faced matriarchs. Around it piles of smoldering juniper emitted clouds of aromatic incense. Something clutched my right forearm. I looked to see a wildly drunk man grabbing my hands and forming them into a cup. Into it he poured cold chang. His look said, "Drink, drink" and I did. He quickly refilled my hands with more liquor.

The whole spectacle was one of affable debauchery, swaying men, dancing women and yelling kids racing around among the grown-ups' feet. Amidst it all a rank of old lay lamas, some as drunk as their congregation, were attempting to guide the festivities.

After my fifth round of chang I was handed a scarf and a green-banded, woolen pillbox Kinnauri hat and forcibly enlisted into the line dance. The steps were only difficult in their delayed movement and I whispered a monotone facsimile of the song. My positioning in the line was pushed forward until, to the delight of the onlookers, I became the leader of the chain.

I was caught in the harvest-time madness. I was bobbing to a half-time, cacophonic rhythm, heading a line of revelling ecstatics, laughing, shouting, holding hands.

The mela was reaching a sensual fever pitch, but my legs were shaking from exhaustion. I relinquished my leadership and moved outside the inner echelon and there I saw an ancient fellow with an unforgettable face, a combination of Mahatma Gandhi and George Burns. He gave me a huge wavering smile and handed me his bottle of chang. I took a few shots, lowered the bottle, and turned to see a hundred faces staring at us. The music had stopped. My initial reaction was that I'd committed some grave indiscretion by drinking from the same bottle and tried to move backwards through the people who had pulled in around us. The crowd, however, was not staring at me but at the old man.

A body brushed by me. The totally inebriated old fellow was escorted by a monk to a small stage on the left of the shrine building where an assistant fed him more chang. An older lama joined them, chanting mantras and throwing blessed barley in the air. In the background the sun was setting. The pale blue sky was stroked in salmon pink. Without warning the old man dropped from standing to squatting. His head twisting back and forth at unnatural angles, he barked like a rabid dog and punched the earth with his fists. The crowd was absorbed by him. His pupils rolled back, exposing the whites of his eyes, and he let out a banshee wail, lifted his face to the blushing sky and threw his arms to the heavens.

Later that evening it was explained to me that the man was being possessed by the local earth goddess. The entity that the people of Pooh believed had infused everyone with harvest joy was about to manifest through him.

The monk who had assisted him onto the stage handed the medium a long, thin nail, the size of a very large hatpin. The old man fumbled with it, then pushed it easily through his left cheek until the tip was far outside his mouth. Not a drop of blood was spilt.

The crowd gathered tighter around the stage. Hundreds of people held out silk offering scarves and hollered questions as the old man now had the power of divination. The people accepted he was speaking from a higher state of consciousness. He stood and his assistant draped a cloak around him. The old man stamped his feet and did a quick jig almost like a mischievous child, waved his hands by his side, rolled his head loosely back and forth and shouted answers to the crowd's appeals. This went on for fifteen minutes and then, with one giant, very controlled step, he dropped down from the stage.

It was only then that I realized a parallel process was underway in the opposite corner of the compound, where a long-haired, rag-clad man was simultaneously being entered by the spirit. I turned to the man next to me and asked in Hindi what was going on. Putting his arm fraternally around me my neighbour pointed at the two shamans and said, "One Buddhist mother. One Hindu mother."

The oracles staggered towards each other in an awkward shuffle and when they came face to face they performed a slow-motion, mirror-image dance, pulling their feet high and stomping in time with some internal rhythm. It was a dance of togetherness, an embrace by two facets of the same goddess.

The population of Pooh then lined up behind the mediums and formed an unbroken line. They followed the hunched, granny-dancing shamans on a drum- and horn-accompanied circumambulation of the temple. I was dragged happily into the order.

Maybe that's what it's like to be tossed in with the faithful rounding the Ka'baa in Mecca or to follow Tibetan nomad pilgrims in their circling of Mount Kailash. Individuality is consumed and enhanced by a whole. For the twenty minutes we circled the courtyard I was lost in the movement.

Finishing the circuit the oracles returned to centre stage and there the chain of people disintegrated into chaos. The mediums returned to their respective corners where the goddess released them from their bondage. Wrenching convulsions ripped them both, as if something was being torn from their bellies; they rolled on the ground kicking, grunting and beating the earth with their fists. Then it stopped and they lay flat out, drained, their arms and legs splayed wide. Eventually, the monks picked them up and physically dragged them off to the side. In the aftermath they sat alone, looking stunned and confused. Around them, in groups staggering back home, the party raged on.

I was left in a small huddle of men who seemed to have adopted me. They all spoke English and were peppering me with questions. All I really remember was one man who kept asking over and over again whether I believed in the power of the oracle. I was drunk and exhausted, in no state to try to give an interpretation of what I had just seen. I told him the oracles appeared very powerful. He grinned and refilled my hands again with chang, then invited me to his house for dinner. It was dark and I had no idea where I would find food so I accepted.

Chander Negi was a small, very well-groomed, serious man, a banker on home-leave from the state capital of Shimla.

I followed him, stumbling back up the village pathways to his family's house. There his mother and sister greeted us and we were joined by one of his friends, Doctor Aggarwal, a resident at the local hospital. I was easily the drunkest of the group. The men and women were all, I discovered later, teetotallers, but Chander's mother and sister happily refilled my glass with an unending supply of barley beer.

Even in my inebriation I was interested in what these two well-educated men thought of the shamanistic possession we had witnessed. They began by emphasizing how important it was to preserve local traditions, talking of the oracles as if they were museum pieces. But as the night wore on both Chander and his friend confessed to having asked personal questions of the spirits and both acknowledged that some of the predictions had come true. They said it was not fashionable for doctors and bank managers to believe in shamans and oracles but there was no reason to discard them.

Chander's mother served dinner. I believe it was tsampa chapatis and several different curries, but my memory gets fuzzy at this point. I do remember Chander leading me back to the guest house, his arm barely reaching around my shoulder and me singing songs. I don't remember which songs and I don't remember if the guest house owner let us in or if the door was open. I do remember lying down on the bed and thinking it was very soft and that inside my sleeping bag was exactly where I wanted to be at that point in time.

October 21

Morning came quickly, and I rose with a thick head. Groggily, I stuffed my household back into my rucksack. I had a cup of tea, paid the guest house owner, took one last look at the temple and started walking. The clouds of yesterday had dissipated but in the deep valley of the Sutlej it was shady and cool. For me this was a gift. As I walked my head recovered from the hangover and by the time the sun had topped the ridges I felt as clear as the sky. I actually felt really good. Whether this was because my body reacted well to chang or because of the strange and wonderful things I'd witnessed the day before I don't know.

The road moved around and over mountains, following the braided path of the river. Not long after I started a red-billed chough followed me for a kilometre, flying ahead, landing, turning to stare, then taking off again when I was two paces away. Up side valleys and at the crest of climbs I glimpsed far-off snow peaks. Below me, the river raced on. It cut a huge swathe through the crumbling mountains yet still managed to look inviting in its back waters and eddies.

The landscape was changing with trees appearing sporadically and patches of grass dotting the hills. The yaks that had grazed by the wayside were replaced by herd after herd of sheep and goats. I was dropping in altitude, moving down out of the alpine zone.

Ten kilometres down the river at the village of Kannum, I climbed off the road on a twisting trail that followed a small creek and arrived forty-five minutes later in a hamlet that wrapped around the hillside and into a lightly treed valley. The village fit the mountainside perfectly. Tight paths between buildings followed along the slope's contours. The houses were multi-storied, wood and stone works of art. Their walls rose three metres, soundly constructed from layers of stone and squared-off logs. The horizontally laid wood was intricately carved with what looked like Celtic knot designs. The houses were like castles, immense, but built for living. Around the exteriors I could not find a single nail; the buildings were secured by friction, mass and craftsmanship.

I followed the alleys farther up in search of the gompa I had been told stood at the top of the village. Past apricot orchards and a pair of grandmothers weaving shawls on large, double-framed looms, I found the building on a south-facing slope overlooking the Sutlej. It was built in the same citadel style as the houses. People had told me it was, like Tabo, founded in the tenth century, but its positioning and fort-like construction was closer in style to monasteries I knew had been built in the fifteenth or sixteenth centuries.

I entered the courtyard to find a sixteen-metre by sixteen-metre space enclosed by wooden balconies on three sides and on the fourth by the prayer room. Climbing the steps to the hall I found four wide-eyed, brightly painted guardian kings greeting me from the frescoed atrium. A flowerpot on the balcony spilled with purple and pink geraniums and golden marigolds. On the doubled-doored entrance was tacked a brass plaque, shiny against the sun-bleached wood. Its inscription brought a smile to my face.

Judit Gulantha
Georgy Norgady
Montreal '92
Alexander Csoma de Koros

Judit Gulantha and Georgy Norgady are Hungarian/Canadian scholars who have traced the path of Csoma de Koros throughout the western Himalayas. To think that in some way I was tracing the legendary explorer brought a lightness to my steps.

I took off my pack and sat down on the balcony of the prayer hall, enjoying the sunshine. The doors were locked, but I didn't feel the need to search out a keyholder. I had been into dozens of monasteries on the trek, and they had all been special in their own way, but Kannum for me was unique for the people who had been there before and for the sense of satisfaction I had just sitting on its front step. I lay there quietly for half an hour, my head on my pack, staring up at an eight-spoked Dharmacakra, or Wheel of Dharma, painted on the ceiling of the atrium above the main door. The paint was peeling and faded but the wheel was still prominent.

Wheels of dharma are everywhere in the Buddhist world because they symbolize the structure of the path to higher consciousness. The hub of the wheel represents discipline, the starting point of meditation. The wheel's rim stands for mindfulness, the state of being which holds the practice together. The circular shape of the wheel refers to the perfection of the Buddha's teachings and the eight spokes represent the noble eight-fold path, the steps of which are right view, right intention, right speech, right action, right livelihood, right effort, right mindfulness and right concentration.

Eventually, I took my head off my pack, pulled the rucksack on and, with gravity helping, ran back down the hill past the village. A few kilometres south of Kannum, not far from the river, I found a campsite that was the perfect blend of mountain views and water at my feet. I made dinner, drank my tea and watched the sun set.

October 22

By mid-morning I had reached Moorang, a village nestled into the slope on the north side of the Sutlej. From a distance its houses were black and white checks against a coarse mantle of deciduous trees. Dominating the skyline on a knoll above the houses was the kila, the village's ancestral fort.

I walked up and circled the abandoned stronghold. The view north and south took in kilometres of the Sutlej River. It would have been almost impossible to slip into the vicinity of Moorang without being detected from the fortress. The building had the same dimensions as a single family home but rose for six stories. It was more of a lookout than a fort. The walls were of a simple log construction, the timbers notched at their ends and slipped one on top of other. Some of the squared-off logs around the base were a metre and a half in diameter. The original trees would have been four times the size of any that I'd seen along the Sutlej.

I sat for a while enjoying a sip of water and watching inquisitive ravens circle the tower. They landed and perched on the upper parapet, staring at me, silently questioning my presence. More and more gathered until the parapet was filled, wing to wing, with large black birds. There were dozens of them staring at me. They sounded like a crowd of commuters in the London underground, the whoosh and screech of trains interspersed with the rumbling murmur of the people in a rush.

At the base of the knoll on which the kila was built I found, each an arm's length from the other, a Buddhist stupa and a Hindu lingam. The lingam, a phallic-shaped stone placed vertically on a pedestal, is an abstract representation of the god Shiva, the Hindu personification of power. The positioning of the shrines indicated I was in a religious transition zone. The whitewashed monuments radiated in the sunshine, both draped in identical garlands of marigolds almost as if the same person was propitiating both traditions.

I pushed on down the Sutlej to Recong Peo, the capital of Kinnaur. It had been a hard day's walk finished off by a long climb to the town. I arrived wearily at sunset.

Recong Peo is a prefabricated government enclave, a larger version of Padum with a maze of concrete paths and broken asphalt roads laid over a deforested, east-facing slope. I quickly found a guest house close to the bus stand; it had that feeling of messy transitoriness that most cheap hotels exude. In the café across the street I ordered rice and dal. The rice was broken-grained and without any of the nutty basmati aroma Indians prefer. The dal was watery and too salty.

I ate with an audience, as a group of men waiting for a night bus stared at me following every spoonful of rice that made its way to my mouth. One of the great differences between India and Western countries is that staring is not considered bad manners on the subcontinent. Being ogled at can even be a sign of respect, indicating the watchers are interested enough to stare. But being gazed at while I tried to eat my dinner was not what I wanted that evening. After a cup of tea and a plate of stale Indian sweets, I made my way across the bus park to my room. I fell asleep almost immediately. The bed smelled of stale beer and cigarette butts.

October 23

I was up before the hotel manager. He was a large man with a massive moustache who the night before had tried to shortchange me when I had prepaid for the room. At the desk downstairs I called for him and rang the little bell next to the register. A man I did not recognize came out from the kitchen. He looked dishevelled. His hair was standing on end and he smelled of whiskey, but he unlocked the front door for me. When I thanked him for getting up, he grunted and closed the door quickly.

Another long day was ahead because I hoped to reach Sangla village, thirty kilometres east in the Baspa Valley, by sunset. This day's walk had dominated my thoughts for the past week, for it would be my first substantial gain in altitude since ascending the Kunzum-la in Spiti two weeks before.

The road twisted through the Sutlej gorge, jumping from side to side on a series of steel truss, cantilevered bridges. At Karcham village the Baspa River merges with the Sutlej. The main road follows the larger river south to Rampur and eventually the state capital Shimla. The road I wanted, which tracked the smaller river east up the tributary valley, climbs almost nine hundred metres vertically, is one-laned and switchbacks dramatically up the 20-degree slope. Hairpin turn after hairpin turn brings it higher. It was pleasant to walk, but nerve-wracking to drive and life-threatening to be a passenger in a sardine-packed local bus.

The route veered away from the line cut by the Baspa River, but returned to it when the gorge opened out ten kilometres before Sangla. The valley brought memories of Kashmir. There were orchards of bare-branched apple trees, crisp cool humid air and the mucky smell of fresh-plowed fields. The faces of the people were less Tibetan and more Caucasian. The houses and temples resembled the wood and stone styles I had seen in Srinagar, Kashmir. On both sides of the little river, towering snow peaks reached up to a cloudless sky. The peaks seemed too big for the narrow space, their flanks muscling into the curve of the valley. The flats along the river were checkered with fields and orchards and although they had already been harvested, it was the most fertile looking land I'd seen since the Kulu Valley.

In Sangla I found a room at an empty guest house on the edge of the town. The old lady who signed me in wore a beautifully embroidered pale woolen shawl. Its borders were patterned in orange and blue interlocking squares, while the body of the fabric featured text in Tibetan and Hindi-Devanagari script and images of stupas and buildings like the tall, mushroom-roofed Hindu timber temples of the valley. She offered to help carry my pack down the hall, but she looked about seventy years old and I insisted I could do it myself.

After Recong Peo it was a pleasure to be in that building. It was dusty and untidy, and an inordinate number of sheet metal trunks were stacked against the corridor walls, but the building was made of wood and stone and the place smelled like a forest. When I walked the hall the structure creaked like a ship bucking along in a light breeze. The window from my little room looked south over the river to the jagged line of sentry peaks that blocked the way from Himachal Pradesh to the state of Uttarakhand.

I went to the bazaar in search of food. The little market was centred around the bus stop, a circular stretch of road lined with wooden-fronted shops. People were staring at me but instead of gawking like open-mouthed, domesticated animals they shouted for me to come to their shops and join them for a cup of tea. I wandered the village's few streets until well after dark, drinking chai, talking and eating sweets in small shops and restaurants.

The customers and owners were all interested in what I was doing in Sangla so late in the year. Tourists had started coming to the valley but by September the locals said all the foreigners had left. When I told them of my walk most of my new friends laughed. I think some of them thought it was a joke and others thought that I must be the joke for undertaking something so silly. Kamran, a young electrician with a jawline beard and a jean jacket two sizes too big for him, slapped me on the back and ordered me another tea, saying, "You need another chai, friend. You have a long way to walk."

From Sangla I planned to move south over the 4,700-metre Rupin Ghatti (in Hindi ghatti means pass). Since the snows of early September I had been debating with myself where I could cross from Himachal Pradesh to Uttarakhand. The Rupin Ghatti is the most direct route but also the highest. I was worried that early autumn's premature storms had left snow too deep to walk through. That evening I asked everyone I talked to what they thought about the state of the pass but no one could tell me the snow's depth, or at what altitude it started. However, the shopkeepers, government officials and farmers I talked to had no reason to know that information. The shepherds were the only group who regularly used the pass, and in late October shepherds would not be spending their evenings drinking chai and eating sweets around the bus park in Sangla.

October 24

I was off early. The old lady was already out in her garden, bottle-feeding some infant goats. She waved and, because I liked her and felt the day had the makings of an adventure, I jumped in the air and clicked my heels. She laughed and waved some more. I dropped from Sangla to Baspa River and started upwards on a hard-packed trail. On the climb I constantly met men and women headed in the opposite direction loaded with bushels of firewood.

I was moving through the first real forest since leaving the Kulu Valley; giant chir pines and deodar cedars graced the draw. I was thrilled to see that the timbers for the kila fortress in Moorang were not history. Stately conifers, almost two metres across at their base, reached for the sky, while a soft bed of green needles lay underfoot. The understorey was cool and moist, so different from my regular midday refuge behind rocks or houses in the open, sunbeaten desert of Lahaul, Spiti, Zanskar and Ladakh. The forest was sheltering.

For the first time in weeks the horizon was out of view, and my focus moved inwards. I was off the road – no cars, no trucks, no crushed and bleeding animals. I was comfortable moving back into my steps. A resinous breeze whipped up from the needles blanketing the ground and cooled my damp forehead.

Where the giant trees thinned around 3,300 metres a group of houses appeared. It was a seasonal village unmarked on my map. The houses were uninhabited, and the fields down the hill from the buildings lay tilled and fallow. Soon they would be under snow. On the far side of the buildings a man was making tea over an open fire. I smelled burning cedar and long-boiled strong brew.

In sign language he invited me for a cup, mixing in sugar and fresh milk poured from an old whiskey bottle. We drank and he talked for five minutes in a local dialect I couldn't understand. Eventually, when I could get a word in, he realized my incomprehension. He laughed and slapped me on the back. We finished our tea in silence.

Then I tried to ask him whether the pass was open by pointing upwards, saying, "Rupin Ghatti, Rupin Ghatti?" and holding my palms open in a gesture of inquiry. He broke into a smile and gave me the thumbs-up. This was great encouragement. I stood to leave and he shook my hand. I threw on my pack and he lay back on the thin grass, watching the wispy clouds reeling across the sky.

The trail levelled off, making the climb easier, and my fears of my body's opposition to the grade melted in the sunshine. It was a delight to be away from the road, walking to higher ground. Mountain sounds came to me: the wind, chirping marmots, the crunch of loose stones underfoot.

The trail I had been following disappeared and I scaled an empty hillside. I was unsure of the route; my map was covered in dotted topographic lines indicating that the cartographers were not a hundred percent sure of the area's terrain. My route-finding relied on intuition and the little I'd gleaned in the Sangla bazaar. By five p.m. I reached the snowline and still there was no sign of the pass. To the south, all around me, snowfields rose in a 180-degree arc. They were smooth, silken-looking curves of ice that ascended into the blue of the sky. My legs felt strong, but I was breaking through ice-crust into knee-deep snow. I decided to camp and cross early the following morning.

I pitched my tent on a snowy knoll. The rice and dal I had for dinner were made with melted ice. As I ate I watched the almost full moon rise and transform the soft contours of the snowfield into a flickering moonscape. With sunset the wind that had whistled off the pass softened until it was breathless, but out of the hush slight noises carried: rustling mice on ice-scabbed crust, the gravitational shift of the snow beneath my body, the beating of ravens' wings. In daytime they would have drifted by, but in the thin, motionless air they came to me clearly. Restlessly, I drifted with them into the cold night.

October 25

I was up before six o'clock and walking soon after, but the sun hit the slope early and the crust was fracturing beneath me less than half an hour after I left camp. My pack felt heavier than normal and uncomfortably weighted to one side. I blamed my uneasiness on a poor night's sleep caused by the bitter cold. The tightened hood of my mummy sleeping bag had been rimmed in ice when I woke.

It was two hours of slogging through knee-deep drifts before the ridgeline came into view and by eleven o'clock I was on the crest of the pass. I stood among haphazard stone cairns above a serac edge and looked far down into a black and white valley. But I was unsure if this was the Rupin Ghatti. After five hours of heavy walking and altitude-enhanced wishful thinking, I wanted it to be the pass but had to be certain. A mistake could cost me days of walking to return to my planned route.

Ten minutes of taking triangulation compass bearings on far-away peaks convinced me I was actually on the Gunas Ghatti, which would lead down the Pabar Nala Creek far to the west of where I wanted to be. The Rupin Ghatti was a drop in the ridgeline two kilometres east. My approach had been too far right. I reproached myself for taking what seemed, at the time, the easier route. I would have to sidetrack across the face and was glad now for the thigh-deep snow because the grade was so precipitous that on the uncovered scree of summer I could not have crossed it. Two hours of sidestepping brought me to the real Rupin Ghatti. I was exhausted.

A blue and white land shivered around me, a flux of titanium and turquoise. In the valley below two lammergeiers, bearded vultures, circled with no thought for what occurred above them. A wind whipped at me from the north. I hid behind a summit cairn of flat stones, gasping for breath, gulping until thin oxygen worked the tightness from my muscles. My head cleared, the cramps in my legs smoothed and I remembered – this was my passage out of the Indus and into the Ganges.

The Rupin Ghatti marks the boundary between two great watersheds. I was moving from the Western to the Central Himalayas, from a desert climate to temperate forest; from a xeriscape to the world of the monsoon, from the watershed of the Arabian Sea to that of the Bay of Bengal, and from Buddhism to Hinduism. I was on top of the world.

I looked in the direction of the far-off plains of India, a land of steamy heat and a billion people. North were the bare mountain deserts of Tibet, thinly populated, cold, wind-chopped lands. The Rupin Ghatti was the last major pass on my route, the last chance for snow and ice to impede my progress. With small steps and a clear mind I was confident I would reach the Mahakali River. I let out a great yell like a drunk teenager and on the wave of that holler dropped from the heavens.

The route fell and fell. My legs, beaten by the upwards slog, now had to contend with a thirty-degree downward pitch. Hard to believe that every year herds of sheep in the thousands crossed this barrier littered as it is with cliffs and icefalls, scree slopes and boulder fields. At the base of the first face I crossed a frozen pond, a circle of ice as flat as an ocean, its symmetry out of place in that tumultuous vertical world.

Following the pond's outlet stream, the water barely trickling over shimmering stones, I came to a cascade. At its base the snow disappeared, replaced by a blanket of tawny grass. Edging along the lip I found a descendable chute and skied the scree using my backside as a brake. This was the source of the Rupin Nala River. I traced the spring, which grew dramatically in size, to the rim of another, even taller set of cascades and sat on a ledge above the fall. Below me billions of water particles mixed with the air, flying against gravity, beating against the cliff, relentlessly transforming the stone.

The sun was only an hour from setting and at that shallow evening angle it caught the levelled stream two hundred metres below me. The silver creek became a ribbon of gold that wound through a jade green meadow before disappearing into darkness. The little river was alive in that light.

As I moved over the brink I realized the cascade was a set of three pitches. The drop was dangerously abrupt and in sections I had to scramble down on all fours. The waterfall was in constant transformation; the bulk of the water dropped with the pull of gravity but sections were frozen in huge translucent stalactites and the air was saturated with cool, free-floating mists. Liquids, solids and gases fused in the sunset.

I reached the lower meadows, my legs shaking from the downhill pounding. Walking away from the cascades I turned to appreciate them one last time. What I saw took my breath away. Arcing across each of the three falls, one on top of the other, was a trio of rainbows, small half circles of vivid colour, steady against the water's quicksilver background, and above the waterfall, the sky was stroked with red and amber, the colours of fire. Through the rainbows, icy ten-metre stalactites plunged, flushed with an internal glow.

With the sun's setting I turned away in search of a campsite. Bitter cold descended from fierce stars.

HINDU HIMALAYAS

CHAPTER 8
Religion in Landscape

October 26

I woke in a dark gorge. The rock wall to my left was black, its face frozen solid. The rim of the right wall was catching the first rays of the rising sun. As daylight edged down the cliff it brought to life a series of tiny cascades. Water leaped from where there had been only ice. The two cliffs were polar opposites; movement and stillness, light and dark, fifty metres of crackling space separated them.

In the chill air I packed my rucksack. The sun crawled across my possessions. I walked the five metres to the creek to scoop water for tea and in the soft mud of the bank saw the paw print of a Himalayan wolf, a mark as big as my clenched fist. Water pooled in the base of the tracks, shimmering in the oblique light. Had the animal been there yesterday? Had the wolf prowled around my sleeping body? Had we shared the vision of the night before?

I drank my tea, made tsampa porridge and finished packing.

Religion in Landscape

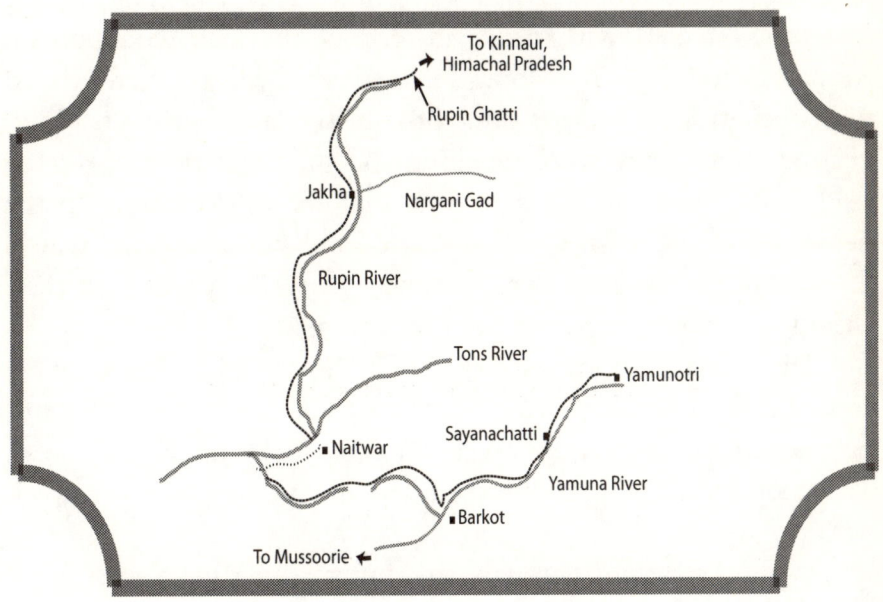

GARWAHL, UTTARAKHAND, INDIA

Within kilometres the alpine meadows had given way to pristine forest. As in the Sangla Valley, deodar cedars and chir pines rose from thick, green moss, the surface scattered with a layer of rust red needles. Mushroom caps, shaggy and fresh, pushed from the earth. Frost iced the early morning shadows. The air had the musty, fresh yeast scent of decay. Other than the rustle of branches and whisper of the river it was shockingly quiet. It was hard to believe I was in India, the country with the second highest population in the world, but the transition from wilderness to human landscape had taken less than five kilometres.

Jakha, the first village in the Rupin Valley, is a settlement of meticulously constructed, two-storey wooden houses aligned along a single dirt path. The houses were different than those over the pass to the north, less stonework in the construction and roofs shaked with cedar instead of the slate common on Kinnauri houses. The slopes around the village were tiered with rock-walled paddies and through the fields grunted plow-bearing oxen. They were breaking soil in the already harvested fields, mixing in the year's store of manure and compost. In the fields below the village millet, scarlet and harvest-ready, waved in the breeze. Barking dogs, chained to walls, yanked at their shackles anxious to investigate the stranger.

The villages downstream on the Rupin River were consistently placed at three- to four-kilometre intervals, but between them there was a pleasant mixture of fields and forest. The people didn't appear rushed and many stopped their work to wave at me.

While walking through an unusually thick section of woods, I was stopped by a high-pitched metallic screech. It grew louder and louder until it filled the air, and then, just as smoothly, it backed away. The sound was repeated again thirty seconds later. It was definitely not a mountain sound.

The clamour passed me three more times before I chanced to look up and there, drifting over my head, was a bundle of a dozen ten-metre-long pine logs suspended from a pair of taut steel cables. The timbers were following a ropeway down to the river. I was in the midst of a forest harvesting operation. I looked down the wires to the dumping ground on the bank of the Rupin Nala and saw a stockpile of hundreds of logs. Without roads in the area I presumed they were going to use the river to transport the trees the next forty kilometres to the trailhead at Naitwar. River running is a mythical activity in North American forestry, but for environmental reasons it's not used anymore. I had never seen a live operation before so I had lots of questions.

Those questions were answered thirty minutes later when I met S.C. Tiwari, a dapper man in his late forties with a carefully groomed moustache and a diligently combed head of thinning grey hair. He was walking with his hunting dog, a fierce-looking black and brown animal with a muscular head that was more jawbone than cranium. It was obvious from his clothes and his brass-tipped walking stick that Mr. Tiwari was not a farmer and when I asked him in Hindi by way of greeting where he was off to he replied in English, "Going to work."

He explained he was a "timber floater," the man in charge of the logging operation. We walked for fifteen minutes, chatting about the mountains. Mr. Tiwari was happy to meet someone who enjoyed walking and had worked in forestry in another country. At the next flattened rock we sat, he lit a bedi, one of the loosely rolled Indian cheroots, and chatted about the business of wood in India.

He told me there is a complete ban on cutting "green wood" in Uttar Pradesh. "Only dead or broken trees can be taken, " he said.

I thought of the stockpile of timber farther upstream. The majority of that wood was alive when loggers felled it. I asked who was enforcing these regulations.

Mr. Tiwari lowered his head, fiddled with his walking stick and told me the foresters were overworked, rarely got out of their offices to check on the harvesting, and that most logging permits were arranged individually between the timber companies and the official.

I thought it was strange that Mr. Tiwari, someone who was profiting from those idle officials, was willing to talk about a system that sidestepped the law. He told me there was such a demand for wood and the officials were so badly paid that the system perpetuated itself. As he said, "In India, so little of the government's planning is enforced. I would like to be more of a conservationist but what is the point? If I don't take the wood, somebody else will. It's first-come, first-served."

A few kilometres farther on, in a particularly rough and shallow section of the river, I saw just how difficult it was to get that Himalayan timber to market. In midstream, along the opposite bank, braced against boulders and a ten-metre-tall cliff, the loggers had built a hundred-metre-long, hewn timber chute through which the logs ran single file above the shallow river. On the lip of the spillway nimble men ran, coaxing the timbers along with spiked poles and well-directed kicks. It was a scene from nineteenth-century Canada, woolen-clad lumberjacks dancing on a river of logs. The men bounded along the frame with the confidence of dancers and the swagger of cowboys.

When we arrived, Mr. Tiwari showed me why the supervisor is called the "timber floater." One of the loggers shouted him a question and the boss yelled back. He quickly shook my hand then jumped boulder to boulder over the river and onto the chute while hollering orders at his crew. He grabbed one of the pikes from where it was stored in the frame and throwing his body weight against it demonstrated, to the man closest to him, how to guide the logs through the man-made rapids. Mr. Tiwari was in control. He turned and waved to me, a huge smile on his face.

Gareth and I had worked together in forestry in Canada for two years. The time marked a change in our relationship, because it was the first time I can remember him as anything other than my little brother. It started when my mother asked, or maybe it was more of an order, for me to get Gareth a summer job with the treeplanting company I worked with. Reluctantly I complied, but I made sure he knew that I wouldn't be babysitting him when we got to the North.

I tried my best to live up to my own promises, but that changed one cloudy afternoon in the early spring when Al the foreman scrambled over to my area of the clearcut.

"Jono, you better get over and check on Gareth," he said.

"I'm not the foreman, Al. That's your job."

"I'm telling you as a favour, Jono. Go and check him out."

I shrugged my shoulders, stuffed my treeplanting bags under a log and, swearing under my breath, started over towards where Gareth had been working. Every minute you're not planting trees you're not making money and if you're not making money then you shouldn't be in the bush, I resented the fact that Gareth was pulling me away from the reason I was on a logging clearcut in the middle of nowhere.

I leaped from stump to log, the steel spikes on the bottom of my boots holding me solid to the slippery trunks. Eventually, I saw the yellow and orange of Gareth's treeplanting bags. Treeplanters fill the bags with the seedlings they will plant and wear them around their waists, but when I reached Gareth's bags all I found were the PVC bags – no sign of my little brother.

I clambered onto a stump and shaded my eyes. I was worried. If you can't see a planter on the planar openness of a clearcut, there's a good chance something is wrong. Then I saw one of his big orange boots sticking out from behind a downed tree five metres away. They weren't moving. I ran to the spot, still swearing under my breath and praying he was okay, and there behind the log he lay – fast asleep.

"Gareth, what the hell are you doing?" I kicked his big boots and he shook his head.

"Oh ... Jono ... How's it going?" He had such a lacksadasical way about him, the words came out in three slow, separate sentences.

"What do you mean? How's it going? You know how goddamn shitty it's going. Al's just been over in my piece telling me to check on you. So the foreman knows you're asleep on the job. You'll be lucky if he doesn't fire your ass."

Gareth sat up. There were twigs caught in his dirty blond curls. He pushed his fingers through his hair.

"Oh, come on. I was tired. I haven't been getting enough sleep. I'm bushed, man," he said.

Gareth's voice was wavering. He'd always been a person who needed lots of sleep. He was massively tall; he'd spent most of his teenage years growing at an incredible rate and when you grow that much you've got to sleep.

"Seriously, Jono. You can't let him fire me." He was talking faster now. I liked the bit of power I had over him.

"Al doesn't have time for lazy asses like you. There's a dozen kids back in town that would kill for this job."

Gareth's eyes opened up. He blinked. I knew that look. It didn't happen often but he was about to cry.

"Jono, please." His shoulders started to shake. "You know I'm trying, but I'm not good at getting up early. I'm trying hard but there's so much to learn."

Silent tears were rolling down his cheeks. I knew he hadn't made any close friends in the camp yet. He was on his own except for his big brother and I was doing my best to ignore him. Guilt rode up on me.

"Okay." I stepped in close to him. He smelled like moist earth. I put my arms around him. "I know you're trying. Just hang in there. I'll make sure that Al doesn't do anything he'll regret. Another week and you'll have the hang of it."

He hung onto me. I was all he had out there. For all his easygoing ways, I realized that Gareth really needed me and I was responsible for him. We held on tight to each other.

I camped close to the river that night on a narrow flat amidst huge trees. When the sun set, the light seeped slowly from the forest and the valley became so dark it felt heavy. It was a stark contrast to the night before when the moon had lit the snow around my tent and created a residual light that flickered through the night.

October 27

I woke to find evidence that I had definitely crossed into the geography of the monsoon; moisture permeated everything.

From my sleeping bag, I unzipped the tent flaps and looked down the river to where fog clung in drifts and wisps to the trees on either bank. I slipped into my humid underwear and damp socks and packed the dripping tent.

Downstream the Rupin River widened and irrigation canals cut to the left and right. The trail was becoming more trafficked and better maintained; government-built steel footbridges spanned its width. The feeling was of a more polished world. Electricity poles sprouted by the side of the trail and more than one polyester-suited walker carrying a cardboard travel case passed me by. Were these the travelling salesman of the foot-bound world?

The day wore on. I stopped in a hayfield for lunch and watched coolies on their way upvalley shouldering one-metre-diameter metal water pipes. They shuffled onwards like overburdened ants, their tiny steps through the meadow's deep grass slow and methodical. The huge loads bent their backs and shortened their breath. One fellow caught my eye as he passed. I waved and he gave me as much of a smile as he could muster with his head twisted under a hundred kilograms of steel.

In the afternoon I followed a man for two kilometres. At first I could only hear him. Up ahead there was a tinkling sound, not quiet, not loud, something like a distant wind chime. Then I saw him – a short, stocky fellow with a khaki canvas rucksack and a woolen pillbox Kinnauri hat. On a section of rocky trail along the river I caught up to him.

He held a short, medieval-looking brass staff directly in front of him, a three-dimensional cross festooned with bells and topped with the head of a Hindu deity. The man walked with an affected, exaggerated gait that made him bob and caused the carillon to ring. He mumbled mantras as he strode along, the words and bells mixing in a way that reminded me of church choirs.

When I caught up to him, he pulled off the trail and sat on a rock, holding his staff before him with a straight arm. I stopped, although I wasn't sure if he had sat down to let me pass or if he wanted me to stop and chat. He looked at me, his chin shaded with day-old growth, his eyes bright from my attention and he shouted, "Baloo, Baloo" while rattling his jingle-stick.

Baloo in Hindi means bear. The man was a human bear scare. We talked in Hindi and he told me how he travelled from village to village offering his bear deterrent services. If a community's fields were being raided by bears, he would use mantras and his magic staff to exorcise the spirits that attracted the beasts. From the top of his canvas pack he pulled out a battered plastic bag and extracted a frayed photo of himself standing almost timidly beside what looked like the carcass of a bear. His name was Chandra Bhaga. He was from Kinnaur but spent most of the summer and autumn on the move, for that was his busy time; the fields were coming to harvest and the bears were down from the mountains.

He pulled a pack of bedis from his bag and offered me one. I don't smoke but in exchange I offered him a piece of chocolate. He asked me if I had ever come across any bears. Since I'd worked in forestry in northern Canada for eighteen years I had had hundreds of bear encounters. This excited Chandra, and he wanted a complete description of the common American Black Bear.

After I had tried my best with limited Hindi, Chandra offered to teach me a mantra that would scare away any bears that crossed my path. I was now more excited than he was. He went through the chant slowly, emphasizing each syllable. I repeated it, trying my best to imitate his intonation. He went through it three times and on the third repeat he corrected my pronunciation, saying if it wasn't pronounced perfectly it could do more harm than good. That was a worrying thought – chanting a prayer for protection and instead it encourages the beast to charge. He complimented my accent, but after the fourth repeat he looked at me gravely and said the mantra was strictly for my own personal use. I was a friend, and he had given it as a gift.

We had lunch together. I made soup and tea on the stove while Chandra made chapatis on a battered pan over a little wood fire. We relaxed for half an hour, Chandra smoking bedis and me lying back and looking up at the clouds. At the next village Chandra stopped to inquire if the residents had any bear problems. They did and so he had business to conduct. I continued on, wanting to get a few more kilometres in before sunset.

Bears have been a part of my life for two decades. In the bush you live with them, and at night in a treeplanting camp there is only the nylon of your tent separating you from the wild. But bears are not stupid; they only interact with people if there's a reason. In a treeplanting camp possibly the most dangerous job is that of the cook as they are left alone all day in base camp. These are the quiet times when bears prowl into the human environment searching for food. I've known camp cooks who have opened up the door of their kitchen trailers to find gangs of bears fighting over waste food in the slop pits.

One of those times I regret something I did to Gareth was when I pretended to be a bear in the area he was planting trees. I could hear him working on the far side of a thick clump of alders, the throw and stomp on his shovel, his exhalation as he leaned over to lay the seedling snuggly in the hole and the gentle tap of his boot closing the earth over the little tree. I snuck as silently as possible through the alder copse and when I was a few metres from him took a branch and rustled it noisily in the underbrush. Gareth stopped.

The silence was excruciating, every bit of his being focused on indentifying the sounds. Holding back a chuckle I rustled the undergrowth again and snapped a couple of small branches. Only a bear or moose would have the size and audacity to make such a noise and not care about it. Gareth knew this.

He screamed, "*Fuck off!*" In defence he threw his metre-long treeplanting shovel through the trees, where it sailed past only centimetres from my head. I heard the pop of the nylex waist buckles on his treeplanting bags open. They fell to the ground, then came the thump, thump, thump of his feet pounding down the hill away from me. I pushed through the patch of trees and shouted after him but he was already gone. I continued on my way, thinking that he would get it was only his brother pulling a trick on him.

An hour or so later when I returned to the crew bus, Gareth was there eating a sandwich. When he saw me he sat up and told me right away about the huge bear that had come at him through an alder patch at the top of his work area and how he was lucky to get out of there without serious injury. I told him to take a good rest, get his head back together and I would retrieve his gear. I didn't have the heart to tell him that the bear was actually me.

October 28

Five kilometres from Naitwar the trail transformed into a rough road. It has a gentle downhill grade. It might have been a lack of sugar or a melancholic funk produced by the long drop from the heights but that afternoon I felt light-headed, not connected with my steps or the landscape. I stumbled along behind an unloaded caravan of pack mules. Ahead I could see the opening in the trees where the Rupin River merged with the Tons River. A low, one-storey wooden Hindu temple marked their convergence. I was in Garwahl, Uttarakhand State, the most sacred area in the Hindu Himalayas.

Naitwar is the trailhead for the Rupin Valley. To the south the road leads to the Gangeatic plain and eventually Delhi, but north there are only trails and mountains. As with so many villages straddling the space between the road-serviced world and that of the foot trail, Naitwar has two faces. By the river the old community survives in elegant rows of wooden houses interspersed with Hindu shrines.

Higher up, lining each side of the main road, is the town's more recent incarnation: a line of open-fronted, corrugated steel stores, a purpose-built community providing for the needs of the highway's traffic. New Naitwar is an interface between cultures. Drunken Garwahlis in coarse homespun stagger past overweight cloth merchants in sloppily built shops and oil-splattered Punjabi truckers drinking steaming chai by the side of the road. Naked fluorescent tubes bathe the strip in harsh white light and Hindi pop, crackling from worn-out speakers, competes with generators, cars and diesel trucks.

I took a room in the half-built hotel at the far end of town. There was no glass in the windows and wooden shutters closed over iron rods. Outside my second-storey door the veranda's floor sprouted rebar like late season wheat. In a café nearby I met P.T. Gose, a merchant from the small city of Rampur just across the border to the west in Himachal Pradesh. He was in Naitwar for a few days to secure stocks of a cork found in the roots of some oak trees, a natural mid-sole material for shoes. His family had been dealing in the substance for decades. Gathered in small amounts by the local people, it provides some side-income for many families.

The material excited me and, after chatting for a while, I suggested to Mr. Gose that such products were the best economic argument to slow the deforestation of the Himalayas. He waved his head in the undulating Indian gesture that accompanies any discussion and told me that the mid-sole cork he dealt with wouldn't play a role in saving the forest because in a few years demand for it would dry up. The oak cork was only inserted in leather-soled footwear and the market for dress shoes was fading as people switched to cheaper, mass-produced vinyl runners.

"Now everything has to be shiny and colourful," he chuckled. "Soon India will be a pink and purple nation."

As he was a major distributor of the new synthetic shoes, he had no regrets about the loss of his old markets. Soon after that Mr. Gose excused himself and I was left alone with the crowds weaving along the roadside bazaar. Night had fallen and the air had contracted around the well-lit line of the road. Outside the fluorescent wash nothing seemed to exist. Beyond the road edge was darkness.

October 29

I started walking early, not because I had planned for a long day but because I wanted to leave Naitwar.

I followed the Tons River downstream. For the first time on the trek I saw women in saris and men in rough, cotton turbans. Chattering monkeys leaped amongst the pines. The population increased rapidly, as villages materialized every kilometre and between them on the valley's flatter sections lay interlocking grids of grey, stubbly, harvested fields. Maybe because it was morning many of the people in the paddocks looked bedraggled, like they'd had a bad night's sleep. When I passed they stared, neither friendly nor aggressive. For the first time I felt self-conscious while walking.

At the village of Nanai I cut east from the Tons, following a stream up a minor pass that would lead to the Yamuna River. The road climbed slowly. There was almost no traffic. People roamed the woods with long wicker baskets thrown over their shoulders, collecting branches and cones for their fires. In a few baskets I saw fresh-picked mushrooms and the odd bundled sprig of herbs. In the well-managed forest along the road there was an obvious system to the division of the forest's produce; every tree had lost its lower branches for firewood to a certain height. Each tree trunk was slashed near its base, a hollow tin rod was inserted in the cut and a small cup was attached to collect resin. The resin is distilled and becomes turpentine, another small side-income for local families. The forest looked used but not damaged.

I crossed the pass and the road joined a stream that led into the Yamuna Valley. I had lunch in a café in the town of Purola. The man who served me my rice and dal smiled but wasn't in the mood to chat. He left and when I wanted to pay I couldn't find him. He returned a half hour later wiping sleep from his eyes. It had been siesta time.

By late afternoon I was on the Yamuna River. From there I should have headed north to visit the Hindu pilgrimage site at its source, but at that point in the trek logistics forced me to turn south. It was strange in the course of such a minimalist walk to have to think about money, but there I was in the heart of the Hindu Himalayas with almost none. To the people I passed I was a stranger and many would invite me to their homes for food and tea. They were generous to the extreme and, unless it was vehemently refused, I insisted on leaving a gift. I had no need to be remembered as a burden. Then, of course, I had to buy meals and beds, rice and kerosene.

So money or the lack of it forced me off my track and onto an early morning bus the next day headed to the hill station town of Mussoorie. There I could change the crisp, clean travellers cheques I had stored in a plastic bag deep in my pack for wads of grubby bank notes and, once again, I could meander off with the Western world's ultimate insurance, a pocket full of cash.

Climbing on board the almost full bus I found a seat on a ripped and sweaty bench near the rear entrance. After so many weeks of walking eight hours a day my body had grown accustomed to dictating its own pace. The vehicle moved faster than my walking-speed mind was accustomed to; scenes drifted by with no time for reflection. Beautiful women stared at me, a buffalo lifted an elegant foreleg, children caught in frenzied play froze then waved at the hurtling bus. To the people outside I was a forty-kilometre-an-hour head without a body. The world floated by in infinite vignettes. I began to understand why so many tribal people have to vomit on bus rides. It isn't just the vehicle's interminable motion, but the vision of a world moving too fast.

The man beside me was excited to the point of agitation at having a foreigner next to him. He possessed little English beyond, "I like you, my dear," but tried energetically every fifteen minutes to draw me into conversation. I tried to speak Hindi with him but either my accent was unintelligible or he was insistent on practising his English. After our first failed attempt at conversation I tried to stay focused on the three-day-old newspaper I'd found jammed between the seats.

The bus dropped me thirty kilometres north and 1,000 metres below Mussoorie at a remote intersection in the midst of a deforested valley. I stepped down from the bus and the men playing cards at the cinder-block café took a momentary pause to stare at me. I nodded, smiled, and went inside in search of rice and dal.

The owner told me there were no more buses for Mussoorie that day, but he gallantly offered to flag me down a shared taxi. Within an hour he'd arranged a ride. I wriggled into a four-door Hindustan Ambassador stuffed to bursting with six adults and four children. The Ambassador is the classic Indian taxi. It has long, arching lines, a look that reminds you of British films from after World War Two. Not surprisingly, the car is a copy of the mid-'50s Morris Oxford and has been produced in India continually since 1957.

The taxi slowly wound its way up through a stark, deforested land. We passed a waterfall that had been given a cement backdrop to insure it kept falling and a spaceship-styled Hindu temple with chrome railings and an antenna that reached for the gods. Both were sightseeing attractions and the queue of tourist buses lined up on either side of them almost pushed us off the narrow route. When we arrived in Mussoorie by the back road, the bustling, Victorian-era shopping strip surprised me with its sudden appearance.

The car came to a stop and everyone stared at me. The driver turned, smiled with his bright red betel juice-stained teeth and said, "Mussoorie, sir. Please leave us."

Mussoorie's origins can be traced to 1825 when Captain Young, a British Army officer who was stationed in Dehra Dun forty kilometres to the south, went exploring and found a ridge that stretched east to west and featured panoramic views north to the Himalayas. He had found the perfect spot to build a hunting lodge. This was the settlement's first building and since then it has grown in fits and starts, depending on the number of people with money enough to climb the ridge and escape the scorching heat of summer.

India is a hot country. The British, who controlled most of it for over a hundred years, enjoy cool weather, so for the Raj administration to function in the sweltering pre-monsoon months of April and May the Anglos migrated to the temperate hills. The entire bureaucracy moved from Calcutta and Delhi to hill towns like Darjeeling, Shimla, Dharamsala and Mussoorie. In a way Mussoorie is a purpose-built community, the progenitor of the late twentieth century's ski resorts and beach-side getaways. Mussoorie is a place to escape the heat and dogged reality of everyday life "down below."

Hill stations are still tourist attractions. When the British left in 1947, many of their properties were seized as summer houses by wealthy Delhi and Calcutta families. With the recent economic boom a new wave of middle-class Indian tourists has descended on the town. Mussoorie is busier than ever and yet the hill station still retains an air of exclusivity and peculiarity. In Mussoorie you see stately Raj residences in various stages of decay alongside concrete-box hotels and corrugated steel shanties.

Over dinner that evening I talked to an Anglo-Indian student who was visiting his extended family from his home in the U.K. Sundar Singh described himself as a modern Sikh. He hadn't grown a beard and he didn't carry a kirpan, the traditional dagger, but he did wear a kara or iron bracelet. Sikhism is a religion that developed in the Punjab under the direction of its founder, Guru Nanak, during the fifteenth century as a bridge between Hinduism and Islam.

Sundar said that being a Sikh for him was not about external symbols but was instead simply about being an honest, hard-working person. He backed this up by proudly telling me his university scores from the past year. Sundar wasn't interested in what I was up to; his eyebrows rose just slightly when I told him of my trek. I don't think he actually believed I was walking the length of the Western Himalayas. He constantly brought the conversation back to whether I thought Canada or the U.K. offered more opportunities for young business graduates.

In the United Kingdom today there are close to three million citizens of Indian descent. It's a long way from the situation in Raj-era Mussoorie when benches along the Strand featured signs on them saying, "Indians and dogs not allowed."

I told him I couldn't tell him which country offered more opportunities as I didn't know much about business and then he said, "Well, I could always come back home. There's unlimited jobs here now. The future is with India."

The next day I changed money, went sightseeing with hordes of Indian tourists, washed my clothes, ate Western food and slept in a bed with clean sheets.

The morning after, I boarded a bus for the long ride back into the mountains. The road traced the rivers back into the Himalayan labyrinth. It was cliff-side motoring. Twice we rounded blind curves and came directly in the path of oncoming transport trucks. The scream of heavy brakes jolted the sixty drowsy passengers from their napping. The driver, a salt-and-pepper-haired man with dark bags under his eyes, would creep the bus past the Tata truck or Ambassador car, so close to the precipice that those of us on the left-hand side could see the tires sending gravel into the abyss. With each of these near misses the driver would touch his forehead with his forefinger and then stroke the head of the small plastic statue of the Hindu god Shiva glued to the dashboard. Six hours of this adrenaline-packed driving and I was back in Barkot on the Yamuna River, the town I had left three days before.

November 2

I walked out of the village before sunrise on a street lined with concrete shops. Behind the shopfronts' bolted iron shutters, the steam engine rumble of kerosene stoves signalled the first cups of chai were on the boil. A line of loaded pack mules was moving north and the clip-clop of their hooves followed me out of town. Fog lingered in the paddies beyond the village. Farmers emerged from the mist, mattocks on their shoulders. The men and women kept their heads down.

The upper stretch of the Yamuna Valley was a pleasant surprise. It was well forested in pine and cedar. Amongst the trees the odd goat foraged on moss and thin grass. At one point, a blue-fronted redstart flitted through the trees and landed with ease on the cracked bark of a deodar cedar.

An hour into the day I stopped to take a sip of water. I looked down the road and two hundred metres away spotted a swaying black and blue nylon pack moving away from me. Indians generally use khaki green army surplus rucksacks so this was anomalous and interesting. I picked up my pace and gained on the walker. As I closed on him I saw the carrier was wearing jeans and a fine pair of leather hiking boots. Closer still I could see he was a tall man with sandy brown hair. I drew parallel and said hello in English. He turned, his eyes wide. We stopped, instinctively shook hands and started walking together.

I suppose to walk was the natural thing to do. Our steps fell together and for the first time in months I talked with someone from my own culture. Our conversation was slow and easy. We had the road to ourselves; there were no buses, no cars, no bicycles, not even other pedestrians. We sauntered down the middle of the asphalt talking and talking, enjoying the opportunity to speak loud and long.

Steve was nineteen years old, a tall man with a quick smile and a lanky gait. Amazingly he was from Toronto, Canada. We had a nation of similarities to fall back on.

At lunch we made a fire and brewed tea to go with the cold chapatis and lentils I'd bought in Barkot. We lay on either side of the ring of stones sipping sweet chai and trying to reduce our six degrees of separation with a mutual acquaintance. The topic of motivations came up, why were we both there, alone in the far reaches of the Himalayas. I gave him the condensed version of Gareth's accident, my childhood fascination with the mountains and my subsequent obsession with the Himalayas. Steve offered his condolences. I shrugged it off. But he insisted he had some understanding as his best friend had died when he was sixteen. Steve still thought about him often. I asked if his friend was the reason he was there.

"Maybe," he said. "It's a few years ago now. I hadn't thought too much about that."

We were two young men far from home in the highest mountains in the world, both in some way nudged there by the death of a loved one. Remarkably, at the time, Steve and I barely touched on the deaths that had so shaped our lives. I regret that now because I see how the walk was a catalyst for my coming to terms with Gareth's death. In retrospect I know I was too fixated on the walk, too focused on situating people and events in accordance with the book I wanted to write. Everyday I was accosted with once-in-a-lifetime experiences. Everyday I could have followed those experiences far off my charted course, but I didn't. I had objectives; nothing was going to stop me.

In a way I had approached the trek the same way I had dealt with Gareth's death, with tunnel vision. When Gareth had died it had consumed me. For months his death was everything; there was no escape. It was going back to work, five months after the event, that freed me from the immediate grief. I threw myself into the job, which is easy when you put in sixteen to eighteen hours a day in the bush. I used work to mask the pain. I created my own tunnel of superficial composure, so much so that even I believed it.

But Gareth was there. I remember once seeing a day pack on the side of a logging road. It was the same brand and colour as Gareth's. Mud was splattered on it, and a stainless steel thermos of coffee lay on top. I started crying, crying so hard I had to stop the truck I was driving and let the wave move over me.

Another time I passed an area where we had planted trees together a few years before. I felt strong, ready to face such a connected landscape. Walking through the young stand of metre-and-a-half pines I could see that the trees were dying; beetles were eating their tender outer bark. The work we had done together had been for nothing. I sat on the moss-covered ground and wept.

That afternoon, north of Barkot, sitting by a fire eating stale chapatis and talking with a man I'd never met about my dead brother, I'd smiled easily. There had been no tears.

I had been so long without dialogue that it was draining to talk for all those hours. After lunch, a few kilometres up the road Steve left me to follow a trail east to Dodit/al Lake. We shook hands and promised to stay in touch. It's a promise I haven't kept.

At the same time I was excited to be moving towards one of Hinduism's most sacred sites, Yamunotri, the source of the Yamuna River. The river starts at the head of the valley I was ascending, and flows south then east across the plains until it joins the Ganges at the great confluence of Prayag in the city of Allahabad. For Hindus this is the meeting point, not just for these two great flows, but also for the ethereal Saraswati River, the river of wisdom. Therefore, Prayag has another name: Tridevi, the three goddesses.

It is at Tridevi where, every twelve years, the Khumbu Mela takes place. The Mela is the greatest Hindu festival and the largest human gathering on the planet. At sunrise, on the most astrologically auspicious day of those dozen years, up to twelve million devotees take a ritual bath in the confluence, immersing themselves in the fused bodies of the three goddesses. The purifying waters absolve the faithful of a lifetime of negative karma and multiply the good deeds accumulating towards their future incarnations.

CHAPTER 9
Balance

November 3

After a cold night in an empty pilgrim's guest house in Sayanachatti village, I spent the morning waiting out some wet weather in the local chai shop. Sayanachatti is the hamlet where the road ends and the foot trail to Yamunotri begins. The shop was ten metres square, roofed with rusty corrugated iron, its sides open to the elements. A low cement wall separated it from the road and over the partition a wind, moist from the river, blew around the dozen tea drinkers huddled around the fire.

The village survives on summer's pilgrimage business but the season ends in September and the place was all but deserted when I wandered up the empty road. The tea shop was the only sign of life. As with most villages in India it was the social centre of the community, a place where business and politics are continually wrestled with by an ever-present gang of happily idle men.

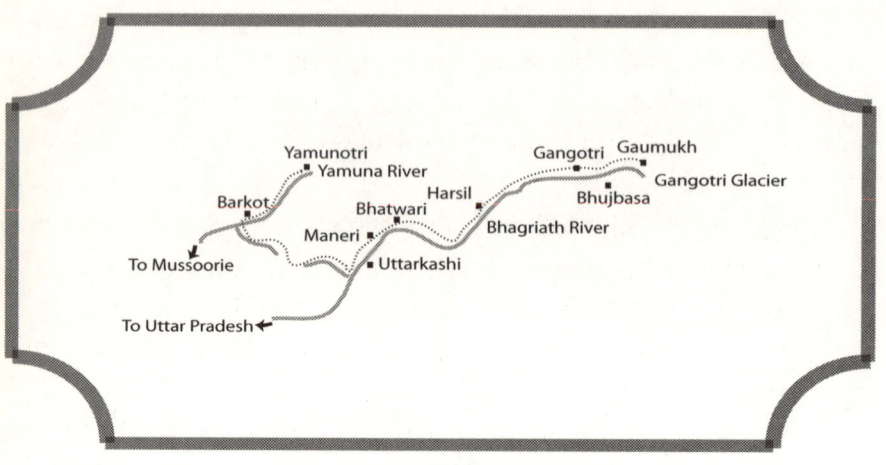

GARWAHL, UTTARAKHAND, INDIA

Politics may trace its etymology to ancient Greece, but I'm confident that India is its true home and the chai shop is the heart of subcontinental politics. Rice and potatoes, the Indian National Congress and the Bharatiya Janata parties, sheep and bridges, roads and buses – all are discussed. Over and over again in Sayanachatti the words rupee and government intersected and became catalysts for the debaters to stand, shout, and wag their fingers. The young shopowner, Prakash, sat next to me. He was bundled in multiple sweaters topped with a woolen sport jacket. A homespun scarf was wrapped turban-style around his head. Between refilling his customers' glasses he provided me with a rapid-fire translation of the local Pahari dialect.

A middle-aged man with tired eyes and a bright red acrylic toque was holding forth. Prakash said, "He is saying his brother-in-law has a new contract repairing part of the pilgrim route. The contract price is much less than last year."

Voices were raised.

Another man with a prodigious belly, his arms spread out on the bench back, shuffled in his seat and replied.

Prakash translated, "The other man is saying that his uncle is an advisor to a big man in the district." The man sat up straight as he mentioned his relative. "He will try and find out why there has been a reduction in cost."

The group nodded.

"Oh, now this fellow," Prakash waved his finger at a bearded man in a purple nylon jacket two sizes too small for him, "is saying that the man's uncle has lost his influence with the public works department because of some bad dealings with the state ministry of roads."

The rotund nephew rose to standing, pointed his finger and shouted to the verge of spitting at the accuser. Prakash did not have to translate. The other man stood and with equal fervour returned the gesture. Two groups rose around the men, and friendly arms reached placatingly around the adversaries, bringing them back to sitting.

Prakash whispered, "These two have never gotten along. Their grandfathers argued about property boundaries back in the British time."

At the Yamunotri trailhead the valley narrows, and a well-maintained path follows it, rising steeply beyond the village of Beef. It was cool and moist, and wispy clouds clung to the hillsides but the climb brought a sweat out on me. The trail was cobbled, the first I'd encountered in the Himalayas, a testament to the importance of the Yamuna pilgrimage. The route winds through a tight, verdant gorge, which was quiet but for the sound of the young river and the whispering tick of dense foliage. Moru oaks and acacias sprouted from the cliffs above and below the trail, their leaves dripping with mist.

From June until September tens of thousands of pilgrims traverse the route, but in late fall it was empty, and from Beef to Yamunotri I saw no one. It was eerie to be the only person on such a meticulously constructed route and I was relieved to round a bend and see, tucked into the cliffs at the river's source, the temple of the Goddess.

But the joy I had in seeing my day's goal was quickly extinguished because on second glance the site looks like a disused mining exploration camp. Buildings that in summer would have been shops and restaurants were roofless, empty and unkempt; ripped canvas tarps flapped in the breeze, concrete flaked off the shops' river-stone walls. As I walked by the skeletal frames, paper and plastic blew by my feet. Woodsmoke marked the interior of each building and the monsoon had stained everything an algae green. These were X-ray buildings, open for all to see but containing nothing worth looking at. It seemed a poor tribute to the Goddess who gives life to such a broad swathe of northern India.

Disheartened, I thought about turning around but decided I could not leave without visiting the hot springs around which the temples are built. Past the line of empty shops I crossed the nascent river on a small steel suspension bridge and climbed to the temple complex that had been built by the Maharani Gularia of Jaipur in the nineteenth century.

On the rusted iron fence circling the steaming, flagstone-lined springs I hung my trekking gear and slipped naked, but for my underwear, into the pool. The faint rotten egg smell of sulphurous spring water mixed with the resinous scent of pines and cedar. I stared at my ghostly pale body under the water. My legs and arms were thin and sinewy from the months of walking. It had been so long since I had taken an extended look at what lay beneath my clothes that it was as if I was looking at a new creation. Muscles I had never seen flexed when I lifted my legs, and new ribs appeared where only fat and muscle had been before. The heat seeped into me. My muscles loosened.

A hundred metres above me new snow glazed the branches of altitude-stunted conifers. The light was turning golden in the magic hour before darkness. I stretched my shoulders and elbows out along the cold stone sill and leaned my head back to appreciate the play of rosy clouds. I looked to the right. Gathered in the ornate stone doorway of a partly completed temple, a crew of ragged construction workers stood and stared. Up until then I had noticed no one in the compound. They smiled between puffs on their cigarettes. Their teeth were the colour of old crispy leaves. The sound of bells and chanting came from one of the shrines. Afternoon prayers had begun and with that the men turned and resumed their work.

In the warmth of the hot springs the landscape around me hummed. Legend has it that Yamuna was the daughter of Surya, the sun god, and the sister of Yama, the god of death. Hindus believe that whoever bathes at the Yamuna's source will never meet a violent death. I exhaled and watched the steam roll off the pool's surface, across the stone-lined courtyard and into the emptiness above the source.

Rivers hold significant power for Hindus. On the surface the silt-rich rivers are the lifeblood of the subcontinent. They ensure the supply of food and provide the water that Indians exist on. At a more subtle level, flowing water for Indians is the physicalization of feminine power. The great rivers – Ganga, Yamuna, and Saraswati – are all female entities. Rivers embody the dichotomy of maternal compassion and parental discipline. They give everything they have and in return demand respect.

The water of the Ganges is the purest element in a purity-obsessed religion; even 1,500 densely populated and polluted kilometres downstream in Varanasi, Hinduism's most auspicious place to die, the water is considered ambrosia, an entity capable of nullifying sins and amplifying good deeds. Devout Hindus consider the water at Varanasi pure enough to drink, an amazing feat considering that by that point the water has passed by and through the 100 million people who call the Gangeatic plains home.

Yamunotri is the first stage on one of India's most sacred pilgrimages, the Chota Char Dham Yatra, the pilgrimage of the four holy sites. Hindus believe that those who traverse the Ganges' Himalayan watershed from west to east, stopping and completing the required rituals at the springs of Yamunotri;

Gangotri, the origin of the Ganges; Kedarnath, the Himalayan home of Lord Shiva, Hinduism's embodiment of power and destruction; and Badrinath, the Himalayan sanctuary of Lord Vishnu, the personification of continuity in Hinduism, will achieve moksha, salvation.

The region of the Char Dham is also known as Dev Bhoomi, the land of the gods. For Hindus the Himalayas are a visionary environment, for the peaks that form the range are not just spires of stone and ice but the thrones of the religion's greatest gods. With the right mindset, one steeped in devotion and good deeds, Hindus can experience the mountains not as an inaccessible labyrinth but as the wellspring of their religion's greatest myths. The Himalayas become a physical medium through which Hindus can connect with their gods. Thus the mountains have been the object of pilgrimage for a pantheon of Hinduism's great thinkers, but it is Adi Shankaracharya, the eighth-century philosopher monk, who is credited with infusing the region with the legends it is so deeply associated with.

In the time of Shankaracharya, Hinduism had been in decline for nearly a thousand years. In the second century B.C.E., King Ashoka had militarily brought most of the Indian subcontinent under his rule. In the midst of his empire building he converted to Buddhism and under Ashoka's patronage India slowly became a Buddhist country.

Shankaracharya was from the south coast of Kerala, an area little touched by Ashoka's Buddhist dissemination. He came north as a pilgrim and a missionary. He wanted to return India to its original belief and travelled widely to achieve his goal. Eventually, he was able to convert most of the central Himalayan population back to Hinduism.

Shankaracharya used landscape as much as philosophy and storytelling to connect the people with the religion. During his time in the mountains Shankaracharya identified not only the Char Dham, but also the Panch Prayag, the five confluences of the Ganges; the Panch Kedar, the five shrines of Shiva; and the Panch Badri, the five temples of Vishnu. By creating a matrix of holy sites in the local landscape Shankaracharya intertwined communities with the religion. To this day Hinduism is connected to the landscape of India in a way that makes the two almost inseparable.

November 4

I camped that night up one of the Yamuna's small steep-walled tributaries not far from the temple and the next morning packed in a frigid gorge unaccustomed to sunlight. I returned down the valley from Barkot and walked east towards the Rari Ghatti that leads to the Bhagriath Valley. It was a long climb. The woods were quiet. Their harvests complete, there was little movement in the few villages along the way. I moved quickly, satisfied with the thump of my rubber soles and the easy breathing that months of hard walking had given me. Every once in a while the sound of children or the rap of an axe would reach me in the echoing way that sound comes to you through trees.

At nightfall I found myself close to the pass and far from any settlement. I pitched my tent in darkness, so accustomed to my portable home that I could erect it by touch. A few hundred metres below I saw the flicker of candles, light from inside a single shanty. Dinner was made and eaten under the beam of my headlamp. I rinsed the dishes with water from my canteen, feeling for the caked-on rice with my fingertips.

My chores complete I lay outside, astounded by the silence. The air was so still it rang in my ears. Not for the first time in those many months I was shocked to think I was in the second most populous country in the world. On all sides were monumental deodar cedars, whose branches reached down out of the darkness, touching the ground by my feet. Through the branches I saw the moon rise. Delicate cedar fronds were silhouetted by the ghostly light and their glossy needles shimmered as a slight breeze danced them round and round. The moon's ascent, the half-time waltz of needles and branches and trunks, the touch of wind on my face – all that movement without sound.

Millenniums of pilgrims had come to the Garwahl Himalayas for exactly that experience, quietude and space. Adi Shankaracharya's identification of the Himalayas' myriad of holy sites became the framework for some of Hinduism's most important pilgrimages.

Pilgrimage, or Yatra in Sanskrit, has traditionally involved a great commitment in time and energy – the slow movement between holy places is a process of spiritual journeying, a time removed from everyday obligations, a period for contemplation. The process of Yatra is as important as its geographic goals. A pilgrimage is a course of inquiry, a long question whose answers evolve in the meditation of walking and the openness that hardship engenders.

I felt the air moving in and out of me, my chest expanding and contracting in motion with the trees. Above me an owl called. Cedar fronds rustled. A rhesus monkey howled at its troupe, a chorus began, and from the valley far below came the answer of barking dogs.

November 5

The morning was chilly and after a quick cup of tea and some biscuits I packed and set off down the road. I walked fast to warm myself. Two kilometres into the day I came across a road crew in torn T-shirts and cotton scarves wrapped tight around their heads. Three of the men stood above a hole, shivering, arms folded over their chests, gazing with sleepy nonchalance at a fourth who shovelled stones into a breach in the road. I stopped. The labourer was sweating. I indicated to the shaking trio that if they joined in they would warm up. They smiled back and raised empty hands, indicating that for them any work was impossible – there was only one shovel.

The sun climbed overhead and the temperature soared. As I moved closer to the Bhagriath River the woods gave way to treeless slopes and haphazard paddies. It was shocking how quickly the transition was made from pristine timber to environmental havoc. On the naked ground the sun worked relentlessly, ossifying hillsides, sealing off the earth to any trace of rain. In a field near the road poor, biscuit-coloured soils were being broken by a crude wooden plow dragged by two gleaming buffalo, their skins rippling in the heat.

To my left diesel-spewing trucks passed on the road, while on my right the paddies were being prepared with 8,000-year-old technology. Behind the plow stalked a withered crone in a cornflower blue, sun-faded sari. The dress was hitched and tied around her leathery thighs. She shouldered a huge mattock, swinging it with precision when the plow missed an unruly chunk of clay. She grunted as she struck, the clods disintegrating in puffs of dust. As I drew level she looked at me but I was not worth a reaction. She returned to her work. It was one of the few times on the walk when my presence produced no emotion at all.

The Bhagriath River is the primary source of the Ganges. Unfortunately, in its lower reaches thoughts of the great Hindu goddess Ganga are drowned by the blare of the road's traffic. Transport rigs and overcrowded buses, share taxis and private cars all barrel down the road honking their horns and laying on their hissing air brakes.

Soon after I started up the valley I passed a roadside café, a dhaba. Vehicles were parked outside and the drivers sat drinking tea and smoking cigarettes. Truckers the world over have the reputation of being a rough-hewn crowd, and the Indian variety are no different. On the subcontinent drivers are thought of as heavy-drinking, promiscuous men. A friend who worked in HIV education once showed me a map of the disease's spread across India, and the virus's path paralleled the country's interstate road system.

Yet for all their hard living truckers hold tight to their religion. In every vehicle outside the café I saw kitschy plastic Hindu icons glued or screwed onto the dashboard: silver and blue Shivas the size of action dolls, Baby Krishnas crawling across the drivers' sightlines, adult Krishnas blowing their magical flutes. The less than holy existences the truckers live and their blatant display of religiosity is no contradiction in Hinduism because the religion adapts itself for every congregation.

Across the country Shiva stares at you from calendars and coffee mugs. People donate enormous sums to wild-haired gurus who claim contact with the gods. Truckers say their prayers and wave incense before their mobile shrines at the start of every day. They are individualized forms of devotion and therefore as acceptable as the learned master who pores over the holy Hindu writings, the Vedas and the Upanishads.

The truckers' approach to Hindu practice is a type of bhakti yoga, one of Hinduism's four Paths to God. Bhakti in Sanskrit means "the way to God through love." Yoga can be interpreted as both union and discipline. Yoga's purpose is to join with God through dedicated practice. The process of this joining and liberation is through bhakti: karma, the way to God through right action; raja, the way to God through meditation and thought; and jnana, the way to God through wisdom.

In the bhakti path by having the image of your chosen god present, not only visually on your dashboard or in your shrine, but constantly on your lips and in your mind, by holding it so close that eventually you are consumed and merge with it, the practitioner uses what the plastic icon represents to move to a higher state of consciousness. The essence of bhakti yoga is held in the three-word Sanskrit mantra, *Tvat Tam Asi*, Thou Art That.

By mid-afternoon I had reached the town of Uttarkashi, the capital of its namesake district and the staging ground for pilgrims travelling farther up the valley to the Ganges River's source at Gangotri. Uttarkashi literally means northern city of light, and it is a miniature version of the great pilgrimage centre of Kashi, or Varanasi, well downriver on the Gangeatic plains. The town is a bustling hybrid of the secular and the saintly; wide-eyed holymen amble by advertisements for Hindi soft-core porn movies, and electrical shops blaring Hindi pop flank centuries-old temples. I saw mechanics chanting mantras while dismantling transmissions and curry cooks waving incense in front of postcard gods. In India Hinduism is everywhere and encompasses everything.

I took a room at a surprisingly comfortable hotel close to the middle of town. Because it is a major stopover on the pilgrimage route, Uttarkashi has dozens of guest houses and on every street there are small restaurants and tea stalls. In an open-air café sandwiched between a shop selling Hindu religious paraphernalia and children's toys, and a travel agency with internet terminals and a side business in water pumps, I had a memorable dinner. There were three different curries – curried okra, palak paneer, and vegetable jhalfrezi – which I ate with fresh tandoori chapatis accompanied by a large bottle of Kingfisher lager.

I was full when I finished but had passed a sweet shop on the way to the restaurant and had promised myself I would return. Good Indian sweet shops understand that presentation is as important as taste. This sweet shop had its products laid out on stainless steel platters in a long, chest-high refrigerated glass display case. The room was brightly lit with halogen lamps and I was suprised to see that when I ordered my gajar halva, carrot semolina pudding, the person who served me wore rubber, surgical-type gloves when he placed the sticky squares in a cardboard box.

I ate my halva as I walked to the Vishwanath Temple, the town's best known shrine. Vishwanath, ruler of the world in Sanskrit, is one of Lord Shiva's personas. Shiva is one of the triumvirate of primary gods in Hinduism, the others being Vishnu and Brahman. As a polytheistic religion, Hinduism has literally thousands of gods, but the vast majority are local manifestations of the trio of dominant male gods or incarnations of Shakti, the embodiment of female energy.

The brick courtyard of the temple houses two buildings, the larger, Vishwanath, built of plain-cut granite and the smaller red painted Shakti temple. The Shakti shrine is famous for the six-metre-tall metal trishul or trident that pushes through its roof. The trident is one of the symbols of Shiva. Legend holds that the trishul was driven into the ground at Uttarkashi by an assembly of gods. Its shaft was wrapped in saffron silk threaded with gold and at its base crumpled garlands of bright marigolds were laid. To Shiva's followers he encompasses the universe. On one level, the trident's prongs symbolize the three forces held by Shiva – the creation, the sustenance and the destruction. On another level, as Lord Shiva's weapon, the trident represents his ability to administer fierce justice on the universe's three planes – spiritual, subtle and physical.

At the opposite end of the compound the Vishwanath temple is focused around a ninety-centimetre-tall lingam, a phallic-shaped stone that stands in the middle of the one-room building. The lingam, Sanskrit for phallus, is an abstract representation of Shiva's male power, and the simplicity of the shape is a reference to the ethereal, attributeless form of the god, a form so elemental it can be imagined and felt in any time or space. I took off my shoes, went inside and sat quietly in a corner of the pale marble-tiled room. Devotees entered and prostrated to the gleaming stone. The phallus, which resembles an elongated egg, looked to be made of highly polished marble.

It was constantly being washed and stroked by an attendant priest. Belief has it that if the stone is not constantly doused with Ganges water, the heat of Lord Shiva would melt the stone and the temple.

Each of the congregation dropped their heads to the floor multiple times, stood with their hands clasped over their chests and whispered prayers to their god. On finishing, a priest offered them a handful of simple white candy, prasad, and a sprinkle of Ganga water, both of which were blessed through their proximity to the stone. The faithful in return offered fragrant oils, flowers, rice, saffron, coins and bank notes.

Beyond the murmur of prayers, the shuffle of sock feet and the splash of sacred water the room was quiet. It was lit by two fluorescent tubes. The cool light, the whiteness of the stone, the muffled sounds, the measured movements of prostration and prayer – all these slowed my senses. After the commotion of the town's traffic and my rush to find a guest house, I relaxed in the chilly corner. I could have stayed longer but with sunset the temperature dropped, darkness seemed to be sneaking in through the doorway and the cold of the marble seeped into my spine. People kept trickling in, but I saw the priest yawning. It was time to go.

Vishwanath is one of Lord Shiva's 1,008 names. In his most popular manifestation he is thought to be a mountain ascetic, a being who lived a reclusive life deep in the Himalyas. But according to legend even the untamed god eventually married. His wife was Parvati, the daughter of Lord Himalaya. Together they emerged on earth at Varanasi, the City of Light, and it was there that the first emanation of the Shiva lingam occurred in what is now the Vishwanath temple. While the lingam represents the raw force of masculine energy, that white-hot male energy emerges from the concave, vulvic form of a stone base. Almost every lingam is seated upon such a stone pedestal, the Yoni or feminine energy. Male and female are reliant on each other for balance. Shiva holds the power of both sexes and the merged stones are a representation of polar energies fused within his body.

November 6

From Uttarkashi I headed north, passing small villages and man-made forests. Hindu monasteries, ashrams, were a frequent sight along the river; some were constructed of plain stone but others looked to be turreted palaces in pink and green, saffron and gold. As I passed I would utter a prayer and put my hands together in respect.

Just before the village of Maneri I was dawdling peacefully along when a pearl white minivan screeched to a halt in front of me. A man in a jean jacket and New York Yankees baseball hat jumped out and strode towards me. By his dress and the swagger of his walk I guessed he was a big city tourist about to ask me to share a cup of tea with them. When he reached me, he thrust his hand in mine, shook it hard and introduced himself: "Jackie Deol, ZEE TV. You're a tourist, right?"

ZEE TV is one of India's new wave of television stations, a non-stop barrage of Hindi movies and music videos. Jackie's enthusiasm was based on his desire to interview me for a news clip. I consented, the camera rolled and I voiced my opinions on Himalayan deforestation, the erosion caused by poorly planned roads and the general lack of infrastructure in the mountains. Jackie wanted to know how Garwahl compared to Kashmir as a tourist destination. I told him there wasn't much comparison because there was a war going on in Kashmir.

It was not what he wanted or expected. He continued along that line of questioning, but by the end of the interview he was making "hurry up" glances at his cameraman. A large crowd of locals had surrounded us: boys in tattered school uniforms, a man with two buffalo in tow, a trio of women shouldering towering loads of hay. Our interview petered out. Jackie gave a weak thank you and offered me a ride farther up the road. I declined but accepted his now limp handshake. The crew jammed back into the tiny van and leaped from the scene in a screech of tires.

North of Maneri I stopped for a cup of tea at a chai stall near the hydroelectric dam across the Bhagriath. The squared-off wave of concrete was painted in geometric blocks of pink, yellow and blue. It was a Piet Mondrian painting holding back the mighty Ganges. From its base shot a stream of foaming whitewater. Behind it the Ganga was stilled. Along its upper edge walked a technician, hard hat on, clipboard in hand. The concrete barrage was surrounded by rusty barbed wire and was shadowed on the roadside by a line of dilapidated chai shops, none of which appeared to have any electricity.

The road climbed out of Bhatwari town and into more scenic country. There were thick deodar forests reaching away from the road and it was heartening to see jagged snow-mountains to the north on the border with Tibet. The traffic had dramatically diminished, and almost all of it now was human: quick-walking men with bulging canvas rucksacks, children for whom the road was a playground and women travelling in gangs of four or five, each of them burdened with a bale of grass three times their own size.

Those women were walking haystacks, their backs bent under loads that would see their cherished livestock through winter. I was impressed and attracted by those women not because of their looks but because of their grace. When they passed they all smiled or giggled and when they were not chatting they were singing. I have seen some translations of those songs by Anjali Capila.

> *The water is cool in the mountains.*
> *Do not go away to a strange land, my Lord!*
> *The Gods abide in this land.*

> *Do not go away to a strange land!*
> *The fields are lush and green.*
> *The Himalayan peaks high and covered with snow.*
> *The forest is dense with tall deodar trees.*
> *The water is cool and clean.*
> *My Lord, do not go away to a strange land.*

A few times old women stopped and asked me questions in the local Pahari dialect, but I would hold my hands up in admission of my lack of understanding and they would shake their heads and laugh. Once a young woman, a beautiful girl with flawless skin, a tiny ruby stud in her nose and stalks of grass scattered across her jet-black ponytailed hair, asked me in surprisingly good English if I had any cigarettes.

I told her I didn't smoke and she nodded her head to one side. I was surprised she smoked, as in the Indian villages it is a social faux pas for young women to do so. Trying not to sound like an older brother I asked her what her family thought of that. She laughed, flicked her head around and walked away without answering my question. She was alone and away from her family, so social norms did not apply. Those women had focus and energy and wit, and through it all their hips swayed and their eyes twinkled.

November 7

The next day I reached an altitude where the forest of oak, sal, acacias and conifers mixed with rolling alpine meadows. The air was cool, with the clarity that comes with a dry cold. I felt loose, happy to be free of the lower valley's heat and human density. Harsil was the first village in the area. I saw five coloured prayer flags like those I had seen through Ladakh, Zanskar, Lahaul and Spiti waving from rooftops in the lower part of town. The upper reaches of the Bhagriath Valley are inhabited by Buddhist Bhotiya people. Originally they are from Tibet, merchants who moved back and forth trading wool and salt from the north for rice and fine cloth from the south. This lucrative trade dried up with the formalizing of borders since India's independence in 1947 and the Bhotiyas have been forced to settle in the villages close to the border.

In that post-harvest season the houses' flat roofs glowed with colour – peppers drying, their redness almost black; amber squash with dried and twisted vines still attached; old green hemp; scarlet millet waiting to be threshed; and sheaf upon sheaf of dusty, golden barley. A Buddhist monk in burgundy robes and carrying a bright yellow shoulder bag paralleled my path for a few hundred metres on the far side of the river. It was a surprising sight in the Hindu heartland.

Harsil was the home, at the end of the nineteenth century, of Raja Wilson, an alleged British army deserter who stumbled upon this piece of untapped wilderness and drained it of all it was worth. Wilson started out killing and stuffing rare birds and animals and exporting them to London. The trade came to the attention of the local ruler, the Raja of Tehri, and in tribute Wilson went before him and offered four hundred gold coins. The Raja was surprised to see so much gold, as his own fortune was based on the meagre grain tithe he received from his citizens. He asked Wilson about the source of the money and when the Englishman explained, the Raja named Wilson his "golden bird." To which Wilson replied, "Oh, there's much more money to be got. Allow me to cut the trees of the Himalayas and the timber can make us a fortune." Thus began the deforestation of the Hindu Himalayas.

Wilson pioneered riverborne timber transport in India; he was the original "timber floater." His discovery initiated the beginning of the Himalayas' commercial exploitation. When he had made his millions, he returned to British society in

Mussoorie, no longer a deserter, but an entrepreneur in a new and needed industry.

That night I camped on a cliff above the Bhagriath River in a small, thinly grassed glen out of which a zen-like garden of small stone monoliths emerged. I ate my dinner at the edge of the abyss watching the late sun streak the turbulent water with flashes of gold, then pink and then red. In the trees I heard the *pi ... you, pi ... you* of a Great Hill Barbet and then the answering calls of a dozen of its mates. Night came and from the slopes behind came the hollow *tock, tock* of axes slicing into wood. Somewhere in the darkness illegal, nighttime loggers were continuing Raja Wilson's legacy.

November 8

I arrived at Gangotri in the early afternoon and the village was a welcome surprise. After Yamunotri I had expected a ramshackle assortment of disused chai shops girdled by a wasteland of gunny-sack outhouses. I was wrong as the place was neat and tidy, like a European seaside resort in winter. The only inhabitants were a core of diehard saddhus, sincere Hindu holymen, and in this was another marvel for me.

Saddhus are Hindu ascetics who have taken vows to follow a strict path towards higher knowledge. They have given up the first three goals of Hindu life – kama, pleasure; artha, wealth and power; and dharma, duty – so as to concentrate wholly on the fourth: moksha, liberation. It is said that in India today there are between four and five million saddhus. Most of these men (and a lesser number of women) are dedicated to their path, but unfortunately there is a scattering of pretenders. Saddhus live on the charity of others. Indians in general are very generous towards their holy men and for the few less than authentic saddhus, donning robes guarantees them an income.

These false holy men have a tendency to congregate in areas frequented by Western tourists, I would guess because it is almost impossible for someone outside of Hindusim to tell the real from the imitation when it comes to holy men. In truth, I don't know whether in the previous five years in India I'd actually met a committed saddhu. But the holy men I met in Gangotri were a different breed because they were immersed in their religion. Unlike the saddhus I'd met in Delhi and Calcutta they generally ignored me. By just going about their business the saddhus gave me the impression that Gangotri was special, a place charged with religious energy. My expectations were heightened for the Ganga-Mai temple that is the centrepiece of the village.

Ganga-mai means Mother Ganges, and this is how Hindus perceive the goddess. She is all-giving but sometimes stern, an energy that is with you always. Almost every Hindu home will have a vial of Ganga water in their household shrine. Ganga water is the purest substance on earth and anything or anyone that comes in contact with it is cleansed. The goddess herself is portrayed as a beautiful, voluptuous woman who carries an overflowing Grecian-looking urn in her hands; she is the personification of abundance.

The myth of Ganga's appearance on earth is a great description of the peculiarly human qualities of the Hindu gods. The legend goes something like this.

King Sagara had two wives. One bore him sixty thousand sons while the other bore him only one, whose name was Asamanjas. The king once wanted to perform a religious ritual that involved a special horse, but the jealous god Indra stole the horse. King Sagara sent his sixty thousand sons to search for the animal. After digging up the entire earth's surface and then the underworld, they eventually found it in a cave close to where the sage Kapila was in retreat. Thinking that the learned man had stolen the horse, the sons hurled abuse at him. This brought the great master out of his meditation. He was angry and with one look instantly burned the sixty thousand sons to ash with his fiery gaze.

The king heard of his sons' fate through Narada, the heavenly wanderer. He sent his grandson Ansuman, the son of Asamanjas, to undo the harm. The grandson met Kapila, who was pleased with the young man's tact. The sons could not be brought back to life, but Kapila granted that the souls of the sons could be released for reincarnation if touched by the waters of Ganga. Ganga-Mai at this time resided in the heavens. However, it was many generations before Bhagriatha, who was Sagara's great-great-grandson, was able to impress the goddess enough with his devotion that she agreed to come to earth.

But Bhagriatha knew that the impact of her fall to the planet's surface would destroy the world, and the blow could only be borne by Lord Shiva. Therefore, Bhagriatha went into meditation again and obtained Shiva's agreement that he would cushion the fall. Finally, the river came down, the thundering descent was absorbed by Shiva's matted dreadlocks (when you look at images of Lord Shiva, you see in his hair a tiny waterfall of Ganga erupting from it) and thence it fell gently to earth. Where Shiva absorbed the flow's impact is the site of the present-day temple at Gangotri. Bhagriatha then used his plow and dredged a course for the water to the south (the path of the present-day Bhagriath/Ganges River) and led the goddess to where the ashes of the sixty thousand sons lay. The souls of the sons were liberated and an ocean formed there. Today, this is Sagar Island in Bengal where the Ganges flows into the Bay of Bengal.

The Ganga-Mai temple is simply designed, a pale stone square with four corner turrets and a central tower. It fits unassumingly into its surroundings. The current structure was built by the Gurkha general Amar Singh Thapa in the early seventeenth century.

When I was there the lack of people and the white-noise rush of the Bhagriath River emphasized its tranquillity. The temple was locked (it is closed for the season on the Indian holiday of Diwali each year and reopened in May), but I could see the whitewashed walls of the inner shrine were covered with thousands of red dots, women's bindis or forehead markings. Bindis mark the area between the eyebrows that is said to be the sixth chakra, or energy centre. In Hindusim it is known as the seat of "concealed wisdom." In a way, each of those scores of women had placed a piece of their being in the guardianship of the goddess. The pattern created by the red marks was endless, like an Australian aboriginal dot painting exposing a community's relationship with gods and landscape.

Then, in true Indian form, reality shifted a little off to one side. I realized the three young men sitting at the far end of the otherwise deserted courtyard were tied together and the two burly, half-naked, fully bearded saddhus standing by them were guarding them with sticks.

In Hindi I asked what was going on and one of the guards explained the trio had kidnapped the teenage son of a wealthy Uttarkashi family and had been holding the boy for ransom in one of Gangotri's deserted shacks. The holy men had known nothing of this but had noticed smoke from the chimney of an empty hut. It would be unreasonable to expect that someone would take over an absent saddhu's hut without informing the others, so they knew something strange was going on. The holy men surrounded the shack and accosted the gang, who made a run for it. The monks went in pursuit and after a wild chase through the deserted village apprehended them. I liked the image: a gang of ochre-robed, barefoot, dreadlocked saddhus pursuing a trio of knife-wielding gangsters. The kidnappers were being held until the police could arrive from Uttarkashi. I had cup of tea with the saddhu guards; the captives stared at the ground.

I stayed that night in a deserted guest house. It wasn't officially open but after I enquired about rooms, one of the saddhus, a heavy-set man with dreadlocks that snaked down his back, touched me on the shoulder and silently indicated I should follow him. He didn't speak the entire time – maybe he had taken a vow of silence – but as we were walking he showed me a key and escorted me into the building and to a room. He didn't indicate that he wanted any money, but I gave him a donation, saying it was for the upkeep of the temple.

The room was musty and damp. I cooked my dinner outside and ate on a stone courtyard, looking across the darkening river at the pale walls of the temple.

November 9

I had breakfast again in the courtyard. I ate my porridge and saw some of the saddhus descending to the river for their morning dips. I decided to join them. It was fantastically cold. I stripped down to my underwear and made a quick dash up to my knees in the surging water. Bathing in the purest substance in the Hindu world seemed a good way to start the day. Most of the saddhus ignored me, but the one who had quietly shown me the room the night before was sitting on the low stone wall by the temple, and through the forest of his beard he smiled and then waved as I left.

Soon after Gangotri the forest ended and the landscape opened out. It was a twenty-kilometre walk up to the river's glacial source at Gaumukh. The valley had a symetrical concave sweep that started with the river at its centre and rose outwards and upwards like an elongated bell curve until the greenness of the valley gave way to the rock, scree and ice of the mountains that cradled its edges. I had heard that meditators inhabited the caves that dotted those mountains. I could understand why. With Gangotri as its anchor and the sky as its limit, it was an environment of direction where the focus was upwards; everything in the valley was directed higher

– to the glacier, to the summits, to the sky. It was terrain epitomizing the focus that the ascetic must have to achieve a higher state of consciousness.

I liked those mountains with their sloughing, disintegrating, re-creating, impermanence. Falling down, getting up. Growing old, being new – they challenged my idea of the unwavering peak. When I had been a climber I had climbed for the challenge, the physical rush. The mountains had always been something *too* solid, almost untouchable in their steadfastness. Now I stepped back and saw their changeability, their death and rebirth and, in the view from afar, how they were like me.

Gaumukh, the cow's mouth in Sanskrit, is the origin of the Ganges, and emanates from the base of the thirty-kilometre-long Gangotri glacier. This is her point of physical manifestation. However, legend has it that the divine source is hundreds of kilometres to the northeast at Mount Kailash in Tibet. Kailash is the mythical Himalayan home of Lord Shiva as well as the cosmological centre of the world to Tibetan Buddhists. It is fitting that she should start there, the Kailash area being the calving ground for a multitude of South Asia's great rivers: the Ganges, the Tsang-po/Brahmaputra, the Sutlej, the Karnali and the Indus. From the mountain's base those waters spread east, west and south to encircle the subcontinent, the fluvial structure for the motherland. Kailash is the heart of a liquid mandala, but only Ganga originates from the peak, from a fountain spilling from the meditating Lord Shiva himself.

I approached at sunset. From Bhujbasa, still six kilometres from the source, I could see the snout of the Bhagriath glacier. I knew I'd have to hurry to reach it before dark. The mother was playing tricks on me, for the closer I got the more fantastic became the light reflected on the circling snow peaks. Darkness was advancing and I wanted so much to see the river's beginning in the transitional light between day and night that I dropped my pack and began to run over the jumbled glacial moraine, leaping from boulder to boulder, agile as a deer. I was a man possessed.

After assuming, a dozen times, that the headwaters were just around the next corner, I suddenly found myself there. I arrived as the mountains glowed in coral red. The infant Ganges emerged from her frigid womb, surrounded by a fortress of ice. The glacier was translucent blue. There again, as on the Phokar River in Zanskar, were the protective colours, turquoise and coral. Again I felt completely at peace in the landscape.

I sat down on a freezing beach at 4,000 metres, the stream an arm's length away. My shirt and fleece vest were soaked with sweat but I was satisfied with where I was. I crossed my legs and stilled my breath until it was soundless. I sat and sat. I felt a warmth rise up my spine. There was a tingle on my eyelids, as tears welled up and stumbled down my cheeks, falling to the sand. The water of me was absorbed by the earth and taken back by Mother Ganga.

My brother had been taken by water and now I was sitting at the source.

The source. Gareth's death was a source of fear for me, fear of not deriving the most out of life and at the same time a source of fearlessness in my drive to transcend that. But his death was also an inspiration for trust, because to get the most out of my many experiences I had to trust the people and the land I came in contact with.

The Ganges flowed on, part of a cycle of transformation. Cloud and sun to ice and water, all leading to the mother flow of a continent and a religion. Gareth's death was the basis of my own transformation, from a world defined by more black and white rules to one ruled by the infinite greys of India. Death was my catalyst for understanding that great paradoxes – why, for example, such a good person as Gareth should die so young – are there not to torment us, but to provoke us into asking more questions, and eventually to accept them for what they are – constant. The world is a matrix of paradoxes and how we navigate the labyrinth is the best definition of our lives.

And the Ganges was faith – the faith of the hundreds of millions of Hindus who believe in the goodness and justice of Ganga-Mai. And again Gareth forced me to accept real faith. His passing pushed me out of the tight, secure world that my life had become and in that movement I gained faith in the goodness of those I met, in India, in the Himalayas, in Europe, in Southeast Asia, in Latin America and across North America. I put myself out there; I had to have faith in their compassion and in the process I gained faith in the landscape, the entity I loved and wanted to walk and ride and paddle through. It was the environment itself, through its unpredictability, infinite variety and constant flux that brought me to understand the permanence of change, the idea that everything and everyone will transform. I learned to accept that this life, this moment, this pain and this joy are fleeting. What is important is to navigate life with goodness.

Most importantly, his passing brought me to look in on myself, to qualify who I am and understand what it is to be good, to live with goodness, in the dozens of cultures I travelled through. Goodness, I understand now, is universal.

My tears dried. Darkness was all around. Where to go? I stood, remembering the night I had learned of my brother's death and had walked alone in the dark rain to Elk Lake, a first small, confused pilgrimage – a walk of dreams, of hope, hoping that maybe it was all unreal, that when I reached the lake Gareth would stride out of the water, intact, dripping like an ocean swimmer. But at the edge of Elk Lake all there was was darkness and wind and the clicking rustle of conifers swaying and rolling, wailing like a line of invisible mourners. At the edge of a stony beach was the water – black, depthless, forbidding. It had my brother and was not about to give him back.

I went to the edge of the infant Ganga. I sat back on my haunches and leaned over. River stones glinted in the moonlight.

I scooped a handful of water, so cold my fingers burned, and drank it. The water was in me.

November 10

I woke the next morning tired and shaky. It had been a hard uphill walk the day before. I had camped on a shaly flat just a few metres above the river's source. I was torn as to whether I should spend more time at the glacier or move on. I decided to walk. I had been given something timeless, and as at Tabo I didn't want to spoil it by trapping it in comparisons. I packed in the cool, icy air and headed downstream.

The sun was out. Small golden birds flitted around me like blowing sparks. A scarlet monarch butterfly, the same colour as my backpack, landed on my arm, billowing its wings to evaporate the morning's dew. The day warmed quickly, and soon I had stripped down to my T-shirt.

I stopped in a grove of chir trees past Bhujbasa and was quietly taking some notes when I looked up. There, three metres away, was a naked man, thin as a stick, with hair that looked like a tattered spray of twigs and wide, piercing eyes. I jumped and let out a scream. The man did a jerky two-stepped dance and chortled hilariously. His laughter brought me back to earth. On a second look I saw he was not naked but wore the skimpiest of loincloths, a rag that barely covered his genitals. He stopped his crazy dance and put one leg up on a boulder, completely exposing his organ, drew a flashing, white-toothed smile across his face and said in English,

"I am Vashisht. You like chillom, my friend?"

A chillom is the hashish pipe used by Shaivite saddhus. In this situation, I decided, it was a good idea.

Vashisht retrieved the needed items from an intricately embroidered lunch box-size bag he carried on his shoulder. He packed a dense ball of black hash into the straight, terra cotta pipe. He held the cylinder, which was a little thinner than a hotdog bun, vertically with both hands wrapped around the tube and lit it by sucking hard while holding a lighter to the hash. It smoldered and he raised the pipe to the heavens offering the first hit to Lord Shiva. He drew deeply and exhaled the smoke upwards shouting, "Bom, Shiva." Then he sucked hard on the chillom himself and passed it with both hands and an air of respect to me. Vashisht demonstrated the proper way to grip the pipe, explaining the significance of the hand gestures, then showed me how to offer the first taste to Shiva, the Lord of the smoke, and eventually how to draw on the chillom myself. I inhaled and coughed most of it back out.

We talked for an hour. He spoke good English in the Indian way, unusual for a saddhu. He was in his late-twenties; five years before, while still at college in the city of Allahabad, he made the conscious decision to become an ascetic. He had become disillusioned with what he called "family life," the interminable circle of wants, desires and money. What he craved, he said, was an "eternally satisfying experience" and so Vashisht renounced his past, gave himself to the spiritual undercurrent of India, and had been initiated as a saddhu.

He was a gentle man with an acute awareness of the world around him. He was a mine of information on the mythical geography of the Dev Bhoomi; he claimed to have witnessed precious stones self-generating into images of gods and he knew of sacred caves and flying saints. He talked about the animals of the area – bear, tiger, leopard, bharal deer – and of his ability to communicate with them. He talked of the elusive musk deer, whose scent sack is the most expensive commodity in the world. The power of the musk, said Vashisht, is derived from a plant the animal enjoys that grows on glaciers. Its roots hold a poisonous snake, the deer absorbs the poison when it eats the plant and its scent sack takes on that potency. He told me he had mixed the oil of the deer in the hashish we were smoking; as he said, we were "joining with the deer."

Vashisht was a practitioner of raja yoga, Hinduism's "royal road to God," the most complex and esoteric of the yogas. Through a series of physical and mental exercises, raja yoga exposes the layers of the self for what they are – ego – and eventually brings the practitioner into contact with a core, non-dual transcendental body that Hindus believe is one with the primordial god Brahman. When you achieve this state, you achieve moksha or liberation.

Vashisht was a captivating storyteller and I could have talked for days, but in the middle of what I thought was a great conversation he stood up, said goodbye, and ran off down the trail.

I was high from the hashish and didn't grasp that he had gone until he was far down the trail. Lethargically, I put on my pack and began walking. A few minutes later I glanced left and saw Vashisht on a moraine field two hundred metres away across the valley. He was barefoot and leaping from boulder to boulder, making his way up to the glacier. He was singing a high-pitched devotional song to Shiva. Ten metres behind him were three full-grown bharal deer.

Late in the afternoon I arrived back in Gangotri and went to the head of the gorge west of the village. From near the temple the river has carved a series of pale granite cataracts, and the water pounds through the tight walls. The stone is sculpted into chambers, pools and caves in organic, flowing forms. It looks as if solid rock is conforming to the goddess's touch. Deep in the gorge three of the chambers are named – Bhrahmkund, Gaurikund, and Vishnukund – and in the winter, with the river's reduced flow, it is said you can see self-generating Shiva lingams in the grottoes. I sat on the edge of the falls and stared and stared, wishing for a glimpse of the phallic stones, but it was not meant to be.

That night at Gangotri, over supper with some saddhus who had invited me to their rooms, I was told the full story of the kidnappers I had seen under guard in the temple courtyard. They had now been arrested and taken by the police to Uttarkashi. The teenage abductors had an accomplice, none other than the victim himself. The boy they had taken had planned the job. He had suggested to his friends they kidnap him, split the ransom four ways and head for Delhi. The plot became even stranger when they arrived in Gangotri as they thought they could steal money from the saddhus who, they presumed, were defenseless and had mattresses full of cash from the donations they received during pilgrim season. Even more ludicrous was their admitted intention to climb the technical ice route up past the Bhagriath glacier to the Tapovan meadows and steal money from the famous cave-dwelling saint Mata-ji.

Their plans were ridiculously flawed. The Gangotri babas have no money because they give everything to their temple committees. The sad result was some rattled holy men, confused parents and cowering boys. Worse, though, was that those petty criminals had even considered stealing from the saddhus. Like the icon thieves of Zanskar and Baltistan they had no respect for their past and no clear concept of the future.

Vashisht, who was on his way up the glacier to inquire about Mata-ji when I had seen him, had some interesting opinions on the teenagers' motivation: "Those boys were rats, sewer rats, but even worse, sewer rats who watch too much television!"

CHAPTER 10
Skirmishes

November 11

I left Gangotri and walked fifteen kilometres back down the Bhagriath River to near Harsil before hitching a ride and retracing the route I had ascended to the village of Malla, twenty-five kilometres north of Uttarkashi. There the traditional pilgrimage route cuts east over a set of high ridges to Kedarnath, Lord Shiva's Himalayan residence.

From Malla, I worked up the pristine Sauri-gad Creek to Belak village. In that valley, for the first time in India, I was shocked by the amount of wildlife. Lower down by the Bhagriath, rhesus monkeys howled and leaped from tree to tree and graceful langur, snow monkeys, stared at me from cedar branches higher up the path. Near Malla dense ringal bamboo stands obscured the view, but I could hear the call of barbets and the tap of a green-backed woodpecker. A brilliant blue verditer fly-catcher glided past and landed on a branch five metres away, silently stared, then dropped from its perch and was gone.

Skirmishes

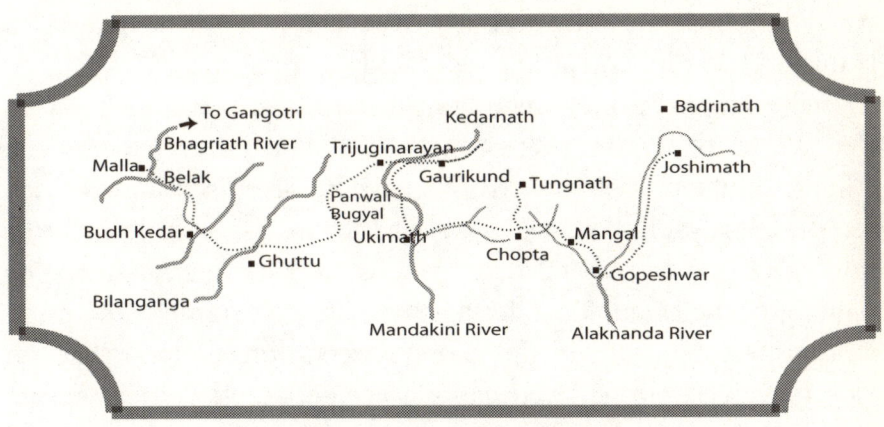

GARWAHL, UTTARAKHAND, INDIA

At one point a great rustling in the underbrush stopped me. I stared at the sound, muscles tensed, waiting for a leopard or bear, but from the thicket burst a Monal pheasant, its metallic purple, blue and bronze-green plumage shimmering. *Cooor ... lew*, it called as loud as it could when it saw me, and exploded in a flash of wings and legs. With groves of maple and tun trees shedding leaves, the ground was thick in rust, yellow, and red. Banj oaks, chinar and horse chestnut gave way farther up to pines and cedars, listing in the hilltop breeze. The Central Himalayas are more temperate than the west and winter comes later. The damp aroma of decomposing matter signalled season's change. In four hours I had moved from a subtropical jungle to a sub-boreal forest.

This trail was the main route between Gangotri and Kedarnath before roads penetrated the Garwahl in the '60s. In the Indo-Chinese war of 1962, when India was embarrassingly defeated and had to concede 15,000 square miles of eastern Ladakh to Beijing, one of the biggest defensive problems was that almost no roads penetrated the Himalayas. The government was compelled to designate all borderland with Tibet as a restricted area and the military was charged with creating a transportation infrastructure as quickly as possible.

The Chota Char Dham pilgrim trail is the antithesis to that burst of engineering activity. The path has experienced a millennium of religious travellers. The area is studded with temples, wayside shrines and dharamsalas, or pilgrim rest houses. Along the way I came across trees covered with coins nailed to their trunks, offerings to the earth spirits. I found stones peaking out of the mossy green forest floor that on closer inspection displayed carvings of gods and deities. Across from one ancient deodar cedar tree, shards of faded scarlet and gold cloth, the same that is used to wrap bodies about to be cremated, fluttered in the breeze. Hinduism is everywhere in the landscape, so you feel that maybe the route has absorbed some essence of the pilgrim spirit.

That night I fell asleep without setting up my tent. The trees were rustled by a wind but the greatest noise was my stove, chugging away as the sun set behind a ridge to the west. As I lay in my sleeping bag, clouds scudded across the moon. In a tree nearby I heard the hooting of an owl, a call echoed in the distance by the whoop of restless snow monkeys.

November 12

From Belak it is a gentle descent to Budh Kedar, the most important religious site between Gangotri and Kedarnath. The centrepiece of the village is a temple dedicated to Shiva. In the chai shop next to the shrine I met one of the priests. He sat, straight-backed in his faded saffron robes. His ears were pierced through the cartilage and hung with thick copper earrings. His face shone with a light application of coconut oil and his cheeks were scarred by some childhood disease, a light puckering that was enhanced by the shine the oil left on his skin. He sipped his tea noisily, looking every part the local king.

In Hindi I asked him about Budh Kedar as it is the source of some conflict for Shaivites. Some Hindus believe Lord Shiva's primary Himalayan manifestation occurred here while others accept Kedarnath as the location. A temple village's reputation hinges on the perceived legitimacy of the god's emanation, and the classification of such subjective events involves an element of politics.

Hinduism, as with all religions, is no stranger to politics. With a profusion of schools and paths within the faith there is bound to be conflict; witness the many orthodox Hindu groups associated with India's national political party, the Bharatiya Janata Party, and the blatantly fundamentalist Hindu policies of the Shiv Sena, or Army of Shiva, whose political wing controls Mumbai. Hinduism is an inclusive religion, but at its core are writings, legends and personalities open to interpretation.

With this in mind I expected the pujari to wax eloquently about the true right of Budh Kedar to be the emanation site of Shiva, but instead he took another slow sip of tea, looked at me and said in perfect English, "My friend, when you are as omnipotent as the Lord you can manifest in infinite forms and infinite locations simultaneously. What is the difference between Kedarnath and Budh Kedar?"

I stayed that night in a small government guest house near the temple. I was the only guest and the caretaker was kind enough to take me in and share his evening meal.

November 13

In the morning on a forested trail between Budh Kedar and Ghuttu, I stopped many times to let groups of five or six women pass me by. They were heading for the hills to collect grass, leaves, and sticks. Over their shoulders hung large wicker baskets. In some I saw calico cloth parcels containing the lentil-filled chapatis they ate for lunch. They chattered noisily, moving lightly almost as if they were gliding – although maybe that had as much to do with the fact I felt sluggish, burdened with my twenty-kilogram pack and tattered boots. The women all wore brightly printed saris and bustiers. When I saw the groups farther up the slope they looked to be flashes of colour floating through the vertical frame of the cedars and pines. Occasionally they would stop, stare at me, and ask abrupt questions in Pahari dialect. When I gestured that I didn't understand they would laugh, skip away and continue their chattering.

In the afternoon I climbed from Ghuttu village to Panwali and there I made way for similar groups returning home downhill. Now they were fully loaded with bales of hay or jagged baskets of firewood. Some of the women were so beautiful they stopped me in my tracks. But they ignored me. I did not exist in their reality of work and family. When they were not talking they were singing. Their songs were, I think, not just to keep the bears away, but to be happy.

> *We are Garwahli, this is our Garwahl.*
> *These mountains are ours.*
> *This is our land of birth.*
> *Our home, our family.*
> *Our lush green fields have abundant grain.*
> *The sounds of our bangles,*
> *The sound of the sickle cutting grain,*
> *creates music, resounding in the hill side.*
> *This is Gandhiji's beloved land.*
> *He spun yarn on a Charkha,*
> *and gave us a message for our lives.*
> (Translation Anjali Capila)

A simple life of duty and devotion, this is the essence of karma yoga, the "way to God through work." The archetypal

Indian wife and mother toils to feed her family, to keep them clothed, to keep them happy. Through their work, subconsciously, the Garwahli women are connected with the eternal, for their daily labours are karma yoga – loving service beyond the self.

A line of the *Bhagavad Gita*, the ancient Hindu text based around a moral conversation between the God Krishna and the warrior prince Arjuna, summed up how I felt about those women.

> *who does the task*
> *dictated by duty*
> *caring nothing*
> *for the fruit of the action*
> *is a yogi*

But the karma yoga of motherhood is universal. I think of my own mother, of what she had given up to raise me and my brothers and sister. Now that I am a parent myself I can understand it better. I think of the aching pain of worry I must have caused her over the years. Would I encourage my two boys to go on a four-month solo trek through the Himalayas? Maybe I would, but I would be anxious the whole time they were away. I think of all the crazy careless things I have done over the years and I realize that a parent, and especially a mother, can never not think about her children. The quietude with which my mother bears my peripatetic existence and the eagerness with which she inquires about my new discoveries is inspirational. I know that losing Gareth was much more for her than I can ever imagine. She had brought him into this life. To realize that he was gone had shattered her. I know she can never fully accept the loss, and yet there are times when she seems to have found some peace. Maybe that state is a result of time or age, but it implies there is much to learn from the gurus who bear us.

November 14

Panwali was a five-hour climb from where I camped, but it was a steady grade, a trail that cuts long switchbacking lines across the open slope. The hillside's grass was sheered to stubble by the summertime migration of goats and sheep. Thousands of hoofprints dotted the slope, and in areas where the grass had disappeared and raw earth was exposed the marks looked to be some kind of vast cuneiform symbol.

Four hours of steady climbing without sight of humans or animals and I was deep into the meditation of walking. One foot at a time, one step ahead, gradually, ever so slowly, reaching for the ridge's horizon. For minutes I would consciously not look up, knowing that the ascent was too long and gradual to measure other than step by step. Instead, I would focus on my feet, the perpetual swing of leg and foot upwards and onwards. I could see my boots were suffering from the kilometres, the leather frayed, the hard rubber soles worn smooth by the days and weeks of constant movement. Yet I felt strong, my muscles loose, no aches or pains to interrupt the flow of motion. Occasionally I would look up, see the ridge and know that, slowly, slowly I was moving to where I wanted to be.

It was a long climb made longer by the lack of water. I had lunch beside the only trickle of a stream on the ascent. In a hollow by the spring, out of the wind, a rhododendron bush grew, its glossy emerald and burgundy leaves reflecting the sun. In the grassy bowl below it a pool of water sparkled.

I began the rituals of unpacking: cleaning my knife, starting the stove – pumping, lighting, placing the pot – spreading cold, hard butter on old chapatis, dipping tea bags, scooping milk powder. There was simplicity and focus. The minimalism of the steps had worked into everything. I was satisfied listening to the rumble of my well-burning kerosene stove.

I drank my tea and began repacking, inverse rituals, and as I did so a pair of lavender butterflies undulated around me as they would around a cluster of flowers. They circled me, a spiral of colour – not floating, not really flying – just a body of erratic wings, kissing my cheeks and forearms. I looked at the spring and saw spiralling eddies, the water rolling behind stones, circling in on itself and disappearing. I looked up. Two crows were caught in an updraft, moving higher together, corkscrewing on an invisible axis, ascending effortlessly. Behind them, even farther up, was a single wispy cloud in a cobalt sky – white, vaporous – and as I watched, it too, almost imperceptibly, spiralled in on itself.

My bag was packed. I stood and tossed my rucksack up and around and between my shoulders, and started walking.

I felt my footfalls, like a metronome, a solid pattern. My breathing was in time with the steps, arms swinging loose, blood circulating. Breath and blood coursing into my lungs, meeting, merging and retreating. I walked and thought of the boiling tea, the butterflies, the water, the birds, the clouds, blood, breath.

Tat Tvam As. Thou art that.

At the end of the climb the ridgetop meadow stretched for miles to the north. The hill crest intersected with a horizon crowded with summits stretching from west to east as far as I could see. From Gangotri's Bhagriath Parbat on my right to Nanda Devi, the second highest peak in India, on the left, the skyline was an infinitely broken line of rock and ice and snow. Between the clouds, the folds of rock, the hanging glaciers and the dark stone chimneys the sun was playing shadow games on the mountains' faces. From my position twenty-five kilometres south, it looked as if the mountains themselves were moving.

Maybe it was the exertion of the climb, or the lack of water or maybe it was just the joy I felt in my everyday movement, but I was transfixed by what lay ahead. It was a wilderness of rock and light – untamed, solemn, something demanding respect but also subtly alarming.

In the *Upanishads*, the Hindu scriptures written almost three thousand years ago, there is a line that talks about the power of the Himalayas: "One glimpse is enough to grant freedom."

November 15

In the morning I continued along the Panwali ridge and from its northeastern edge dropped down towards Trijuginarayan and the Mandakini Valley. The trail was in shadow most of the way. The air was cool. Patches of snow caught in dark clefts between poplar and sal trees. There was the rich decomposing smell of humus about the place and layers of fallen leaves and withered grass lay by the trailside.

According to legend, Trijuginarayan was the capital of King Himvat, the lord of the snows, and is revered as the site of Lord Shiva's marriage to the king's daughter, Parvati. Parvati means daughter of the mountains in Sanskrit and she is considered by many Hindus as the personification of Shakti, female energy. It was astrologically predicted early in her life she would wed Lord Shiva. Shiva was at that time in deep retreat on Mount Kailash and Parvati set herself on a course of extreme religious devotion so as to impress the god she wanted to marry.

Kalidasa, the great Hindu poet of two thosand years ago, wrote the definitive interpretation of Shiva and Parvati's marriage. Arthur Ryder, one of Kalidasa's first English translators, described Parvati's penance in these words in 1912.

"She [Parvati] therefore resolves to lead a life of religious self-denial, hoping that the merit thus acquired will procure her Shiva's love. Her mother tries in vain to dissuade her; her father directs her to a fit mountain peak, and she retires to her devotions. She lays aside all ornaments, lets her hair hang unkempt, and assumes the hermit's dress of bark. While she is spending her days in self-denial, she is visited by a Brahman [high caste Hindu] youth, who compliments her highly upon her rigid devotion, and declares that her conduct proves the truth of the proverb: Beauty can do no wrong. Yet he confesses himself bewildered, for she seems to have everything that a heart can desire. He therefore asks her purpose in performing these austerities, and is told how her desires are fixed upon the highest of all objects, upon the god Shiva himself ... In response to this eloquence, the youth throws off his disguise, appearing as the god Shiva and declares his love for her."

The Trijuginarayan temple is a relatively small square building. Inside the entrance was a courtyard, twenty metres by twenty metres surrounded by a three-metre-high wall. The walls and temple were of grey stone while the roof and floor were laid in dark slate. In the middle of the courtyard, before the small temple, a fire burned. Pilgrims to the temple traditionally bring wood to feed the fire and those ashes are purported to insure a happy marriage. Fire and water are the purest elements in Hinduism. According to the Rig Veda, the earliest and most important of the Hindu sacred writings, Agni, the sacred flame, arises from the water. Even today the most important part of a Hindu wedding are the four circumambulations the bride and bridegroom make around a sacred fire while reciting mantras and making offerings. Agni is the most auspicious witness to any of life's great ceremonies.

The courtyard was cool but the walls kept at bay a brisk wind funnelling down from the northwest. Inside the open front door of the temple I could see the saffron robes of a priest, but I had no desire to meet him. I was satisfied just being by the fire. Over the top of the temple, past the brass spire that crowned its roof, I could see snow peaks. From far below the village I could hear the rushing Mandakini River. Trijuginarayan is felt to be at the centre of Hindusim's five elements – earth, wind, fire, water and, with the place's overwhelming sense of myth and mystery, ether.

The Mandakini is the Himalayan river most associated with Lord Shiva. Its upper banks are dotted with temples and shrines commemorating his infinite appearances in the area. The most significant of these is Kedarnath at 3,600 metres, close to the river's source. It lies in a steep valley nestled between the Dudhganga and Bisall glaciers. According to legend, the significance of the site goes back to the time of *The Mahabharata*.

The Mahabharata, one of the major Sanskrit epic poems, is a discussion of Hinduism's four human goals – wealth, pleasure, duty and liberation – set within the context of a dynastic struggle between two branches of a royal family, the Pandavas and the Kauravas. The rivalry culminated with the battle at Kurukshetra where the Pandavas killed their brothers the Kauravas. The Pandavas felt guilty about this and went in search of Lord Shiva to seek his redemption. However, Lord Shiva eluded them and took refuge in his Himalayan home, Kedarnath, in the form of a bull. The Pandavas pursued him and on being found, he dived into the ground, leaving only his hump on the surface. His remaining parts appeared at four different locations in the area: his arms at Tungnath, face at Rudranath, belly at Madhmeshwar and hair at Kalpeshwar. These four shrines along with Kedarnath are the Panch Kedars, the five places of Shiva.

In the eighth century, Adi Shankaracharya came to the area and claimed the headwaters of the Mandakini River as the earthly location of the legend and there he built the present-day temple.

I was excited to visit a place where so many interconnected legends merge, but on this trip fate would interfere with my pilgrimage. About two-thirds of the way up the fifteen-kilometre trail from the village of Gaurikund to the main temple, I was stopped by a group of three dishevelled-looking policemen. They informed me the area was off limits for winter.

I was more than a little surprised and asked how they could close a site that was sacred to 900 million people. The shrine was within sight; I could see the cluster of buildings and the bulbous granite three-storey tower above the Shiva temple. To be told I was not allowed to reach one of my major goals was beyond frustrating. In Hindi I let loose with a barrage of questions, one of which was why one of the most sacred shrines in Hinduism was closed to pilgrims.

The policeman in charge had a scraggly beard and his black woolen watch cap was pulled down close over his eyes. He looked at me and gave an answer memorized from a Hindi film: "Sorry, sir. It is Top Secret!"

I was dumbfounded. What could be top secret about a holy site venerated by twenty percent of the world's population? My mouth dropped open.

I know now the shrines at Kedarnath and Badrinath are closed from late October until May to insure the safety of the pilgrims, but it still strikes me as strange, in a land where saddhus walk naked up glaciers, that a well-outfitted, much experienced trekker should be told to turn around on a sunny day five kilometres from the temple.

I tramped back the way I had come, muttering profanities under my breath. I camped on the banks of the Mandakini not far from Gaurikund and in that foul mood the river was my solace. After a dinner of rice and dal I sat on its banks, sipping tea and listening to the water rush by. To be frustrated with my turn around was only natural; to fight it in the complexity of India was insane. Realizing this helped evaporate my anger. There was no need to be upset by things beyond my control.

November 16

I moved south on the Mandakini River and stopped early at the town of Ukimath. The strip of concrete shops along the road was closed, which seemed strange since it was already late in the morning, so I found a guest house and took a dark and rather dingy room. I was tired, still a little frustrated from the day before and decided to take a nap. An hour or so later I was snatched from my sleep by the sound of distant waves. In a place so far from the sea it was a dreamy arousal. It was coming from outside. I threw on my clothes and staggered out into a bright but overcast day. There, by the line of shops in the town centre, close to a hundred men had assembled, shouting, waving banners and throwing their fists in the air. I went back inside. I had learned from years in India to steer clear of anything that resembled a demonstration; I have seen protests transform into riots in a matter of seconds.

I asked the guest house proprietor about the rally. He explained that recently two Garwahli activists had been found dead near the town of Srinagar in the southern part of the district. They had been on a hunger strike in support of the creation of Uttarakhand, a separate mountain state sliced from the larger entity of Uttar Pradesh state. Weeks before the police had taken the men, in their starved condition, into custody. The pair were never heard from again. A few days previous their bodies had been found, washed up on the banks of Alaknanda River. Police said foul play was suspected. The Garwahli separatists were furious and called for an immediate general strike. That day shops and government offices were shut and all public transport halted.

After lunch in the kitchen of the guest house I ventured back outside. The rally had subsided and the assembly had shifted to the chai shops. I went in search of tea and in a grimy dhaba just off the main street I sat in the only available seat at a table with three men poring over a newspaper they had sectioned up between themselves. They eyed me suspiciously. I smiled at them and they smiled back. My tea came and after a few calming sips I asked their opinion on the situation. In reply I got a short lecture from each of them. But their speeches were too excited and I lost track of their thoughts in the mix of too-fast Hindi, Pahari dialect and hot emotion. I bought us all another round of tea and biscuits and the group cooled down.

Prasad Singh, a student in his twenties with a well-trimmed moustache, clear dark skin and ears that seemed too large for his head, was the most literate of the group. I asked him to go through again what the demonstration was all about. He said, "For years we Garwahlis have been slaves for people on the plains. We were the ones they would import to do the dirty work and we would diligently send our paychecks home ... All we want is control over our land. We want a Garwahl administered by Garwahlis."

It seemed a strange fight in a way. Two men had died, possibly from police brutality, maybe from their own hunger strike, over the splitting of a state. It was not that Uttarakhandis were agitating to join China or Pakistan; it would still be part of India. Prasad Singh and his friends were ardent in their conviction that they would not stop fighting until Uttarakhand was free. I asked if they were nationalistic Indians. Narsingh, one of the other students, piped up, "I love my India. Absolutely!" Then I asked why they were fighting other Indians. Prasad looked at me sideways and turned the question back to me. "Mr. Lineen, I believe that some people in your country Canada have a different language and also want to have their own country?" I obviously had no sense of the intensity of the feelings around the table.

After returning to the guest house and reading for an hour or so I went outside again. It was late afternoon. Shuttered businesses had been painted with slogans, and leaflets printed on cheap paper fluttered in the breeze and lay in the puddles at the edges of the road. The sun was setting and the bronze hills to the north of town were framed by glowing snow peaks. Down the road towards me a bus swayed, loaded to bursting with cheering young men. On its roof rack people stood, precariously balanced, waving red and silver banners. The bus roared through the village. As the protesters passed the chai shops the patrons spilled onto the street. A wave of encouraging cheers greeted the bus, but it didn't stop or even slow down. The movement disappeared in a blare of horns and Hindi music.

As I write this now I can report that in November 2000 the state of Uttaranchal, later to be renamed Uttarakhand, was formed out of the mountainous 50,000-square-kilometre northwestern corner of Uttar Pradesh. Thirty-one people died in the struggle for statehood.

November 17

The road climbs from Ukimath to Chopta. It's a pleasant grade, not enough to make vehicles drop to first gear but just right for the body to find an agreeable tempo. About halfway up I came across an old bridle path, a stone-paved trail probably part of the old pilgrim route. Moss framed each cobble, and bracken ferns leaned in from its borders. I left the asphalt and entered the trees – banj oaks, cassia, tun and maple. Once again autumn leaves crackled underfoot. The path moved into meadows then back to forest. Abandoned buildings appeared by the wayside, refuge for summer herders and shelter for foot-bound pilgrims. But summer was over, yatra season had passed and the wind blew through their open doorways.

By two o'clock I'd reached the village of Chopta. From there the road moves east from the Mandakini into the Alaknanda River watershed while north from the village a foot trail continues up to the Saivite temple of Tungnath at 3,700 metres. Tungnath is one of the Panch Kedar sanctuaries. Here, according to *The Mahabharata*, Lord Shiva's arms appeared while the Pandava brothers searched for him in Kedarnath.

The trail moved out of deodar cedars and into high altitude meadows. It was a steep climb on a dirt track that, like the ascent up to Panwali, was a series of long, even switchbacks.

Tungnath temple is built into a natural amphitheatre. It is a smaller version of the Kedarnath temple, a Spartan, uninhabited, three-storey tower of rock and slate. It fit well with the stony cliff to its right, the lines of the tower gathered into the contours of the earth. On the outer edge of the amphitheatre the land climbed a little further and then dropped away in a sheer cliff.

On the way up, close to the temple, I was caught by a British man, Mike Asola, a tall, thin fellow with deep lines on his forehead and amiable crow's feet around his eyes. He was on a solo cycling marathon from Srinagar in Kashmir to Assam in the far northeast of India. It was peculiar to meet a kindred spirit in such a remote place. He was the first Westerner I'd met in over two weeks.

We talked, admired the temple and climbed another two kilometres above the shrine to the peak of Chandrasila, the mountain of the moon. We stopped only momentarily on the frigid summit. A wind was pushing south from the high Himalayas and the temperature on the peak was well below zero. Returning to the temple we sat out of the breeze in its little courtyard and from there we gazed over the foothills to the south.

As evening wore on, the light became more angular and each ridge farther back took on a lighter shade of grey, blue, or green, until the land dissolved into the sky. Thin clouds ran parallel to the horizon and as the sun set they absorbed the last rays of light and formed a golden strata echoing the hills' layered earth tones. We sat quietly watching the play of light and out of the silence Mike uttered something that Shankaracharya could have said 1,200 years ago: "It's easy to believe in God in a place like this."

Mike did not have the gear to stay the night. I offered to let him share my tent, but he was worried about his bike and had no sleeping bag. So we had a quick cup of tea and some biscuits and he headed back to Chopta by the light of his torch. I watched him walk down the slope, a wavering beam moving farther and farther away through the darkness. I pitched my tent on the edge of the cliff. We had spent as long as possible watching the sky and in the dark it was the only flat spot I could find. The thought that three metres away birds were hovering on the precipice's updraft brought sleep on in a mild rush.

November 18

In the morning it was all downhill, so what had taken me a long day to climb was reversed in four hours. At lunch I was in Mangal, a pleasant village with orange trees full of fruit and a winter wheat crop green in the fields. When I had awoken that morning at Tungnath the water left overnight in my cooking pot was frozen solid.

At the little café I ate rice and lentils in the company of Neemchand Narayan. He wore apricot-coloured robes, a heavy wool blanket was neatly folded beneath him and a khaki rucksack lay off to one side. He had long unkempt hair and a thick beard, both peppered in grey. His demeanour was quiet and confident.

When I entered he looked up from his tea and asked in good English how I had enjoyed Tungnath. How did he know where I had been? I asked him and he said, "Well, you're coming from that direction, you're on foot, you're alone – so I assume you must be on yatra." He smiled and invited me to join him for lunch.

Neemchand was incredibly chatty. He was in his early sixties and described himself as a sunnyasin rather than a saddhu, although he had been a wandering ascetic for fourteen years. He explained how he had progressed through Hinduism's four phases of life and in the fourth phase had become a renunciate or sunnyasin. Traditionally, devotees follow the four stages of Brahmacarya, the period of education and discipline; Garhasthya, the time of family and work; Vanasprasthya, a period of retreat to bring oneself closer to the spiritual life; and finally, Sunnyasa, the time of the ascetic.

Previously Neemchand had been a sergeant in the army. It was there that he had learned his English. He had also been a family man with a wife and three children, but said he had gradually turned to the spiritual life because of "discoveries" made in his yoga, the prayers and meditations he undertook every day. With those revelations pushing him on Neemchand had progressed to the third phase, the initial stage of devoting your life to Hinduism.

As a sunnyasin Neemchand was removed but moving through this world. He described his youth and education as fruitful, his family life rewarding and with his army pension his wife and children were financially secure. In the third stage he had studied with a pundit, or teacher, and meditated in a cave near Gangotri. Now in the final period of his life he drifted from pilgrimage site to pilgrimage site, getting, as he said, "close to God."

When I asked him if he missed his wife and family, he replied, "My head is so full of Shankar that I don't think about it. Fourteen years is a long time."

I inquired if there was anything he missed from his previous life; he raised his eyes to the rough concrete ceiling, then looked directly at me and answered, "No."

After lunch I continued another eight kilometres down the valley to Gopeshwar. The town is the headquarters of Chamoli district and like most of the mountain district headquarters I had visited it appeared poorly planned. Houses on the far edge of town looked to be sliding down the slope to the Alaknanda River. The hillside was cloaked in cement boxes. I went in search of a guest house. There was nothing encouraging about the room I found: more unpainted concrete walls latticed with spiderwebbed cracks. A window that wouldn't close properly and a dog in a nearby side street that howled and howled. I had a meal and went to bed.

November 19

Gopeshwar had no hold on me. I was gone before dawn, tramping down narrow brick lanes onto the road, across the Alaknanda River and through Chamoli town on the other bank. I followed the river north towards the town of Joshimath, the gateway to Badrinath, the fourth site of the Chota Char Dham Yatra. Badrinath is the Himalayan abode of Lord Vishnu. Where Shiva represents the power of destruction and Brahma encompasses the power of creation, Vishnu embodies the continuation of life. He has many emanations, from Krishna, the personification of male love, to Ram, the prototypical hero of the *Ramayana* epic. The Buddha is considered an avatar of Vishnu and so too is the deposed King of Nepal.

It was forty kilometres to Joshimath and it was a dull route. The road is carved out of the hillside far above the river. The drone of transport trucks battling their way up the valley outdid the call of the water. I tried to switch off the external world and focus on walking. I was moving quickly, swinging my arms, letting old pop songs dart though my head, happy in my motion-filled world, but then the chaos of India pulled me back.

Just after the village of Biri I stopped for a sip of water and caught the interest of a dozen boys playing cricket in a stubbly field. They hopped over a low stone wall and ran to the road, gathered round me in a tight circle and stared intensely at me. I smiled, finished my drink and stood to go.

A bigger boy, with the start of a moustache darkening his top lip and acne dotting his cheeks, stood with a cricket bat on the edge of their circle hitting rocks in my direction. I put my water bottle back in its container and swung my pack up and onto my back but the boy stepped into my path and blocked the way. He grabbed my forearm and said, "Five rupees!"

I stared at him. I felt a tingle on the back of my neck and replied, "Begging is bad!"

Immediately I felt a fool for saying that. With their limited grasp of English they wouldn't have understood what I had said and begging, I think, wasn't his real purpose; he only wanted a reaction out of me.

The older boy's face broke into a huge grin. It was as if I had spoken for his entertainment alone. The huddle of boys started to buzz, and they all began chanting, "Five rupees, five rupees," like some kind of mantra.

I pushed past them. The group had no idea what I was talking about, but my reaction had encouraged them. I was a white-faced colonial, the sort of character in Hindi films who always loses. I realized my mistake. I was playing their game. The kids upped the volume. Now they were screaming, *"Five rupees! Five rupees!"*

To them, it was the mantra that made me say things so the logic was, the louder they shouted the more I would say. Extra kids from the village joined the crowd. I was surrounded by two dozen boys jumping up and down, working themselves into a frenzy. It was a miniature exaggeration of the demonstration in Ukimath three days before. I strode off, a dozen boys in tow.

I thought they would grow tired and disappear back into the fields, but in retrospect I was much more amusing than a game of pick-up cricket. I was a strange white guy who had descended to their village to give a private performance. They wanted more. They jeered at me, shouting the insults their

Bollywood heroes spat at film villains: "Bahin chod," sister fucker; "Mata chod," motherfucker.

I ignored them and tried to walk faster. They slowed down but then replaced the words with stones. First they threw pebbles at my feet but then, when I ignored them, they grew hungry for more and began pitching rocks at my head. I had to do something or they would really hurt me. I couldn't chase them – they were faster. Shouting abuse was the cabaret they desired and if I went back to the village I could do nothing without their names. There was only one choice: give them what they wanted – my death, the death of the Bollywood bad guy. I waited for another stone to whiz by my ear and dropped hard to the ground, hands loose, my head lolling to one side, my pack driving into the back of my head.

From my prone position I looked back through half-open eyes and saw the gang leaping up and down as if they had just won the World Cup. I lay still. The young hoodlums stopped their celebrations and stared. Thirty seconds, a minute passed. They talked amongst themselves in sharp, whispered sentences. They stared again, their eyes now the size of saucers. Then the biggest boy, the troublemaker with the cricket bat, shouted three quick words and the group sprinted up the road away from me. The verdict was out; they had murdered a movie star, and the punishment for such a crime would not be worth waiting around for.

I lay another minute then got up, dirty and frustrated. I started walking again, the anger coursing through me like hot steam. Yes, I was angry, not for what they had done to me physically but more for how they had spoiled the months of generosity and kindness from everyone I'd met. I was annoyed with their breaking the spell that had been cast over my time in the mountains.

I was walking fast. I didn't stop for lunch, I just kept walking, moving steadily, putting distance between myself and the whole embarrassing situation. Unconsciously I was channelling the anger into my legs, and the consistency of the movement was a way for the heat of memory to dissipate. I was working the futility out. My feet thudded against the broken pavement. My breath worked in time with the footfalls. I could feel my pack swinging, evenly, on either side of my spine. Time moved with the steps. The blacktop ahead shimmered and in the distance faded to grey. After a few hours of almost running I stopped, thirsty. I drank deeply from my water bottle, the liquid spilling over my cheeks. I gasped for air. The trees on the slope above undulated in the breeze. The gravel underfoot crunched. Clouds scudded. I slipped my bottle back into its pocket and started walking again. I walked fast, the motion cleansing me. Walking is my yoga.

November 20

Joshimath is a steep town. The place seems to fall in layers to the Alaknanda River. It didn't look unsteady like Gopeshwar – it had more permanence about it – but it was still the kind of place where a bicycle would be of little use. I stayed in a guest house in the upper end of town. The building was the usual fractured concrete and rusting rebar, but the rooms led out onto a broad shared balcony that had a 180-degree panoramic view of the Himalayas to the north. In the morning I had tea and porridge at a rickety table while sitting on an unsteady chair. I counted the peaks to the north but lost track after thirty.

A young man came up the stairs from the office. This was strange as I knew I was the only guest in the hotel. He was a short, compact fellow with a broad moustache and a baseball hat that had Ski Auli printed on it. Auli is the ski area just above Joshimath. He walked with a slight limp and when he caught my eye he smiled unabashedly. He asked if he could sit at a free chair at the table and brought out a tattered map and a brown plastic book, the kind of cheap picture holder you get for free when you process photographic film in the developing world. He held out his hand and said, "My name is Bhim Thapa. I am wondering if you would like to go trekking."

My heart sank. The last thing I wanted while trying to take in such a memorable view was to be sold a trekking excursion. As politely as possible I told him that I would not be needing the services of a guide. The fellow was far from dissuaded. "Where are you going?" he asked with a smile on his face. I ignored him, although he was less than a metre away from me. Then he said, "I am only here to help."

Over the years in India I had become hardened to the salesmen of Delhi, Varanasi and Kolkata, but I was the only tourist in town and I felt sorry for him. I offered him tea. He took a cup and sat quietly. After a few sips he apologized for interrupting but said he had had little business that trekking season and two children to feed so he had to try. When I told him I had walked from Pakistan his eyes opened wide and he asked me, "Are you Pakistani?" I laughed and told him no but that I'd met some nice people there. He stood, left his business card on the table, excused himself and apologized again for disturbing my breakfast.

Joshimath's importance to Hinduism can once again be traced to Adi Shankaracharya. It was there that he founded the most northerly of his monasteries or maths. He established four monasteries, one in each of the cardinal directions within India, at Sringeri in the south, Dwarka in the west, Puri in the east and Joshimath to the north. The maths were established to insure the transmission of Adi Shankaracharya's Advaita Vedenta philosophy. This is the master's great contribution to Hindu thought; it is a summation of the doctrine of Advaita or non-dualistic reality, the idea that there is no differentiation between the individual, the world and God. The saint possibly surmised his philosophy best in a line from his *Viveka Chudamani* treatise, saying, "Brahman (God) is the only truth, the world is illusion, and there is ultimately no difference between Brahman and individual self."

I had dinner at a small, messy dhaba. The place was almost empty; two men were drinking chai and talking to a large man behind the desk. Behind them was a poster of Shiva and Parvati standing side by side in a mountain landscape. The white plastic chair I sat in swayed backwards when I put too much pressure against the backrest. The table had an arborite top with a pattern of intertwined cricket bats; cigarette burns and breaks in the laminate interrupted the design. I ordered vegetable curry and dal from the man behind the counter. He transferred the order by shouting it back to the kitchen. A few minutes later a small boy came out bearing a tray with the food. The big man indicated with a nod of his head where the food was going and the child placed the steaming bowls before me.

Soon after I started my meal an old man walked in. He had a flowing white beard and long silvery hair. He had on worn but clean sienna-coloured robes and slippers made of wood that clip-clopped across the concrete floor like horses' hooves. He gathered his robes before him and sat on a similarly shaky plastic seat at a table off to my right. The swami ordered his meal in Hindi. He ate his meal methodically, dabbing at the little piles of curried vegetables and dal delicately with his chapati. When he finished his meal, I plucked up the courage and asked him across the table if I could buy him tea. He nodded, and I inquired if he would mind if I asked him a few questions. He nodded rather gravely and answered in English, "My pleasure."

Swami Chindabaram was from Karnataka in the south. Swami in Hindi is an honourific title meaning master, as in master of religious understanding; it is bestowed on people who are considered Hindu teachers as opposed to renunciates like the saddhus. He told me there was a tradition of swamis from south India coming to Joshimath because Adi Shankaracharya was from Karanataka. I wanted to ask him about Hinduism but realized soon into our discussion that I understood so little about the religion that I couldn't phrase intelligent questions. The swami was used to a higher level of discussion. He was patient; it must have been like dealing with a child for him. Eventually, I felt the need to tell him of my confrontation with the kids from the day before.

I recounted the events, feeling my blood again begin to rise and when I had finished he wagged his head and said simply, "Boys!"

Then he asked if I had been hurt in the process. I shook my head and added, half-comically, "Only my ego," to which he broke out laughing. I took his good humour personally. "What's so funny?"

The pandit replied, "What is funny is the lesson you have received. I think you should be thanking those children, not berating them, for helping you to realize you possess this thing called ego that can be hurt without actually being touched."

Ego is a strange concept; when I was younger I thought of it as something that sports stars or TV personalities had an inordinate amount of. Having a big ego wasn't such a bad thing in a society that appreciates self-promotion. Either way I understood it as something integral to who I am.

Years later, after that discussion with the swami and some years of studying the basics of Buddhist philosophy, I grasped that what the swami was saying was the ego is not a core element of the self. It is the part of a human being that feels a need to fight for its place in the world, but it has no understanding of a deeper, more universal being that Adi Shankaracharya claimed is connected in a non-dual way with God and the universe.

I don't think if I had more of an understanding of the teacher's non-dual reality it would have stopped the kids from throwing stones at me, but I do think I wouldn't have held onto the thought that some injury had been done to me. Simply put, having a superficial understanding of those Buddhist and Hindu concepts has helped me move through life with less baggage, less resentment, less regrets.

At the time, though, I remember leaving the café with more questions than answers. Outside it was cold. There were mountains all around. They were solid things. After the mental gymnastics of trying to understand what the swami had to say, I remember thinking they were even more beautiful – great heaps of rock and ice that rewarded you for simply looking at them.

November 21

In the morning I dropped a thousand metres from Joshimath to the river. From there I wanted to climb not only the 2,400 metres to Badrinath but also to Hem Kund, a small alpine lake, ten kilometres east of Vishnu's shrine, sacred to the Sikh religion, but on the way up I came to a roadblock.

On the left side of the route a corrugated steel hut sat wobbling in the breeze. A delimbed birch pole painted in flaking red and white lay horizontally across the road. As at Kedarnath I found my progress barred by a policeman; he sauntered out from the shack holding a cup of tea in his hand. He was wearing what looked like three sweaters piled one on top of the other and a thick burgundy balaclava rolled down so it framed his face. He greeted me and seemed quite happy to have me there, but when I told him I wanted to get to Badrinath he apologized profusely and, holding his hands together in the gesture of prayer, said he could "not let that happen." The road to Badrinath was closed until May and the only person who could give me permission to continue on was the sub-district magistrate back in Joshimath.

I had almost expected this, but still had to ask why. The policeman, who was making an effort to be accommodating, replied, "Most sorry, sir, but it is very cold, extremely dangerous for the unqualified right now." I shrugged my shoulders. Clearly, the gods were working against me.

The guard was kind enough to tell me where in Joshimath I would find the sub-district magistrate who he emphasized again was "the only man authorized to qualify your ability to manage sub-zero temperatures."

I returned to town and went in search of the magistrate. His office was in a typical Indian government building, a square concrete block that looked to be weeping with monsoon residue. Inside, the place was shockingly quiet other than the roar of a kerosene stove blasting blue flame from a corner at the far end of the hall. There seemed to be no one at work except the man tending the stove's flame. He wore a towel wrapped turban-style around his head and half a cigarette dangled unlit from his lower lip. I asked where I could find the magistrate. He was pushing hard on the little stove's pressure pump. Without saying anything he pointed down the hall. I thanked him and turned to go. Then he said in Hindi that the magistrate was not in the office but "on tour." I asked who I could talk to instead and he said maybe his assistant magistrate could help. He pointed to the room next door. Again I thanked him and again he told me that he wasn't there. It was lunchtime; everyone had left the building.

I would have ordered a tea from him and waited for the deputy to return, but it seemed he only made tea for the government officials and it was lunchtime so he too wanted to go outside.

I came back an hour later. I nodded at the chai man as I went by. He nodded back, in that slight tilt of the head way that said, "I know you." I knocked on the door of the assistant's office and someone said, "Enter" in Hindi.

Inside the assistant's office was as uninspiring as the building, a damp, concrete cubicle with a few metal lockers lined against one wall. One of the cupboards had glass doors and I could see the cabinet was full of paper; sheaves of the stuff were held in manila folders and tied with binding twine. On the wall behind the assistant's desk was a frayed poster of the Auli ski area. A man in a bright red, '70s-style one-piece suit was schussing down a tree-lined trail with a huge smile on his face. The secretary was not smiling; he looked a little confused when I came in. He indicated for me to sit in the chair opposite him.

"How can I help you?" he asked in English.

Even while sitting down he was quite a tall man. He wore a dark blue hand-knit sweater with the collar of his light blue shirt tucked out over its neck. He had a long thin face and wide eyes that seemed too soft for a bureaucrat. On his head he had a woolen peaked cap, the kind I remember my grandfather wearing and immediately I felt an affinity with the man.

I told him my situation and tried to emphasize that although I wasn't a Hindu pilgrim I considered myself to be on pilgrimage and it would be a great favour if he could grant me the special privilege of going to Badrinath in winter.

I had spoken for two or three minutes. The secretary sat behind his sprawling desk nodding, his hands folded in his lap. When I finished, he laid his hands gently on the table and asked if I would like chai. In my politest Hindi I said that would be very nice. He clapped his hands and shouted, "Devgan." The chai man came in and stood ramrod straight without even looking at me. Tea was ordered and the lackey backed out of the room. Mr. Rao was the assistant magistrate's name and while we waited for tea he asked me questions about my country, mentioning that he had relatives in England and was planning to visit them someday. The chai arrived, steaming, in glasses that were too hot to touch.

Mr. Rao drank his almost immediately and my first thought was that his mouth must be made of asbestos. I sipped mine slowly and when I was done he announced, "Mr. Lineen, I believe the magistrate can help you but he is out of station right now."

I inquired where he might be. Mr. Rao said he had appointments in Chamoli, Gopeshwar and Lucknow, but "did not know where in this schedule the magistrate might be at that moment." The assistant wound his head back and forth in the flowing, prototypical Indian motion. I imitated the movement and asked when he thought the magistrate might return. The deputy smiled, still rolling his head, and told me he wasn't sure; it could be in the next few days but definitely within the next two weeks. We were waving our heads in matching patterns.

Now that I've had time to think about my years in India, I've been able to give the intensity of the head rolling gesture some perspective. I realize that the head rolling motion, the universal gesture of the subcontinent, the movement that implies, acceptance, understanding and acknowledgement, actually sketches the sign of infinity: ∞. The motion itself is a recognition of the infinite. What better image could there be for the eternal complexity of India?

Mr. Rao could not help me. The magistrate would be away for an unknown length of time. I accepted that I would not be going to Badrinath on this trip.

That evening I boarded a bus that would take me south, back down the Alaknanda River, the way I had come, to the village of Nandprayag.

CHAPTER 11
Gratitude

November 22

Prayag in Sanskrit translates as meeting. Nandprayag is one of the five major river confluences on the pilgrim route from Badrinath to Rishikesh where the river exits the mountains and enters the plain. It marks the joining of the Alaknanda and the Nandakini, a small stream that drains the peaks in the Nanda Devi region.

I was up early. I wanted to see the merging of the two watercourses at sunrise. The air was damp and cold, the kind of clammy nip that enters your bones, and I shivered in the mist that hovered on the water. The rivers moved together easily. It was too early for the clamour of trucks from the road twenty metres above, so there was only the sound of water and stone: hissing, grinding, thunking, rushing, swishing. The rounded boulders lining the bank were glazed by the river's spray, glistening like semi-precious jewels.

An old man, naked but for a cloth around his waist, stood at the water's edge, exhaling steamy breath and ladling the

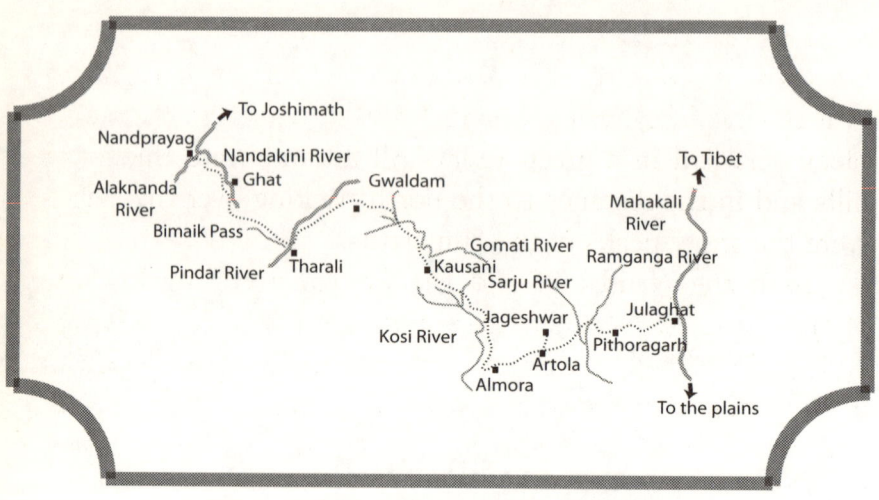

GARWAHL AND KUMAON, UTTARAKHAND, INDIA

freezing water over himself. I could hear the mumble of his morning prayers. The words and the water falling from his body were both taken by the current. He was solid, his body rooted against a fluid background.

In the sacred geography of Hinduism, river confluences are a common metaphor; in relation to Shankaracharya's philosophy, they represent the individual merging with the supreme. The tiniest trickle dropping from an icicle on Nanda Devi joins the stream that feeds the Nandakini; the Nandakini meshes with the Alaknanda, which in turn couples with the Bhagriath to form the Ganga. Ganga irrigates and nourishes hundreds of millions on the Gangeatic plain, but eventually even she joins with the ultimate, the Indian Ocean at the outlet in Bangladesh. Thus it is with the devout Hindu; after lifetimes of meetings and understandings, of integrations with knowledge and experience, the spirit finally coalesces with the one and enters a higher state of consciousness.

I moved east twenty kilometres up the Nandakini River to the town of Ghat. It was a one-lane settlement, an ugly town in a beautiful landscape, a single row of disintegrating concrete blocks cradled in a green valley. All around were thickly treed hills and in the distance to the north peeking over the ridgetops were the snow peaks of the Himalayas.

Both the Nandakini and the Pindar rivers are key routes of the Nand Raj Jat. The 280-kilometre pilgrimage takes place over eighteen stages ranging in altitude from 900 metres to 5,337 metres. For the orthodox it is a journey that should be undertaken barefoot. It is the largest religious undertaking in the Hindu Himalayas and must rank amongst the most arduous mass pilgrimages in the world.

The trek has no regular date but occurs on average every dozen years. The event is the ultimate form of devotion to the region's patron goddess, Nanda Devi. Nandi Devi means Goddess of Bliss. She is a manifestation of Parvati, Lord Shiva's wife, and resides on the peak of the mountain named in her honour. Nanda Devi is surrounded by a circle of peaks more than 6,000 metres that are integrated into her mythology: Nanda Ghunti, Nanda's veil; Nanda Kot, Nanda's fortress; and Nanda Khat, Nanda's bed.

The Uttarakhandis see the goddess as a lifesaving force. According to Hindu myth, a flood once covered the entire world. The sage Manu had a premonition of the event, built himself a boat and along with his family survived the disaster. Vishnu then transformed himself into a fish and towed the master to the summit of a mountain. When the waters receded Manu and his family descended the slopes and repopulated the earth. Garwahlis believe the mountain in their midst is Nanda Devi and the people of the area see themselves as the first people.

The timing of the Nand Raj Jat is dependent on the Devi herself. She channels herself through oracles in villages around the mountain's base to reveal the starting date for the pilgrimage. Once the start has been set, a miracle occurs as before each event a rare four-horned ram is born in the southwest of Chamoli District. The ram is ritually invested with the spirit of the goddess and thereafter leads the procession. The trek passes through dozens of villages along its route and in each one the local temple's image of the goddess is removed from her place of privilege, dressed in fresh silks, placed on a palanquin and shouldered by the men of the village to join the procession. By the climax of the festival, up to three hundred idols have joined the trek followed by thousands of her devotees. The pilgrimage reaches the high altitude, Hemkund Lake, in late August or early September. There the ram is set free to return to Nanda Devi.

However, I am wary of such mass showings of faith. My doubt stems from childhood experiences at the July 12 Protestant marches in Belfast. The massive parades celebrate the Protestant King William of Orange's victory over the Catholic King James II at the Battle of the Boyne in 1690. Willam had deposed James in 1688 and the campaign was a key event in the ousted king's unsuccessful attempt to regain the British throne. The victory ensured the continuation of the Protestant hierarchy in Ireland and so is commemorated to this day by hardline Protestants, primarily through the orthodox Orange Order movement, who intentionally organize marches through Catholic areas of the country in a show of historical force.

When I think about the marches I can still feel the pounding of the big lambeg bass drums thumping in my chest, a hammering so ferocious it threatened to throw my heartbeat off-kilter. The energy of the parades was something I was uncomfortable with even as a boy. They were and still are a demonstration of communal bullying. They highlight one of the great contradictions of faith, the conviction of the one side's interpretation of God melding into a hatred of another side's understanding of the same God. Superficial belief is too easily mutated. I know now that I need a faith based in logic, an analyzed trust. The words of the Buddha have stuck with me. He said, "Be lanterns unto yourselves."

He was constantly searching and exploring. The philosophy he created is one of intense self-effort, an ideology of analysis. "Question everything," he told his followers. Even if his own words were proven baseless, they too should be discarded because to cling to them was to hide from the truth.

As I ascended towards the Bimaik Pass, the houses thinned and again I entered coniferous forest where the scent of resinous needles of blue pine, chir, and deodar and the whistle of a breeze came through sharp trees. I stopped in a meadow. It was another clear night. I made tea, rice, dal. I ate my dinner in silence and watched the sun paint the peaks around Nanda Devi to the northeast.

November 23

On the far side of the pass I descended the Pranmati River towards Tharali. Ten kilometres into the day I caught up with a young man wearing a baseball hat, Nike sport shoes and a nylon pack. He was much too modernly dressed to be local. We were surprised by each other's appearance; he did a double take when I came up behind him. I smiled, he greeted me in English and after an impulsive handshake we sat on a nearby rock and shared some water.

Prem Singh was nineteen years old, with skin the colour of perfectly brewed milk tea and the dark down of a first moustache gracing his top lip. He spoke such excellent American-accented English that initially I presumed he must be a non-resident Indian, someone who had grown up outside the subcontinent, but he was actually from the industrial city of Ludhiana in Punjab state. He was a student taking a year off college and had walked the Curzon Trail, so called after the

British viceroy who trekked in the area in 1905, from Joshimath to Ghat, and now he was continuing on to the Pindar River.

We chatted for an hour about Indian interpretations of America. It was the first time in a week that I had had such a chance and was more than willing to listen. I was impressed by his knowledge of Western music and films.

I asked him if there was much of a rock music scene in Ludhiana, wondering where he had acquired such an encyclopedia of knowledge, but he shook his head and said, "Naw, but me and my friends watch a lot of MTV."

Prem was travelling by himself. Other than saddhus and sunnyasins, he was the first Indian solo trekker I had ever met. India is a densely populated place, but in my years there I rarely saw people travelling alone. Security on the subcontinent lies with family and caste, so for him to be on his own was a radical departure. I had to ask him about this. Again he returned to satellite TV as he said, "Man, I watch a lot of American movies and the ones I love are the ones where the guys go out and do stuff on their own. They don't wait around, they just do it."

As we were about to start walking again Prem asked if he could take a picture of us together. I agreed and as we stood, shoulder to shoulder, waiting for the camera's self-timer to click, he said, half under his breath, that it was for his father. "I told him I wouldn't walk by myself. If he knew I was trekking on my own he'd kill me."

We continued down the valley. In the river seething whitewater churned over spray-shot boulders. Across a long chute of broken rapids I saw goats, their wool the same colour as the waves. Rusty red and saffron leaves from oak and sal trees still held to some of the branches and shook in the breeze. For many kilometres we tracked a caravan of mules. The donkeys threw up clouds of dust and by the time we reached the road both of us were powdered in a pale coating of silt.

In Tharali we shared a room at a guest house on the main road. The room was another concrete cave with an internal skin of peeling paint. The next morning Prem was planning to get a bus to the nearest railhead at Haldwani and then back home to Punjab.

Sleep came easily but late in the night I woke suddenly – someone was speaking in the room. I sat up with a jolt and listened intently, but it wasn't someone else talking. Prem had been whispering song lyrics in his sleep. It was 'Come as you are', a Nirvana song I knew well.

The next morning I was up early. I would be walking before Prem caught his bus. We chatted over a cup of tea, but I made no mention of the song from the night before.

November 24

I followed the Pindar River five kilometres east and then climbed south on a road that switchbacked to a ridge where the route eased its ascent and contoured the land. I only wanted to reach the town of Gwaldam on the border between the Garwahl and Kumaon districts. It would be a relaxed twenty-kilometre day.

After Garwahl, Kumaon is the smaller of the two administrative divisions of Uttarakhand state. The area was annexed from Nepal by the British after the 1815 Gurkha war and for seventy years the entire area was administered by British bureaucrats before it was partitioned into Garwahl, Terai and Kumaon. The Kumaonis claim a different origin and dialect than the Garwahlis. Legend has it that the Kassite Assyrians left their homeland of Kummah near the Euphrates River in the fifth century B.C.E. and settled in the area as the Kumaoni Koliyan tribe.

I arrived at Gwaldam in late afternoon. It is a substantial village straddling the ridge between the Pindar and Gomati river watersheds. Thousands of Indian tourists make the trip there every summer as the village has a famously unobstructed panorama of Nandi Devi to the northeast. But it was early winter now, the air was cool and the one main street was empty. Fortunately, there was a good Indian sweet shop still open and after settling into a nearby guest house with a worthy view to the north, I happily sat in the café with my book, a cup of chai, and a plate of sweet milky treats.

I sipped my tea and the sun moved towards the horizon. The shadows on the street lengthened and I looked up to see Nandi Devi's glacial flanks take on the heated colours of sunset. I hurriedly paid for my food, left the restaurant and clambered up a nearby hill searching for the best view.

In Hinduism what I was doing would be called darshan, the practice of being in the presence of a holy entity. Merely the process of sitting quietly and observing a beatific, religiously charged object, whether a living being, an image, a river or a holy mountain, is enough to be gifted its energy. I was in search of darshan from the Goddess of Bliss, Nanda Devi. What made my audience even more powerful was that in her form as Nanda Devi, the goddess is considered to be at her most beautiful and therefore most beneficial.

I found a vantage point a few hundred metres above the village and sat on a smooth boulder beneath a pine tree. The mountain was transforming from a thick fin of snow and ice to a vaporous mirror of the day's last light. The amber shadow play moved across the peak's sheer south face in slow, almost imperceptible waves. Nanda Devi absorbed the sunset's colours seamlessly, individually. The light was changing so subtly that it appeared to be moving independent of the transition from day to night; colour was displacing time. I lost track; sky and earth worked together for those precious seconds to prove the

Goddess of Bliss's true divinity, her place of supremacy on a horizon studded with remarkable peaks.

I waited and waited for the mountain to be absorbed by darkness and when finally she was only a black outline against an even blacker sky, I slowly made my way down the hill through the dark of the new moon night. I stumbled to my guest house door, fumbled for the room key deep in my pocket and for a minute was unable to find it or the lock. Temporary blindness – maybe that's a by-product of darshan with the goddess.

I have sometimes wondered if my time in the hospital morgue when I first saw Gareth's body after the accident was in some way darshan. The room, silent, cool and only half lit, had a sense of the temple around it. Gareth wasn't a holy spirit, but he was a good, gentle soul, whose path to somewhere better, I have no doubt, was facilitated by having lived a life that caused so little pain to others. The reaction of us all, Mum, Katrina and I, was emotional in the extreme; tears were the only response to seeing Gareth lifeless and yet so peacefully there before us. I think of darshan in that instance because of the effect seeing him had on me. There was relief – he was no longer lost. Just knowing that cleared a path. There were many unseen, unknown obstructions in the way ahead but I could move forward now, stumbling, ever so slowly out of the shadows.

November 25

In the morning, descending from the heights at Gwaldam I came to the Gomati River. The valley widened, the trees disappeared and were replaced by a checkerboard of paddies. It was almost December, but at that lower altitude the temperature soared as the noon sun beat down relentlessly. The villagers wore sweaters and woolly hats. I suffered in a T-shirt.

I climbed again, this time towards Kausani, another ridgetop village, this one between the Gomati and Kosi rivers. Kausani is best known as the home of the Anashakti Ashram, a community set up by Mahatma Gandhi's disciple Sarala Ben to put into practice the great man's principles of truth, non-violence, vegetarianism, brahmacarya (asceticism), faith and simplicity. Nowadays, however, it is a destination like Gwaldam that swells in summer with an influx of tourists hungry to see Nanda Devi at sunset.

Again I entered forest; the shade cooled and brought me back in tune with my steps. I dropped into the thump of my feet and the motion of my pack. I was walking intently, but just below the village I heard mumbling from my left and in my distracted state I looked up to see a severed head on a concrete wall. I stopped and stared. The head summoned me three times before I realized who it was talking to. The face was that of a bank clerk, slightly jowly but well sunned, the bald head meticulously shaven. It was telling me in English of a shortcut to Kausani on the far side of the compound. The head came out from behind the wall and was joined with a body. The man made small talk and offered to show me the path. I followed him through a small, well-organized vegetable garden where spinach, peas, carrots, potatoes and late season tomatoes still bloomed. He pointed to the shortcut trail, then gave a Cheshire cat grin and said, "But come on, there is no rush. You must come in for a cup of coffee."

From outside it was a fine-looking house. I expected to be escorted to a well-appointed living room, but instead he brought me around the back to a tiny cell; the ceiling was criss-crossed with electrical wires, the floor was uncovered concrete, and a single rope-strung bed stood propped vertically against one wall. He offered me a seat in a patio chair that looked to have been salvaged from a dumpster and recovered with burlap. I sat and was shocked at how comfortable it was.

"Call me Baba," the man said.

On his bookshelf, which, from the bags of rice and lentils interspersed with the books must have doubled as his larder, I noticed a picture of the Indian saint Ramakrishna. I commented on this and quoted a passage I had recently read: "Māyā (Sanskrit for illusion), that is the ego, is like a cloud. The sun cannot be seen on account of a thin patch of cloud; when that disappears one sees the sun."

The Baba erupted into ecstatic laughter and gave me a smothering bear hug. He was a man full of emotion. My Ramakrishna quote was enough to send him into a half-hour talk on the significance of the saint and the importance of the quote.

The Baba was a follower of Swami Vivekanda, a late nineteenth-century Hindu philosopher and the premier disciple of Ramakrishna. The swami believed that Advaita Vedanta was not just a religious way of thinking but a way to approach social and even political issues. Vivekanda invented the concept of "Daridra narayana seva," the service of God through poor human beings.

Baba-ji was from a wealthy Kolkata family. He had been raised in a cosmopolitan household, his relatives visited from around the world and in his boarding school the students were the children of diplomats and international business people. From the Bible to Buddhism, Sufism to Shiva he had studied all the world's great religions, but had settled his practice in the roots of his Hindu background.

The Baba summarized his conviction in one word, "Joy." His instructions for life were simple: "Search for the bliss that is endless." I asked what he meant by this and he explained the bliss that is endless "is the bliss that knows no self."

He was boundlessly cheerful and appeared to be more interested in my happiness than his own. He barraged me with questions, tea, biscuits and commentary. I couldn't help but be caught in his exuberance, for when he talked his whole personality brightened.

He was fascinated by my walk, my encounters with people, my understanding of the landscape and my interest in religions. He harangued me to tell him more and more about the trip, but eventually he grew serious.

"Jono," he said, "you are walking all over, meeting so many people, discovering so many things, but please remember the most important journey is the pilgrimage to understand the heart. When you are confident enough to undertake that trip, then you will find a joy that is boundless. Confidence is faith and faith is joy."

Evening was darkening his little garden, and though he offered me a sleeping space on his floor, I declined. There was really nowhere for my long body in his tiny room. I thought we would both be happier if I found a room in the village. He gave me a huge bear hug and I left. Other than Baba-ji, which means uncle in Hindi, I never learned his full name nor did he ask me mine.

November 26

Another morning and the path led downwards again, this time to the Kosi River. As on the upper reaches of the Bhagriath, the Kosi has cut a deep, winding path through a narrow sandstone valley. Its current has formed smooth curls and holes in the malleable silt stone. Every now and then I would stop and gaze, caught in the water's movement. There was no end to the flow.

In the afternoon, after a lunch of tea and chapatis on the side of the road, I could see far above me the outskirts of Almora. It would be another long ascent to end the day. The climb, however, gave me the chance to see the town from the bottom up. Almora is a community of layers. Lower down I moved through an area of government offices. They looked neglected, their foundations wasting away, walls splattered with urine and betel nut juice, the exteriors raw and bony, as if everything had been pilfered from the shells. With no character in them and no admiration for them, those buildings seemed the woeful by-product of an uncaring bureaucracy.

Above this lay a strata of decaying relics, one-hundred-year-old architectural memories, vestiges of a time gone by: the mansions of the British Raj. They were once regal slate and stone villas. From below they looked to be a matrix of peaked roofs and arched windows, steep-roofed fantasies transported from Surrey and Kent. The remains in Almora are distinguished but sad; hand-worked brick walls fall inwards, chimneys have been toppled by winds, leaded-glass windows are missing jigsaw-puzzle pieces.

On the town's crest was a last layer, where the old bazaar tops the ridge; it is an avenue of masterfully laid paving stone lined with rabbit hutch shops. Each ground-floor storefront is similar in size and design to the last, yet their interiors teem with a great jumble of different products. Upstairs from the retail space are the merchant's living quarters and from the intricately carved and endlessly diverse window grills and tiny balconies families look down upon a scene unchanged for hundreds of years.

In Almora I found that people in some strange way reflected the architectural layering of the town. I met Mr. Verma in a local chai shop that surprisingly served brewed coffee and tasty gulab jamun sweets. He was an assistant engineer with the electrical department and a talkative man, interested to know my impressions of all the places I had visited within India, but he had little curiosity about the world outside. He was obsessed with cricket and the army and was somehow able to relate the places I had been to throughout the Himalayas to those two topics; a certain cricketer who was born in Kashmir had these scores in a test match from decades before, or a general made a particular decision in Ladakh that affected the outcome of the 1962 Sino-Indian war. Mr. Verma loved India, and he believed in its superpowerdom, but he was not interested in judging his convictions against anything outside the subcontinent.

In the stratum of neglected mansions Mr. Shah owned the dilapidated one-hundred-year-old hotel I stayed in. The building must have been beautiful in its day, full of nooks and crannies and secret passageways. But now it was a wheezing skeleton of cedar and stone; I would wake at night to the moan of the wooden superstructure and the scuffle of small animals through the room. Taking a shower involved obliging unknown powers of plumbing. It was fitting the hotel was managed by that spritely octogenarian. He had been in the hospitality business since the time of the British and was an effortless schmoozer. Mr. Shah had an amazing talent for sizing up customers and, with his toothless smile, separating you from your money: a bottle of mineral water here, a guided tour of old Almora there, all the while making you feel he was providing an essential service.

Mr. Shah's antithesis was his servant, Pradeep Dabar, a young Nepali who lived in a room behind a shop near the bazaar. He had left home when he was nine years old after the death of his father and had worked in a succession of cafés and chai stalls, making his way west along the Nepali Terai and Kumaon until he arrived in Almora and had secured work with Mr. Shah. He had started working for food alone but now made a small wage. Pradeep had the contorted body language of a defeated man but the twinkling eyes of a pixie. He really seemed to enjoy helping. Yes, I tipped him well, but unlike Mr. Shah he never reminded me that ten percent was the usual rate on all transactions.

The only other guest in the hotel was a young Finnish man, Juha Pukkola. Like many Finns he spoke perfect English so we talked well into the night. Juha was from Helsinki, but spent most of his time now in India. He was a tall fellow with dark, narrow eyes and the thick, straw-coloured hair you would expect from a Finn. He was a chain-smoker, with a slight tremor in his fingers, and when he smiled his teeth were a jagged mash of yellowing stumps. I presumed, since he spent so much time in the country, that he worked for a non-governmental organization but when I pressed him he admitted he was a drug runner.

Juha transported hashish from the Western Himalayas to Copenhagen, Stockholm and Helsinki. It's something I could never do – I don't have the nerve for it, and therefore have a vicarious fascination with the people who do. We talked about the logistics of smuggling, an intricate process of trusting, paying and deceiving a multitude of officials. He acknowledged it was a stressful career. I was shocked when he called it a career, but he insisted that if the "transits" were well-planned there was little to be worried about and he thought he could continue smuggling for many years to come. I probed him more on this and he admitted that he felt trapped by the huge amounts of money he could make on every trip. "It's a gamble," he said, "and there's a rush in that. And when it works I get a shitload of cash and feel like a king."

November 27

From Almora to Artola the road interconnects and traverses a long series of ridges through southern Kumaon. At Artola I headed north on a branch road to Jageshwar, one of the most sacred Saivaite temples in the region. The path descended through a forest of mixed conifers. Up until then the entire route from Almora had been devoid of timber. The slopes had mostly been entirely cleared and rice paddies were everywhere, but where in Garwahl the fields had been framed by trees, in Kumaon there were only bushes and vegetable gardens. I decided that the integrity of the Jageshwar watershed must be the result of the population's reverence for the shrine. Beside the road a pristine creek jumped between mossy boulders. At the wood's edge was a web of the deepest green; barberry and rhododendron, silver weed and ferns waved in the breeze. The trees – chir, deodar and a few miniature oak – were an emerald reflection of the forest floor. The woods were surprisingly dense. By the road, colours were lightened by the sun but the deeper into the trees you looked, the darker it became until it disappeared into earthy blackness.

Seven kilometres on, the forest opened onto a quiet hamlet where woodsmoke hung in the cool air, creating a blue-tinted ceiling. On first impressions there appeared to be an order, a sense of balance about the place; the temple complex straddled the creek and was offset in the fore- and background by an unbroken, curving line of woods. It was late afternoon and the light was mellowing. I headed for the main compound, a group of more than one hundred carved stones and half a dozen temples, the most important of which holds what some devotees believe is a Jyotir Linga – a rare, spontaneously created Shiva phallus in stone.

The temple's interior was a crisp stone cavern. Roof openings directed shafts of light, silver funnels against the dark stone, into the dim space. Everything glimmered from constant washing. It was crowded with brass and copper religious utensils; lustrous, pregnant shapes glowed in the shadows. In and out wandered the priests, who seemed absorbed in the business of propitiating Shiva. The main lingam was draped in fresh flowers. A bright red silk cloth stiched in gold encircled the yoni base of the moist phallus.

I sat on a stone bench off to one side and stared at the lingam. The place was humid and cool. I had been walking for twelve hours and was tired and hungry, but my mind was focused. The lingam stood in the middle of what felt like a medieval cathedral, and as I concentrated on it, it seemed to pulse, to beat almost as if taking in and exhaling breath. Had the thousands of years of devotion lavished on the stone given it some form of life, transformed it into what the community wanted it to be, a living, breathing emanation of the deity who ruled their lives? The coldness of the bench and the damp floor on my bare feet had no register because I was focused on the organic nature of that inorganic object, but a clatter of metal plates against the slate floor broke my concentration. The stone's breathing dissipated and I was once again in the moist interior of a Hindu temple.

There were so many times on the walk when I had been struck by what had seemed to be the living spirit of inanimate objects – mountains, rivers, architecture, painting, stones, sculpture. No doubt the months of walking, day after day of being alone with only my thoughts and the manic consistency of my steps, had opened me to those possibilities. I was ready to accept what before I would so easily have dismissed. The weeks of walking meditation and the constant interaction with what I wanted to learn had opened me in ways I couldn't understand. There was no logic to so much of what I had experienced. I was the freest and happiest I had been since Gareth's death, but in the back of my mind I worried that the magic of what I had felt would not transfer to my life beyond the Himalayas.

To one side of the temple a group of congregants started chanting, deep, pulsing tones that reverberated and amplified around the chamber. The temple walls echoed the mantras, and they became louder, more imbued with the wild spirit of Shiva. The chanters were rooted in their place, and the building trembled with their devotion for the god.

November 28

When I left Jageshwar at dawn, mist clung to the lower branches of the trees. It was a murky morning. I was walking in an interzone, in a time before daylight in an ancient forest.

Back at Artola I again headed east, following the road along endless ridges. The day wore on, the light grew stark and the details of the land became hazy, obstructed by heat and dust. Then after lunch, the process reversed itself as the light mellowed with afternoon progressing to evening.

Village after village floated by, nameless clusters of huts, their name signs rusted to incoherence. Each one melted into the next. Every hamlet appeared to be just a slight variation on the last. In each village I drew a swarm of youngsters. Like hungry mosquitoes the kids followed me, sometimes for thirty or forty minutes. Although it was incredible to think that a red rucksack and faded yellow sleeping pad could provide so much amusement, I was hardened to my followers now and could ignore the superfluous chatter of a dozen gossiping kids for as long as I needed. I focused on the next footfall. Being stared at and talked about was a reality I had to accept. I was the reluctant ambassador of a far-away world.

But one man didn't stare. I was between villages on a treeless section of road that ran along a barren ridgetop. He came up out of a paddy field. He was old, had thin grey hair and a patchy beard. He wore a battered woolen vest and an off-kilter Nehru hat. On his shoulders rode a small child of five or six years old, maybe his grandson. I was impressed by the way he moved, one footstep to the next with considered precision. It was continuous motion but stuttered as if he tested every step before committing to his forefoot. There was something meditative about his progress.

I stopped. He moved towards me, his eyes straight ahead. The child was speaking quietly, his head moving this way and that, an inquisitive little boy. The couple came broadside and I could see the old man's unblinking eyes. His pupils were clouded with cataracts – he was blind. The child's words were coded directions, and every step they made was carefully planned. The pair moved by and as they passed the little boy turned and smiled.

It's hard for me not to think of Gareth when I remember that image. There was never that symbiosis between us, but still when he passed away something abandoned me. I was emptier. Part of me was gone and it has never truly returned. At first it manifested as an almost physical pain in my stomach; it honestly felt as if there was hole boring into my guts. Over many months that bodily ache left me, but the psychological damage took years to reconcile.

Last year my older brother was contacted by a friend who directed him to a website that had a video of Gareth on it. Strangely, in this age of ubiquitous recording, this is the only moving image we have of him. Peter sent me the link and nervously I opened the clip. It's a grainy black and white scene of a few teenagers on a rain-soaked outdoor basketball court talking amongst themselves. The camera pans shakily around the kids and then settles on a tall wet young man with tight dirty blond curls and a shy smile. He laughs and adds a few comments to their personal conversation. My jaw dropped. There he was again after all these years, walking, talking, the same jovial yet timid teenager who left us all those years ago. I immediately burst into tears. I haven't been able to go back to the clip. The emotion it brought up was shocking, and I could feel the empty void in my belly opening ever so slightly again.

I've spent years thinking about what that emptiness is: lost potential, the destruction of expectations, the damning of innocence, the ruin of a carefully created worldview, the undermining of a family, the pressure of knowing that no matter how good you are it can all end in a flash – all these have fed that black hole in my soul. Yet out of that nihilism and pain I have stumbled into being a happier person. Gareth's death was the bottom of the barrel and to climb out demanded strength that has held me in good stead. I've pushed myself to the edge in so many ways that I now understand my own limits – what

I can and cannot do, what I'm capable of in this life. Gareth is gone, part of me is gone, and I accept there's no way to get that back and yet he's left something with me. His legacy is timeless. It's simply to get the most out of the time I have in this body. Every day, find the beauty.

My admirers in the Kumaon villages drifted away as evening approached – suppertime was calling them – and as the light faded I searched for a chai shop. It was dark when I found what I was looking for. The white glare of a kerosene lamp called out of the blackness. Inside the bamboo hut was warm. Three men were seated by a crackling fire, but they squeezed down the bench and made room for me.

An expressionless old lady in a threadbare, burgundy salwar khamiz appeared. The man farthest away inquired in Hindi if I wanted potato or spinach curry. I hadn't asked about food. I replied I'd like both and he and the man sitting beside him laughed. Within ten minutes the food appeared, a small mountain of rice and vegetables. Three sets of eyes were glued to my every move. They were happy when I asked for more of the old lady's hot lime pickle. I finished the meal and set the plate on the dirt floor beside me. The old lady came silently and took it away. The man who had asked me if I needed food talked to her. She said nothing but nodded. When she came back she placed a bottle of cloudy liquid and a glass near my feet. Each of the men received a glass. The man at the far end leaned forward, held his up, pointed at the bottle indicating I should pour the alcohol and smiled. He had three gold teeth and in the firelight his eyes glinted the same colour as the precious metal.

I poured a finger's worth of the smoky liquid into my glass, nodded my appreciation and handed it down the line. Each in turn filled his glass and on the prompting of the far-end man, we raised our glasses and called, "Cheers." It turned out that this was the extent of my new friends' English.

We were up until very late that night. I'm sure we talked about many things, and I know we must have laughed a lot because my sides hurt, but those are the things you generally do when you get drunk. However, the specifics of the evening elude me because my mind is a blur from not long after we started on the local liquor to when I woke the next morning, horizontal on the bench with three snoring bodies lying at obtuse angles from the smoldering fire. The old woman was nowhere to be seen.

November 29

Starting from the Ramganga River it was a long climb thirty kilometres to the district capital of Pithoragarh. The road clings to a hillside devoid of cover, its surface viciously channelled by hundreds of monsoon rains. I floated, oblivious to the diesel-reeking transport trucks and the buzz of overhead transmission lines. Villages melted in my passing as the road levitated from its stony bed. I saw children playing games, exuberant and full of energy, ignorant of the torn landscape around them. I saw winter vegetables, chard and spinach, bursting through the thin soil. On rooftops I saw sheafs of drying chilies, red peppers and millet laid out across terra cotta tiles, red upon red upon red. Two magpies cackled at me as I passed their roost, telling jokes in a language I didn't understand. An old lady sat on a flattened stone by the roadside. She smiled, pressed her hands together in prayer and shouted her greeting, "Namaste" – I bow to you. There was a hurry about my movements now. Inside I knew the walk was ending and there was an uneasiness in my steps.

Before I realized it night was falling and I was on the outskirts of Pithoragarh. I found a room in another concrete-box guest house and went in search of dinner.

The dhaba next door was overpopulated with employees and absent of customers. The making of my curry, dal and rice was a labour of a half dozen men, all moving at a snail's pace. It must have been the gloomy mood I had been in all day but, although it had not bothered me for all the years I had been in India, that night I was frustrated by the great waste of potential in the men I saw standing around the café doing nothing and in that microcosm I saw something of India and Hinduism.

The Vedic concept of Varna or social categories was developed with an understanding of the differences between people. Everyone's path to realization is individual and this is reflected in the Sva-Dharma, or code of practice. As the *Bhagavad Gita* says, "Better to do one's own caste duty, though devoid of merit, than to do that of others, however well performed."

Unfortunately, the idea of duty, the performance of one's practice, has become synonymous with specialization, and obligations to caste have become so codified that creativity has been squashed. Caste has been polluted by its bureaucracy and transformed into feudalism.

The making of my cup of tea that evening was an example. One man took my order for chai; another, and not the man who made chapatis or the man who made dal, made the tea. The making of tea is a ritualized ceremony in an environment of repetition, and yet he could not deliver it three metres to my table. That function had to be performed by his underling, a boy of maybe ten years old who was summoned from across the road where he was watching Hindi films in the display window of an electrical shop. He shuffled over, moved the chai, and in the process spilled it on my table. He shrugged in apology and returned to the movies. Neither he nor any of the cooks could clean it; for that, a separate, even younger, member of the crew was summoned from the rear of the restaurant. He appeared lethargically, barefoot, clutching a greasy rag, and proceeded to move the spill around the arborite tabletop, not so much sopping it up as dispersing it over a wider area. He then shuffled back to his corner accompanied by a chorus of unwarranted abuse from the sweaty chai-wallah.

I went back to my room trying not to think about the loss of human promise such a system engendered. As I passed the electrical shop on the other side of the street, I could see the boy who had moved my tea from the kitchen to the table dancing in time with the Bollywood movie he and a friend were watching. He saw my reflection in the mirror, turned and waved excitedly. "God night, Mister," he shouted, still gyrating his hips like a dance star. Considering the service at the dhaba had been far from good and we were in the land of the ever-present God, it was a fitting farewell.

November 30

The landscape I moved through on the thirty kilometres between Pithoragarh and Julaghat on the Mahakali River forecasts the apocalyptic future of the Indian Himalayas. The rocky slopes were dotted with scattered low-lying brush. The forest had disappeared long ago. There is nothing to hold it back, so the monsoon slides off the hills as fast as it falls and in the process takes with it what little topsoil is left. The land's thin veneer of fertility is stripped away. Even in December, the sun routed the land; the heat felt like an oppressive weight. That environment, at 1,500 metres, looked less healthy than valleys I had walked through at 4,500 metres.

The road moves due east and the route itself is a travesty of engineering. Washouts emerged every kilometre or so, and great chunks of its surface had slipped away. I saw boulders, gravel and flattened lumps of ashphalt sitting in village gardens. I suppose the road was another example of entropy; everything constructed and left to its own accord will deconstruct.

Julaghat is a typical frontier community, a haphazard, shantytown tenanted by a disproportionate number of little shops all catering to the Nepali population freely crossing the border. Because there are no roads on the Nepali side, traversing the river on a thin, steel cable footbridge is the fastest way for people for thousands of square kilometres inside Nepal to access a road-serviced market. The main bazaar was a bustle of activity. Business is the lifeblood of borders and the lines of stores and open stalls traded everything from cheap tin spoons to computer software. The market was framed at either end of its 400-metre stretch by open sewers.

I left the bazaar and went in search of the river. I followed a trail past a cluster of concrete, monsoon-stained government buildings and down onto a grey beach. I took off my pack, boots and socks and wriggled my toes in the freezing grey sand, feeling the grit rise comfortably around my feet. It was as if the land was conforming to my touch.

Before me was the Mahakali River. It originates on the Tibetan border at the southern edge of Mount Kailash's watershed, another river like the Indus and the Ganges that reaches south from the mountain that Hindus and Buddhists believe to be the subcontinent's axis mundi. The Mahakali is the river of Great Kali – the goddess of death. Kali is the ferocious aspect of Parvati, but on that silent inlet I saw nothing predatory. The river was quiet, smooth, unrushed, almost patient. There was no whitewater on that stretch, just constant movement, an interminable current. It was the emerald-blue of glacial streams. The ochre cliffs on the Nepali shore reddened in the evening's dwindling light. Turquoise and coral – the protective colours. Refuge in landscape.

To my right an old woman washed. A wet cotton white sari clung tight to her thin body. Shampoo foam fell as white clouds from her hair. I could see the frothy drifts like tiny icebergs rounding a further turn in the river. They were moving south to merge with the Ganges and eventually reach the ocean: the mother spirit. Noticing me the woman smiled, which was strange because women in India usually turned away if I looked at them. I smiled back, rolled up my pants and waded in to knee-depth. I spread my arms wide, curled my toes into the riverbed sand and turned to face the heavens. I closed my eyes, breathing deeply. I let the river run and roar through me. I slowed and tried to make my breath as tranquil as the stream. I scooped water – liquid blessings from the mountain's heart – and doused myself. Now I was surrounded by the river that had been my focus for those four months. I felt enveloped by so much water that my mind itself was becoming fluid – unfettered – clear, moving with grace, without fear, without end.

Gareth was lost in the water, and his remains are still there. I remembered back to the year after his death. My family had gathered at the National Rowing Centre at Elk Lake on the anniversary of his passing. It had been a difficult year, the most gruelling in my life, but for others in my family it had also been a traumatic twelve months. My parents had divorced, although the process had been underway before Gareth's death, and my sister, who had been trialling for the Olympic field hockey team, had been cut in the very last stages of the selection process. All our lives had been changed forever.

We borrowed a boat from the rowing centre, an inflatable Zodiac – an unsinkable coach boat – some lessons had been learned from the tragedy. The five of us motored out to the far end of the lake where the rowing shell had capsized. It was a cool, cloudy day but the surface was glassy smooth, an opposite extreme to the night of the accident. I trailed my fingers through the water; it was cold and silky smooth, almost inviting. With us, in an urn, were Gareth's cremated ashes. We were giving him back to the lake. We each took a turn in releasing him to the water. It was the first time I had seen bodily ashes and was shocked to realize how a physical being could be reduced to a few handfuls of dust. There were tears again; his passing was still too close for any understanding. The ashes were taken by the breeze wafting across the surface and spread wide – an entire life reduced to a mottled tinge on a black glass surface.

The motor throbbed behind the boat. We hugged each other; few words were spoken. The western lakeshore was bordered with dense conifer forest, dark and ominous, like the only future I could imagine for myself.

Above the Mahakali River the sun was setting. Violet and saffron streaked the thin cirrostratus clouds skitting just above the horizon. Rocks pulled by the current thunked and banged in an invisible rolling dance along the riverbed. Every cloud was perfectly different. Bright Mars shone in the west, the first star.

I made a silent wish.

I scooped more water.

I thought of Gareth, completely, putting him back together piece by piece, filling out the shattered puzzle that had lain in my psyche for so long. Months of walking, of being alone with him in the mountains had gifted me the chance to view him from every angle, to grasp him again in an innocent embrace. He was gone but that loss, I realized now, could not destroy the love I would always have for him. In the end, all we have is love.

I absorbed myself in the process of gratitude, simply recalling Gareth, family, friends and events while watching the river.

Every good thought is a prayer.

I don't know how long I stood in that thigh-deep backwater, but when I looked again, the woman in the white sari was gone.

No book is written alone. This one would never have made the transition from manuscript to book without the love and belief of Trish and the restless nights and long hours of thought induced by my amazing sons Liam and Connor.